✿ A cookbook to use for every meal, every day. Hundreds of tasty appetizers, brand-new main dishes along with important dress-ups for old favorites, the new ways with vegetables, all kinds of salads, luscious desserts—plus all these bonuses... A FRENCH CHEF IN YOUR KITCHEN : the secrets of cooking *en papillon*—"package-prepared" specials that taste better than anything you've ever made, thanks to the cooking magic of aluminum wrap... FOIL AND YOUR FREEZER : all you'll ever need to know about freezer cooking and storing... COME-AND-COOK PARTIES : a wonderful way to turn kitchen chores into fun—give a good cook's get-together and reap a surprise reward in ready-to-serve meals for your family when the party's over!... LUNCH BOX LUXURIES : making packed-at-home lunches an eater's treat... THE GREAT OUTDOORS : taking the sameness out of backyard cookery... A WHOLE NEW WORLD OF CASSEROLES : for a whole new world of meal-time enjoyment... THE COOKIE JAR : best kinds to bake, best ways to store...'ROUND THE WORLD KITCHEN : exotically delicious foreign meals, with easy-to-follow, step-by-step directions for every dish.

Mealtime Magic COOKBOOK

Margaret Mitchell

Director of Home Economics,
Wear-Ever Aluminum and
Alcoa Wrap Kitchens

PUBLISHED BY POCKET BOOKS, INC. NEW YORK

MARGARET MITCHELL'S MEALTIME MAGIC COOKBOOK

A *Pocket Book* edition
1st printing......September, 1964

This original *Pocket Book* edition is printed from
brand-new plates made from newly set, clear, easy-to-read type.
Pocket Book editions are published by Pocket Books, Inc., and
are printed and distributed in the U.S.A. by Affiliated Publishers,
a division of Pocket Books, Inc., 630 Fifth Avenue,
New York, N.Y. 10020.
Trademark of Pocket Books, Inc., 630 Fifth Avenue,
New York, N.Y. 10020, registered in the United States
and other countries.

W

Grace Before Meat

Let all of us
  In full accord
Give grateful thanks
  Unto the Lord—

A very kind
  And gracious Lord,
Who gives us more
  Than our reward.

—NEW ENGLAND PRIMER

Contents

Aluminum foil is one of the wonders of modern home-making. Uses for versatile Alcoa Wrap can be found in every room in the house—but it is in the kitchen that foil's magic comes to full realization. Use of Alcoa Wrap makes possible better-tasting, time-saving changes in old favorites and, better still, the invention of wonderful, never-before recipes that open up a whole new world of kitchen minor miracles.

Best Ways with Meat

Meat's likely to be the most important thing on the menu, both from the point of view of the diners and from the homemaker's budget . . . so doesn't it make sense to know the very best ways to deal with whatever kind and cut of meat you're going to serve?

METHODS OF COOKING MEAT

There are seven specific methods of cooking meat—roasting, broiling, panbroiling or griddle broiling, panfrying, deep fat frying, braising, and cooking in water. It's generally the cut of meat that determines the cooking method.

How to Roast:

True roasting is a dry heat method of cooking. It is done in a shallow pan. No water is added. Basting is unnecessary. All tender cuts of beef, pork, lamb and veal are best cooked by this method.

1. Season as desired. It makes little difference whether a roast is salted before or after cooking because when done, the salt has penetrated only to a depth of about one half inch. 2. Line shallow open roasting pan with Alcoa Wrap by shaping piece of foil over outside of pan then fitting it into pan. 3. Place meat fat side up on rack in pan. The rack holds the roast out of the drippings and with fat on top, roast will do its own basting. 4. Insert a meat thermometer so that its bulb is in the center of the thickest part. The bulb should not rest on the fat or touch the bone. 5. Add no water; do not cover. If the pan is covered or water added, the meat will be a pot roast. 6. Roast according to time and temperature given in chart.

How to Broil:

Tender beefsteaks, lamb or mutton chops, sliced ham or bacon and ground beef or lamb are suitable for broiling. Fresh pork and veal are seldom broiled. Steaks and chops should be cut at least one inch thick for best broiling and a slice of ham at least one half inch thick. To broil:

1. Turn oven regulator to "broil." Pre-heat or not as desired. **2.** Line broiler pan with Alcoa Wrap by shaping piece of foil over outside of pan, then fitting it into pan. Drop rack into place. Do not cover rack with foil, so that excess fat can drip down into pan. **3.** Place meat on rack of broiler pan, 2-3 inches from the heat; the thicker the meat the greater the distance from the heat. **4.** Broil until top side is thoroughly browned; season with salt, pepper (except ham, bacon). **5.** Turn; brown second side; season; serve at once.

How to Panbroil:

The same tender cuts of meat suitable for broiling may also be panbroiled. An aluminum fry pan or griddle is particularly good for this type of broiling.

1. Place pan over medium high heat. **2.** Place small piece of white paper in bottom of pan. When paper turns a golden brown, add meat; reduce heat to medium. When the cold meat hits the hot pan it will stick but as it cooks and browns it will loosen itself. If juices start to cook out of the meat,

increase heat slightly.   **3.** When meat is brown on one side, turn; brown second side. Do not cover and do not add water.   **4.** When meat is cooked to desired degree of doneness, season and serve at once.

How to Panfry:

Comparatively thin pieces of tender meat, meat that has been made tender by pounding, cubing, scoring or grinding, or meat that is breaded are best suited to panfrying, which is the cooking of meat in a small amount of fat. To panfry:

1. Place fry pan over medium high heat; add small amount of fat—usually two tablespoons will be sufficient.   **2.** When fat starts to bubble or sputter, add meat; cook as in panbroiling.

How to Deep Fat Fry:

This method of cooking is almost always used for breaded meats or croquettes made from leftovers. To deep fat fry:

1. Place about one pound fat in French fryer or a deep kettle. Heat fat to correct temperature. Most accurate temperature control is obtained by using a thermometer. Temperatures for deep fat frying of meat range from 300 to 350° F., dependent upon size of pieces and whether it is uncooked or left over meat.   **2.** Place a few pieces of meat in fry basket; lower slowly into hot fat.   **3.** If fat covers meat, no turning is necessary; allow meat to brown thoroughly and cook through.   **4.** When done, raise basket; let meat drain; remove from basket.   **5.** In this type of frying, best results are obtained when only a few pieces are fried at one time.   **6.** Fat may be used again if it is strained and stored in refrigerator.

How to Braise:

Braising, also known as pot roasting, is the method most frequently used for cooking the less tender cuts of meat. Some tender cuts are also better if braised. These include pork chops, pork steaks, pork cutlets, veal chops, veal steaks, veal cutlets and pork liver. To braise:

1. Brown meat on all sides using fat if necessary.   2. When brown, season; cover; reduce heat to low; cook until tender, turning frequently.   3. *Oven Pot Roasts:* The less tender cuts of meat such as chuck, shoulder, rump, breast or sirloin tip can be made deliciously tender by the Alcoa Wrap method of oven pot roasting.

1. Pre-heat oven to 425° F.   2. Place meat in center of large piece of Alcoa Wrap. Season as desired. Bring torn edges together over meat; fold, then fold again bringing fold down close to meat. Fold ends over and over, pressing in close to meat.   3. Place wrapped meat on rack in shallow pan. 4. Roast 35-45 minutes per pound.   5. Forty-five minutes before meat is done, open foil; push away for browning.

How to Cook in Water:

Large cuts of meat may be browned or not as desired. However, browning helps to develop flavor and improves the color. Corned beef and cured pork need not be browned.

1. Brown meat on all sides.   2. Cover with water or stock; liquid may be hot or cold—it makes no difference.   3. Season with salt, pepper, spices and vegetables.   4. Cover; simmer until tender.

Small pieces of meat such as are used in stews are prepared as follows:

1. Cut meat into 1-inch cubes; roll in seasoned flour; brown on all sides in hot fat. 2. Add just enough water, stock or vegetable juice to cover meat. 3. Season as desired; cover; simmer until meat is tender. 4. Vegetables are added about one hour before cooking time is completed. Liquid is thickened just before serving.

COOKING FROZEN MEAT, POULTRY, FISH

To thaw or not to thaw frozen meat, poultry or fish is entirely a matter of time and convenience.

If thawed, they should be cooked the same as when fresh and as soon as possible after thawing.

The best way to thaw meat, fish or poultry is in the storage compartment of the refrigerator. To prevent surface drying, food should be covered or left in its original wrapper.

A more uniform degree of doneness is achieved, especially with large roasts, if thawed before cooking.

Small pieces frozen together must be thawed if they are to be browned.

Roasts started in the frozen state require 1½-2 times longer to cook rare, 3 times longer to cook well done. The larger the piece the longer the cooking time.

One-inch frozen steaks or chops require 3-4 minutes longer; two-inch steaks or chops take 16-18 minutes longer.

When using frozen poultry, it is best to thaw the fowl and then cook it the same as a fresh bird.

Whole fish or fish fillets are best if they are thawed and then cooked while there is still a little ing.

Frozen uncooked or cooked lobster, shri oysters and clams are thawed or not dep are to be used.

If there are thawing and cooki or the package, they should b

If using a meat thermom state, insert after center about half done.

Best Ways with Beef

Tender, rich in its own juices, perfectly cooked to the exact degree of doneness you like—that's beef at its best. With the help of Alcoa Wrap your beef dishes will always be better than ever before, and your clean-up time will be cut to the bare bones!

BUYING GUIDE FOR BEEF

Characteristics	Cut	Weight	Number of servings
Color when ish brown ing ra chang- cherry bright posed firm, fine ex- marbled n, bones red white, bri	Short Ribs	1 lb.	1–2
	Sirloin Steak	1 lb.	1–3
	Round Steak	1 lb.	2–3
	Standing Rib	5 lbs.	8–10
	Boneless, Stewing	1 lb.	3–4
	Hamburger	1 lb.	3–4
	Brisket	1 lb.	2–3
	Flank Steak	1 lb.	2–3

6

TEMPERATURE-TIME CHART FOR ROAST BEEF
325° F. Oven Temperature

Cut	Approximate Minutes Per Pound 3–5 Pounds	Approximate Minutes Per Pound 5–8 Pounds	Meat Thermometer Reading When Roast Is Done
Rolled Rib			
Weight after boning, rolling			
Rare	31–36	27–32	140° F.
Medium	36–40	32–36	160° F.
Well Done	40–45	38–43	170° F.
Standing Rib			
Rare	21–26	17–22	140° F.
Medium	26–30	22–26	160° F.
Well Done	30–35	28–33	170° F.

BROILING TIME TABLE FOR STEAKS

Turn meat after broiling ½ the time

CUT	THICK-NESS	TOTAL APPROXIMATE TIME		
Beef		Rare	Medium	Well Done
Club Steak	1 inch	8–10 minutes	11–13 minutes	13–15 minutes
	1½ inches	16–18 minutes	19–21 minutes	21–25 minutes
Filet Mignon (or tenderloin)	1 inch	5–6 minutes	7–8 minutes	8–10 minutes
	1½ inches	8–10 minutes	11–13 minutes	13–15 minutes
	2 inches	11–13 minutes	15–17 minutes	17–19 minutes
Hamburgers	1½ inches		8–10 minutes	10–12 minutes
Porterhouse Steak	1 inch	8–10 minutes	11–13 minutes	13–15 minutes
	1½ inches	16–18 minutes	19–21 minutes	21–23 minutes
	2 inches	27–30 minutes	34–36 minutes	36–40 minutes
Rib Steak	1 inch	8–10 minutes	11–13 minutes	13–15 minutes
Sirloin Steak	1 inch	10–12 minutes	12–14 minutes	14–16 minutes
	1½ inches	18–20 minutes	20–24 minutes	24–26 minutes
	2 inches	34–36 minutes	36–40 minutes	40–42 minutes
T-Bone Steak	1 inch	8–10 minutes	11–13 minutes	13–15 minutes
	1½ inches	16–18 minutes	19–21 minutes	21–23 minutes
	2 inches	27–30 minutes	34–36 minutes	36–38 minutes

BROILED STEAKS

1. Turn oven regulator to "broil" or to highest degree of setting. If no regulator, turn heat on full.   2. Pre-heat broiler 10 minutes or as directed by range manufacturer.   3. Trim surplus fat from meat; if meat is very lean like filet mignon, brush surface with fat.   4. Slash fat edge of meat at 2-inch intervals to prevent curling.   5. If desired, steak may be rubbed with cut side of clove of garlic or spread thinly with prepared mustard.   6. Line broiler pan with Alcoa Wrap by shaping piece

of foil over outside of pan then fitting into pan. 7. Grease broiler rack; add steak. 8. Place broiler pan at least 1½ inches below heat. The thicker the steak, the greater the distance. 9. Broil about ½ the approximate time; season; turn. 10. Broil second side remaining time; season; serve at once.

STANDING RIB OR ROLLED RIB

1. Wipe meat with damp cloth to remove any small loose pieces of bone. 2. Rub meat on all sides with the cut side of a clove of garlic. 3. Sprinkle with salt, pepper if desired, but never flour it. It makes little difference if meat is salted before or after cooking because salt only penetrates to about ½ inch depth. 4. Line shallow open roasting pan with Alcoa Wrap by shaping piece of foil around outside of pan, then fitting it into pan. 5. Place meat—fat side up—on rack in pan. 6. Do not flour; add no water; do not baste during roasting period; do not cover. 7. If using a meat thermometer, insert into center of thickest meaty part of roast, being certain bulb does not rest on bone, fat or gristle. 8. Roast according to chart.

BECKER'S ROAST RIB OF BEEF

1. Early in day remove roast from refrigerator so it will be room temperature when placed in oven. If frozen, it must be completely thawed and at room temperature. 2. Six hours before dinner, pre-heat oven to 375° F. for 10 minutes, then place standing rib of beef in Alcoa Wrap lined shallow roast pan; season as desired. 3. Place in oven; roast one hour. 4. Turn off oven. *Do not open oven door.* Allow roast to remain in oven. 5. 45 minutes before serving time, turn oven on to 375° F. 6. Roast meat 30 minutes. *Do not open oven door.* 7. Remove roast from oven. For easier carving, allow roast to stand 15 minutes, then carve.

Good to know: *Oven door must not be opened at any time while meat is inside. To ensure that this will not happen, seal it shut in several places with adhesive tape and attach a sign to the door—DO NOT OPEN.*

STUFFED STEAK ROAST

6 servings

2 pound slice round steak
1 teaspoon salt
¼ teaspoon pepper
2 cups dry bread crumbs
3 tablespoons grated onion

1 teaspoon sage
⅓ cup milk
2 tablespoons ketchup
1 egg, beaten

1. Wipe steak with damp cloth; season with salt, pepper.
2. Combine remaining ingredients.   3. Spread stuffing on steak; roll as jelly roll; tie with string.   4. Place roll on rack in Alcoa Wrap lined open roasting pan; roast 45 minutes at 350° F.

CUBE STEAKS PARMESAN

6 servings

3 eggs
1½ teaspoons salt
½ teaspoon pepper
1½ cups fine, dry bread crumbs

9 tablespoons grated Parmesan cheese
6 cube steaks
½ cup shortening
2 8-ounce cans tomato sauce

1. Combine eggs, salt, pepper; blend thoroughly.   2. Combine bread crumbs, 5 tablespoons Parmesan cheese.   3. Dip steaks in egg mixture, then in crumbs.   4. Sauté steaks in shortening.
5. When steaks are brown on both sides place in Alcoa Wrap lined baking pan; add tomato sauce; top with remaining 4 tablespoons Parmesan cheese.   6. Bake 25 minutes at 325° F.

POT ROAST OF BEEF

6 servings

3–4 pounds beef rump, chuck or shoulder
2 tablespoons shortening
Salt, pepper
½ cup water

6 medium potatoes, peeled, cut lengthwise
6 carrots, cut lengthwise
12 small whole onions

1. Wipe meat with damp cloth to remove any small pieces of loose bone.   2. Melt shortening in fry pan; add meat; brown

well on all sides; sprinkle with salt, pepper. **3.** Fold two pieces of heavy duty Alcoa Wrap together lengthwise, using a double fold. **4.** Place meat in center of foil; add water. **5.** Bring the two torn edges together over meat; fold, then fold again, bringing fold down close to meat. Fold ends over and over, pressing in close to meat. **6.** Place in shallow pan; roast 35–38 minutes per pound at 425° F. **7.** Open foil 45 minutes before roast is done; add potatoes, carrots, onions. **8.** Re-seal package; return to oven; roast 45 minutes longer.

BARBECUED POT ROAST

6 servings

4 pounds blade-bone pot roast,
  1½ inches thick
  Salt, pepper
1 recipe Barbecue Sauce

2 stalks celery, cut in diagonal
  slices
2 carrots, cut in diagonal slices
1 small onion, thinly sliced
½ green pepper, thinly sliced

1. Brown meat slowly 20–30 minutes; season with salt, pepper. **2.** Tear off a 2½ foot length of 18-inch heavy duty Alcoa Wrap. **3.** Place half the Barbecue Sauce in center of foil; place meat on top of sauce; pad sharp bones with pieces of foil. **4.** Cover top of meat with celery, carrot slices, remaining sauce; top with onions, pepper slices. **5.** Bring up torn edges of foil in tight double folds; fold ends up using tight double folds. **6.** Place package on baking sheet. **7.** Bake 1½-2 hours at 400° F.

Good to know: For outdoor cooking—use double-thick sheet of heavy duty Alcoa Wrap; place package on grill over low coals for 1½-2 hours or until tender; turn once during cooking.

Barbecue Sauce

2 tablespoons butter or margarine	2 tablespoons Worcestershire sauce
1 onion, chopped fine	2 tablespoons brown sugar
½ cup chopped celery	1 teaspoon dry mustard
¾ cup water	1 teaspoon salt
1 cup ketchup	¼ teaspoon pepper
2 tablespoons vinegar	
2 tablespoons lemon juice	

1. Melt butter; add onion, celery; cook until tender.   2. Add water, ketchup, vinegar, lemon juice, Worcestershire sauce, brown sugar, dry mustard, salt, pepper; simmer 15 minutes.

DEVON STEAKS

8 servings

3 pounds round steak, cut 1 inch thick	1 cup sliced onion
1 clove garlic, cut in half	1 cup sliced mushrooms
½ cup flour	¼ cup fat
2½ teaspoons salt	½ cup hot water
1 tablespoon paprika	1 cup commercial sour cream

1. Cut meat into 8 serving pieces.   2. Rub each piece with cut side of garlic.   3. Mix flour, salt, paprika together; pound into meat.   4. Brown onions, mushrooms in fat in heavy fry pan; add meat; brown on both sides.   5. Add water; cover; cook over low heat 40-45 minutes or until meat is tender; add more water if necessary.   6. Pour sour cream over meat; recover; simmer 10 minutes longer.

Taste Tip: Extra good with noodles.

PEPPER STEAK

4 servings

2 tablespoons fat	1 cup canned beef bouillon
1 pound round or flank steak	1 cup drained canned tomatoes or 3 tomatoes, quartered
1 teaspoon salt	
⅛ teaspoon pepper	1½ tablespoons cornstarch
2 tablespoons minced onion	2 teaspoons soy sauce
1 clove garlic, minced	¼ cup water
2 green peppers, diced	

1. Melt fat in fry pan.   2. Cut meat into 1 inch strips; sprinkle with salt, pepper.   3. Place meat, onion, garlic in fry pan;

brown.   4. Add peppers, bouillon; cover; cook 30 minutes.
5. Add tomatoes; simmer 5 minutes.   6. Combine cornstarch,
soy sauce, water; add to meat mixture; cook 5 minutes, stirring
constantly.

SWISS STEAK

4 servings

1½ pounds round steak, 1½ inches thick	⅛ teaspoon pepper
2 tablespoons flour	2 tablespoons melted fat
1 teaspoon salt	1 cup hot water
	3 large onions, peeled, sliced

1. Trim excess fat from meat; cut into serving size pieces.
2. Combine flour, salt, pepper.   3. Place meat on breadboard;
sprinkle with half of flour mixture; pound it into meat using
rim of saucer.   4. Turn meat; pound remaining flour into second side.   5. Melt fat in heavy fry pan or Dutch oven.
6. Brown meat on both sides over medium heat.   7. Add
water, onions; cover; cook over low heat 1½-2 hours or until
meat is tender.   8. More water may be added if necessary
during cooking.

Variations: 1. Use 1½ cups canned tomatoes instead of water.
2. Substitute tomato sauce or vegetable juice for all or part of
water.   3. Add 2 tablespoons ketchup, ½ teaspoon prepared
mustard to water.   4. Add 1 green pepper, seeded and cut
into thin rings.

CORNED BEEF

4-5 pounds mild cure brisket of beef	1 bay leaf
3 sliced onions	1 clove garlic, peeled, quartered
3 whole cloves	1 stalk celery
6 peppercorns	1 peeled carrot
	2 sprigs parsley

1. Wipe meat with damp cloth; place in large deep kettle;
cover with cold water.   2. Add remaining ingredients.   3. Cover; bring to a boil; reduce heat to low; simmer 3½-5 hours or
until meat is tender; remove any scum which appears.   4. Remove from stock; slice; serve with horseradish sauce.

MAGGIE'S CORNED BEEF HASH

2 servings

4 slices bacon
1 can corned beef hash, sliced into
  4 pieces

4 slices canned pineapple
Juice from canned pineapple

1. For each serving: Lay 2 strips bacon crisscross. Place 1 slice corned beef hash on top of bacon; add 1 slice pineapple; top with second slice hash, pineapple. Bring bacon up over sides; fasten on top with a toothpick or skewer.   2. Place both servings in Alcoa Wrap lined 8 x 8 x 2-inch pan; pour juice into pan.   3. Bake 25-30 minutes at 350° F.

ROAST BEEF HASH

4 servings

3 tablespoons butter or
  margarine
2 tablespoons minced onion
3 tablespoons flour
1½ cups beef stock or left-over
  gravy
½ teaspoon bottled meat sauce
½ teaspoon dried parsley

¼ teaspoon salt
⅛ teaspoon pepper
3 cups ground cooked beef
2 cups finely diced cooked
  potatoes
2 tablespoons butter or
  margarine
2 cups soft bread crumbs

1. Melt butter; add onion; cook until lightly browned.   2. Blend in flour, stock; bring to boil.   3. Blend in bottled meat sauce, parsley, salt, pepper, meat, potatoes.   4. Spoon into Alcoa Wrap lined 1½-quart casserole.   5. Melt butter; add bread crumbs; toss; place on top of mixture.   6. Bake uncovered 30 minutes at 350° F.

BEEF STEW
4 servings

1¾ pounds beef, 1½ inches thick, chuck or round	1 cup canned tomatoes
⅓ cup flour	½ teaspoon salt
¼ teaspoon pepper	½ teaspoon Worcestershire sauce
½ teaspoon salt	3–4 medium potatoes, pared, quartered
3 tablespoons fat or drippings	12 small white onions, peeled
¼ cup diced onion	12 carrots, peeled, cut into 2-inch pieces
1 minced clove of garlic	
2¾ cups boiling water	1 cup frozen peas (½ package)

1. Trim excess fat from meat; cut into 1½-inch cubes. 2. Combine flour, pepper, salt in paper bag; add meat; shake until pieces are coated. 3. Melt fat in Dutch oven; add meat; brown on all sides. 4. Add diced onion, garlic, boiling water, canned tomatoes, salt, Worcestershire sauce. 5. Cover; reduce heat to low; simmer 2 hours or until meat is tender. 6. Add potatoes, onions, carrots; cook 20 minutes. 7. Add peas; cook 15 minutes longer.

Variations: 1. Potatoes may be mashed and served as a border around stew; sprinkle potatoes with parsley.

2. Drop dumplings may be added when peas are put in to cook.

3. Stew may be served over cooked noodles, in which case omit potatoes.

4. Place stew in Alcoa Wrap lined casserole; top with baking powder biscuits or flaky pastry; bake 20-25 minutes at 450° F.

HEAVENLY HAMBURGER DISH   6 servings

1 pound ground beef	½ cup sliced ripe olives
½ teaspoon onion salt	2 cups very fine, dry noodles
½ teaspoon salt	1 No. 2 can stewing tomatoes
¼ teaspoon pepper	¼ cup water
½ pound American cheese, sliced	Salt, pepper
1 cup chopped celery	

1. Brown beef in fry pan. 2. Season with onion salt, salt, pepper, mix well. 3. Place a layer of cheese over beef. 4. Add celery, ripe olives, dry noodles, stewing tomatoes, water in order given. 5. Sprinkle with salt, pepper. 6. Cover; cook over high heat until steam appears; reduce heat to low; simmer 30 minutes. ··

BEEF ROLI POLI   8 servings

Part One:

3 tablespoons fat	2 eggs, beaten
1 pound beef, ground or	1½ teaspoons salt
2 cups ground left-over beef	⅛ teaspoon pepper
1 cup chopped mushrooms	1 tablespoon minced parsley
1 medium onion, minced	

1. Melt fat in fry pan; add meat, mushrooms, onions; cook until brown, stirring occasionally. 2. Add eggs, salt, pepper, parsley; mix well; set aside to cool.

Part Two:

3 cups sifted all purpose flour	2 tablespoons sugar
4½ teaspoons baking powder	½ cup shortening
1 teaspoon salt	1 cup milk

1. Sift dry ingredients together; cut in shortening; add milk to make a soft dough. 2. Roll on lightly floured board to ½ inch thickness. 3. Spread with meat mixture; roll up as for jelly roll. 4. Cut into 1-inch slices; place in Alcoa Wrap lined shallow baking pan; brush with butter. 5. Bake 20-25 minutes at 425° F. 6. Serve with a sauce made by adding 1 cup leftover cooked vegetables to 3 cups mushroom soup or to equal amount of gravy.

BEEFBURGER PIE WITH CHEESE PUFF   6 servings

Meat Mixture

2 tablespoons shortening	3 tablespoons flour
2 tablespoons chopped onion	1 No. 303 can tomatoes (2 cups)
1 pound ground beef	½ teaspoon Worcestershire sauce
1 teaspoon salt	1 cup diced cooked carrots
⅛ teaspoon pepper	1 cup cooked green beans

1. Melt shortening in fry pan; add onion, meat; brown well.
2. Blend in salt, pepper, flour. 3. Add tomatoes, Worcestershire sauce; cook until slightly thickened, stirring occasionally.
4. Add cooked carrots, green beans. 5. Shape six individual casseroles from squares of heavy duty Alcoa Wrap; pour meat mixture into casserole.

Cheese Puff Ingredients

1 cup sifted all purpose flour	2 tablespoons shortening
1½ teaspoons baking powder	¼ cup grated sharp cheese
½ teaspoon dry mustard	½ cup milk
½ teaspoon salt	

1. Sift together flour, baking powder, mustard, salt. 2. Cut in shortening; add cheese, milk; blend to a soft dough.
3. Spoon topping over meat mixture in casseroles; spread evenly. 4. Bake 25-30 minutes at 350° F.

CREOLE STUFFED PEPPERS   6 servings

6 medium green peppers	1½ cups cooked rice
2 tablespoons butter or margarine	1 teaspoon salt
	½ teaspoon pepper
1 pound ground beef	3 8-ounce cans tomato sauce
½ cup chopped onion	

1. Wash peppers; cut thin slices from stem end of each; remove seeds. (If necessary, cut very thin slice from bottom of peppers so they will rest evenly and not topple over.) Place peppers in boiling salted water; remove from heat; let stand 5 minutes; drain. 2. Melt butter in Dutch oven, add ground

beef, onions; sauté until brown—about 5 minutes.   **3.** Place meat mixture in bowl; add rice, salt, pepper, 1 can of tomato sauce; combine thoroughly.   **4.** Stuff peppers with the mixture; place in Dutch oven.   **5.** Pour remaining cans of tomato sauce into Dutch oven, spooning some on top of each pepper; cover.   **6.** Reduce temperature to low; simmer 20-25 minutes or until peppers are tender; baste occasionally.

STUFFED CABBAGE

8 servings

1 large head cabbage	1 large onion, sliced
1 pound ground chuck	2 8-ounce cans tomato sauce
½ cup raw regular rice	2 No. 2½ cans tomatoes
1 small onion, grated	Juice of 2 lemons
2 eggs, slightly beaten	1 teaspoon salt
1 teaspoon salt	¼ teaspoon pepper
¼ teaspoon pepper	½–1 cup brown sugar

1. Remove 12 large leaves from cabbage; wilt with boiling water.   **2.** Combine meat, rice, grated onion, eggs, salt, pepper.   **3.** Place mound of meat mixture on each cabbage leaf; roll loosely.   **4.** Place remaining cabbage, diced, in bottom of Dutch oven.   **5.** Alternate layers of rolls and sliced onion. **6.** Combine remaining ingredients to make sauce; bring to boil; pour over rolls.   **7.** Bake covered 1 hour; uncovered 2 hours at 375° F.

CHIPPED BEEF IN WINE-MUSHROOM SAUCE

4 servings

(Chafing Dish)

2 tablespoons butter or margarine	½ cup white wine
¼ pound sliced dried beef, shredded	½ cup grated American cheese
2 tablespoons flour	¼ cup mushrooms, sliced
1 can condensed cream of mushroom soup	2 tablespoons chopped parsley
	1 tablespoon Sherry wine

1. Melt butter in blazer pan of chafing dish; add shredded dried beef; sauté 3 minutes.   **2.** Blend in flour.   **3.** Combine mushroom soup, white wine; add to dried beef mixture; cook until mixture is thick. **4.** Place pan over hot water; add cheese, stir until melted. **5.** Add mushrooms, parsley, Sherry. **6.** Serve over baked potatoes or toast.

ROLLED STUFFED MEAT LOAF

8 servings

2 pounds ground beef
½ cup milk
1½ cups dry bread crumbs
2 teaspoons salt

⅛ teaspoon pepper
¼ cup finely chopped onion
2 eggs, beaten

Stuffing

2 tablespoons butter or
   margarine
1 4-ounce can mushrooms,
   drained, chopped

1 tablespoon chopped onion
2 cups soft bread crumbs
½ teaspoon poultry seasoning
¼ teaspoon salt
1 tablespoon chopped parsley

1. Place ground beef in bowl; add milk, dry bread crumbs, salt, pepper, onion, eggs; mix thoroughly. **2.** Place meat mixture on sheet of Alcoa Wrap; shape into an 8 x 14-inch rectangle. **3.** Melt butter; add mushrooms, onion; brown lightly. **4.** Add soft bread crumbs, poultry seasoning, salt, parsley; mix well. **5.** Spread stuffing over meat; roll as for jelly roll; press overlapping edge into roll. **6.** Place rolled meat loaf on double-thick square of Alcoa Wrap. **7.** Bring torn edges together in tight double fold on top of meat; fold ends up using tight double folds. **8.** Place on rack in shallow pan. **9.** Bake 1½ hours at 450° F. **10.** Fifteen minutes before meat is done, open foil; push down away from meat to allow for browning.

SLOPPY JOES

4 servings

¼ cup sliced onions
½ cup diced green pepper
2 tablespoons fat
2 medium tomatoes, peeled
¾ cup diced mushrooms

½ pound ground beef
1 cup tomato juice
¼ teaspoon paprika
¼ teaspoon pepper
¾ teaspoon salt

1. Sauté onions, green pepper in fat in heavy fry pan until lightly browned. 2. Cut tomatoes into eighths; add. 3. Add mushrooms, beef, tomato juice, paprika, pepper, salt. 4. Cover; cook over low heat 15-20 minutes. 5. Thicken juice if desired; serve over split toasted buns.

MEAT LOAF

6 servings

2 eggs, beaten
1½ pounds ground beef
½ pound ground pork
2 cups soft bread crumbs
¾ cup minced onion
¼ cup minced green pepper

2 tablespoons bottled horseradish
1 tablespoon salt
¼ cup milk
¼ cup ketchup
1 teaspoon dry mustard

1. Add eggs to meat; blend lightly with fork. 2. Add remaining ingredients; mix thoroughly but do not stir more than necessary as it tends to toughen loaf. 3. Shape into an oval loaf; place in Alcoa Wrap lined shallow pan. 4. Bake 1 hour at 400° F.

Good to know: Line 9 x 5 x 3-inch loaf pan with foil allowing edges to extend up over top of pan; pack mixture into pan. Bake as above. To remove from pan, drain off liquid; use foil "tabs" to lift meat loaf onto heated platter; then turn right side up on heated platter.

Variations: 1. Spread top with ½ cup ketchup before baking. 2. Place ½ of meat mixture in loaf pan; make three depressions using a tablespoon; place a shelled hard cooked egg in each depression; add remaining meat. 3. Pack mixture into ring mold. To serve, fill center with mashed potatoes.

MEAT BALLS WITH VEGETABLES
6 servings

¾ pound ground beef
¼ pound ground pork
¼ cup raw rice
¼ cup milk
1 egg, beaten
  Salt, pepper
¼ cup finely chopped onion

2 tablespoons chopped parsley
2 cups canned tomatoes
1 teaspoon bottled meat sauce
1 cup hot water
1 cup diced carrots
1 cup diced celery
1 cup cooked peas

1. Combine meats, rice, milk, egg, seasonings, onion, parsley.
2. Form into 18 balls; brown on all sides.   3. Add tomatoes, bottled meat sauce, water, carrots, celery; cover; simmer 25 minutes.   4. Add peas; cook 10 minutes longer.

DELICIOUS MEAT BALLS
12 servings

2 pounds round beef, ground twice
1 pound pork tenderloin, ground
6 eggs, beaten
2 teaspoons salt
¼ teaspoon pepper
¼ cup all purpose flour

½ cup salad oil or shortening
3 tablespoons all purpose flour
2 10½-ounce cans condensed beef consommé, undiluted
1 tablespoon bottled sauce for gravy
1 cup Sherry wine

1. Combine ground beef, pork, beaten eggs, salt, pepper, flour; toss together lightly.   2. Heat salad oil or shortening in large fry pan.   3. Shape meat into small balls, ¾ to 1 inch in diameter.   4. Brown, a few at a time, in hot fat; remove each ball as soon as it is well browned.   5. When browning is complete, add 3 tablespoons flour to fat in fry pan; stir until smooth.   6. Add consommé, bottled sauce; cook, stirring constantly until thickened.   7. Add Sherry; blend; pour over meat balls in serving dish.

Good to know: To freeze, pack meat balls into foil pie pans. Pour gravy over top; set plates level in freezer; wrap in foil after they freeze. To serve, slip meat balls and gravy block from foil pan into chafing dish or fry pan. Cover; heat over low heat until meat balls are hot.

HAMBURGER PATTIES
With Roquefort Spread

4 servings

1 pound ground beef
2 tablespoons fat
½ cup hot water
¼ cup Roquefort cheese, crumbled

3 tablespoons soft butter or margarine
1 tablespoon prepared mustard
Few drops Worcestershire sauce
Salt, pepper

1. Shape meat into eight thin patties; brown lightly on both sides in hot fat in heavy fry pan. 2. Add water; cover; cook over low heat 10 minutes. 3. Combine cheese, butter, mustard, Worcestershire sauce, salt, pepper. 4. Spread over patties; cover; cook 5 minutes longer.

DOUBLE DECKER HAMBURGERS

4 servings

1½ pounds ground round steak
¾ cup cold water
1 teaspoon salt
½ teaspoon pepper
¼ cup ketchup

4 large stuffed olives, sliced
3 tablespoons soft butter or margarine
1 medium onion, sliced, broken into rings

1. Combine meat, water, salt, pepper; shape into 8 flat patties; brown in fry pan. 2. Cut 4 six-inch circles or squares of double-thick Alcoa Wrap. 3. Place one browned patty in center of each piece of foil. 4. Spread patties with ketchup, olive slices. 5. Top with remaining 4 patties. 6. Spread with butter; insert a toothpick through the center of each double patty. Hang onion rings over toothpicks. 7. Bring Alcoa Wrap up around bottom patty in cup shape. Place cups in shallow pan. 8. Bake 40-45 minutes at 375° F.

BEEF PATTIES WITH ONION SAUCE   *4 servings*

1 pound ground beef	2 cups boiling water
1 teaspoon salt	1 teaspoon bottled thick
¼ teaspoon pepper	condiment sauce
¼ cup butter or margarine	¼ cup cold water
3 cups sliced, peeled onions	2 tablespoons cornstarch

1. Combine meat, salt, pepper; shape into 4 patties.   2. Pan-broil patties on both sides until brown; remove from pan.
3. Melt butter; add onions; cook until deep brown.   4. Add boiling water, condiment sauce; stir.   5. Combine cold water, cornstarch; stir into sauce; cook, stirring constantly until clear and thickened; add salt, pepper to taste.   6. Place patties in sauce; cover; reduce heat to simmer; cook 5 minutes.

WIENER CROWN ROAST WITH HOT POTATO SALAD

12 servings

1. Completely cover a 10½-inch dinner plate or large round platter with Alcoa Wrap.   2. Run a string through 24 wieners 1 inch from top.   3. Tie together forming a circle; stand on foil-covered platter.   4. Fill center with Hot Potato Salad.
5. Bake 25-30 minutes at 375° F.

Hot Potato Salad

½ pound sliced bacon, diced	¾ cup water
¾ cup chopped onion	½ cup vinegar
2 tablespoons flour	8 medium potatoes, cooked, diced
1 tablespoon salt	

1. Fry bacon, onions until bacon is crisp, onions tender.
2. Combine flour, salt, water, vinegar; add to bacon-onion mixture; stir until mixture boils and is thick, smooth.   3. Add potatoes; toss gently.   4. Put into center of Wiener Crown Roast.

BOBOTIE
(Meat Custard)   6 servings

1 pound ground beef	1 slice white bread
2 medium onions, sliced	2 cups milk
1 teaspoon curry powder	2 eggs
1 teaspoon salt	½ teaspoon salt
1 tablespoon sugar	⅛ teaspoon pepper
1 tablespoon vinegar	2 tablespoons butter

1. Brown beef, onion in heavy fry pan; add curry powder, salt, sugar, vinegar; mix well. 2. Soak bread in milk; drain off milk; set aside. 3. Combine bread, one egg; beat well; add to meat mixture; mix. 4. Place meat mixture into lightly greased Alcoa Wrap lined casserole. 5. Add enough milk to milk drained from bread to make ¾ cup; add remaining one egg, salt, pepper; beat well; pour over meat mixture; dot with butter. 6. Place in pan of warm water. 7. Bake 35-40 minutes at 350° F.

HUNGARIAN GOULASH WITH NOODLES   8 servings

1 pound beef, cut into cubes	3 tablespoons Worchestershire sauce
2 medium onions, minced	¾ teaspoon cider vinegar
¼ teaspoon dry mustard	6 tablespoons ketchup
1¼ teaspoons paprika	1½ cups water
2 tablespoons brown sugar	3 tablespoons flour
1¼ teaspoons salt	1 6-ounce package noodles

1. Brown meat on all sides in fry pan or Dutch oven; add onion. 2. Combine mustard, paprika, brown sugar, salt. 3. Combine Worcestershire sauce, vinegar, ketchup; add to mustard mixture; add to meat; add 1 cup of the water; stir; cover. 4. Cook over low heat 2½ hours or until meat is very tender. Add more water if needed. 5. Blend flour with remaining ½ cup water; add to meat mixture; stir until thickened. 6. Boil noodles in salted water until tender; drain. 7. Serve meat mixture over noodles.

BEEF STROGANOFF WITH RICE

6 servings

3 tablespoons butter or margarine
½ pound fresh mushrooms or 2 4-ounce cans, sliced
1 large onion, cut into ¼-inch slices
1½–2 pounds flank or round steak

1 tablespoon bottled horseradish
½ cup water
1 teaspoon thick meat sauce
1¼ teaspoons salt
⅛ teaspoon pepper
1 cup commercial sour cream
4 cups cooked rice

1. Melt butter in fry pan; sauté mushrooms, onion 5 minutes; remove from fat. 2. Trim fat from meat; mince; add to butter in pan. 3. Slice meat crosswise into 1-inch strips; roll in flour; brown on both sides. 4. Place onions, mushrooms on top of meat. 5. Combine horseradish, water, meat sauce, salt, pepper; pour over meat. 6. Cover; cook over low heat 1½-2 hours or until meat is tender; add more water as needed. 7. Add sour cream just before serving. 8. Serve over cooked rice; garnish with spiced fruit.

Good to know: To freeze or store for later use, line 8 x 8 x 2-inch pan with Alcoa Wrap; pour meat into pan; cover with foil. Wrap rice in Alcoa Wrap. When ready for use place both in oven; bake 30 minutes at 425° F.

GREEN PEPPER STEAK

4 servings

À *La Chinese*

1 tablespoon soy sauce
1 clove garlic
¼ cup salad oil
1 pound round steak, cut into 1-inch cubes
1 green pepper, cut into 1-inch cubes

1 large onion, coarsely chopped
½ cup diced celery
1 teaspoon cornstarch
¼ cup water
2 tomatoes, cut into eighths

1. Mix soy sauce, garlic, salad oil together; pour over steak; let stand one hour. 2. Pour into fry pan; allow meat to brown thoroughly on all sides. 3. Add pepper, onion, celery; cover; cook 5-10 minutes over low heat or until vegetables are

tender.   **4.** Stir in cornstarch dissolved in water; stir until thickened; add tomatoes; cover; cook 5-10 minutes longer or until meat is tender; serve over boiled rice.

SAUERBRATEN

6 servings

3 pounds beef, round or shoulder
½ cup vinegar
½ cup water
1 small onion, thinly sliced
2 bay leaves

3 whole cloves
2 teaspoons salt
⅛ teaspoon pepper
4 tablespoons fat
1 cup water

1. Place meat in bowl.   **2.** Combine vinegar, ½ cup water, onion, bay leaves, cloves, salt, pepper; blend.   **3.** Pour over meat; let stand 18-24 hours.   **4.** Melt fat in fry pan or Dutch oven.   **5.** Add meat; brown thoroughly on both sides.   **6.** Add 1 cup water to liquid in which meat was soaked; pour over meat.   **7.** Cover; simmer over low heat 3 hours or until meat is tender.   **8.** Remove meat; make gravy from juices in pan.

Best Ways with Lamb

Often neglected, lamb—properly cooked, deliciously seasoned—deserves to come to American tables more often. Whether your family prefers lamb just-barely rare or well done, these recipes will make lamb a welcome treat for everybody at company meals.

BUYING GUIDE FOR LAMB

Characteristics	Cut	Weight	Number of servings
Color, dull pink; lean, firm, fine grained, tender, well marbled with fat; fat firm, white, thin, weblike; bones soft, red.	Chops, thick	1 lb.	2
	Leg-Roast	6 lbs.	10–12
	Shoulder-Roast	4 lbs.	7–8
	Breast	1 lb.	2
	Shanks	1 lb.	1–2

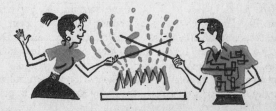

TEMPERATURE-TIME CHART FOR ROAST LAMB
325° F. Oven Temperature

Cut	Weight Pounds	Approximate Minutes Per Pound	Meat Thermometer Reading When Roast Is Done
Leg			
Unboned	4–6	35–40	182° F.
	6–7	30–35	182° F.
Boned, Rolled	3–5	45	182° F.
	5–6	40–45	182° F.
Loin	2½–3	50	182° F.
Cushion			
Shoulder, Stuffed	3–4	40–45	
Rolled Shoulder	3½–5	40–45	182° F.
Sirloin Half of Leg	2–3	60	
Crown of Lamb (no stuffing)	3–4	40–45	182° F.

BROILING TIME TABLE FOR LAMB CHOPS AND PATTIES
Turn after broiling ½ the time

Cut	Thickness	Approximate Total Time
Patties from Ground Lamb	¾ inch	14–15 minutes
Rib or Loin Chops	¾–1 inch	14–16 minutes
Double Chops	1½ inches	20–25 minutes
	2 inches	36–40 minutes

BROILING TIME TABLE FOR LAMB CHOPS
AND PATTIES—CONT.
Turn after broiling ½ the time

Cut	Thickness	Approximate Total Time
English Chops	1½ inches 2 inches	20–25 minutes 36–40 minutes
Shoulder Chops	¾–1 inch 1½ inches	14–16 minutes 20–25 minutes

ROAST LAMB

1. Wipe meat with damp cloth; do not remove the "fell," a thin papery skin from a leg of lamb.   2. Rub with cut side of a clove of garlic.   3. Sprinkle with salt, pepper.   4. Line shallow open roasting pan with Alcoa Wrap by shaping piece of foil over outside of pan, then fitting it into pan.   5. Place meat fat side up on rack in pan.   6. If using a meat thermometer, insert it into thickest part, being sure bulb does not rest on bone, fat or gristle.   7. Do not flour; add no water; do not baste during roasting period; do not cover.   8. Roast according to chart.

CROWN ROAST OF LAMB

1. Have butcher shape two or more rib sections into a "crown."
2. Remove any ground trimmings butcher may have placed in

center; use these for patties or meat loaf.   3. Cover ends of bones with cubes of bread, salt pork, or pieces of foil; remove these before serving.   4. Sprinkle with salt, pepper.   5. Line shallow open roasting pan with Alcoa Wrap by shaping piece of foil over outside of pan, then fitting it into pan.   6. Place meat fat side up on rack in pan.   7. Roast according to chart. 8. To serve: fill center with mashed potatoes, buttered peas, buttered peas and carrots, buttered cauliflower or buttered peas and mushrooms.   9. Allow 2-3 ribs per person.

POT ROAST OF LAMB   8 servings

4 pounds lamb shoulder boned,   Clove of garlic
   rolled, tied   Salt, pepper

1. Rub meat with cut side of clove of garlic.   2. Heat Dutch oven over medium high heat until piece of white paper placed in bottom turns golden brown.   3. Add meat; brown thoroughly on all sides.   4. Sprinkle with salt, pepper.   5. Cover; cook over low heat 2-2½ hours or until meat is tender. 6. Potatoes, carrots may be added during last hour of cooking. *Good to know: May also be prepared by the Alcoa Wrap method of oven pot roasting.*

BROILED LAMB CHOPS

1. Turn oven regulator to "broil" or to the highest degree of setting. If no regulator, turn heat on full.   2. Pre-heat broiler 10 minutes or as directed by range manufacturer.   3. Trim surplus fat from meat.   4. Slash fat edge of meat at 2-inch intervals to prevent curling.   5. Line broiler pan with Alcoa Wrap by shaping piece of foil over outside of pan then fitting into pan.   6. Grease broiler rack; add chops.   7. Place broiler pan at least 1½ inches below heat. The thicker the chops, the greater the distance.   8. Broil about ½ the approximate time shown on chart; season; turn.   9. Broil second side remaining time; season; serve at once.

ORANGE GLAZED LAMB SHOULDER CHOPS   6 servings

½ cup flour
½ teaspoon salt
¼ teaspoon pepper
6 large shoulder chops, cut ¾ inch thick
2 tablespoons shortening

1½ cups orange juice
2 tablespoons grated orange rind
¼ cup brown sugar, firmly packed
½ teaspoon nutmeg
1 cup peeled, sectioned oranges (about 2 oranges)

1. Combine flour, salt, pepper. 2. Dip chops in flour mixture.
3. Melt shortening in fry pan; brown chops on both sides.
4. Place in Alcoa Wrap lined pan. 5. Mix orange juice, grated orange rind, brown sugar, nutmeg together; pour over chops; cover with foil. 6. Bake 1 hour at 350° F. 7. Baste chops several times with orange juice mixture. 8. Add orange sections; return to oven for 10 minutes or until orange sections are heated through.

MAGGIE'S LAMB CHOPS   4 servings

4 loin lamb chops, 1 inch thick
Salt, pepper
4 slices American cheese

4 slices Bermuda onion
8 tablespoons commercial sour cream

1. Wrap tail end of each chop around thick part to form a flat round patty; fasten with toothpicks. 2. Sprinkle with salt, pepper. 3. Place chops in Alcoa Wrap lined shallow baking pan. 4. Place one slice cheese, one slice onion on each chop.
5. Put 2 tablespoons sour cream on each chop. 6. Add no water; do not cover. 7. Bake 1 hour at 375° F.

FRY PAN KEBABS   4 servings

6 tablespoons wine vinegar
6 tablespoons water
1 pound leg of lamb, cut in 1-inch cubes
2 green peppers

2 tomatoes, cut in eighths
¼ cup butter or margarine
½ teaspoon salt
¼ teaspoon pepper

1. Combine vinegar, water; pour over lamb; cover; refrigerate 45-60 minutes; turn meat once or twice. 2. Wash peppers;

cut thin slice from stem end; remove seeds; pour boiling water over peppers; let stand 5 minutes; drain; cut into 24 1-inch squares. 3. Melt butter in fry pan; brown marinated lamb thoroughly on all sides—about 15 minutes; remove from pan; cool slightly. 4. Place meat, green pepper, tomato alternately on 8 short skewers; sprinkle with salt, pepper. 5. Place kebabs in fry pan; cover. 6. Cook 15 minutes, turning occasionally.

Good to know: 1 pound sirloin steak may be substituted for lamb.

IRISH STEW
8 servings

3 pounds lamb cut into small pieces
Water to cover
4 allspice berries
2 tablespoons minced parsley
1 cup sliced carrots

¾ cup diced turnips
3 cups cubed potatoes
½ cup sliced onion
Salt
Pepper

1. Place meat in Dutch oven; add water to cover; add allspice berries, parsley; cover; simmer 2 hours. 2. Add vegetables, salt, pepper. 3. Cover; cook 35-45 minutes longer. 4. Thicken gravy if desired.

Good to know: Drop dumplings may be added 15 minutes before cooking is completed.

LAMB AND RED BEAN GOULASH
4 servings

2 teaspoons salt
½ teaspoon pepper
4 tablespoons flour
2 pounds lamb shank, cubed
2 tablespoons fat
1 clove garlic, minced

¼ cup diced onion
2½ cups canned tomatoes
1 green pepper, diced
1 teaspoon salt
2 cans red kidney beans

1. Combine salt, pepper, flour; add meat; toss until coated. 2. Melt fat in Dutch oven; add meat; brown on all sides. 3. Add garlic, onion, tomatoes, green pepper, salt. 4. Cover; simmer 1½ hours. 5. Drain kidney beans; add; cook 5 minutes longer.

LAMB CURRY

6 servings

1¼ cups washed uncooked rice
1 cup sliced, peeled onions
2¼ cups diced celery
4 tablespoons fat
1 tablespoon flour

4½ cups cubed, cooked lamb
1½–2 teaspoons curry powder
1¼ cups lamb gravy
½ cup hot water
Salt

1. Cook rice in boiling salted water until tender; rinse; drain.
2. Sauté onions, celery in fat in heavy fry pan until tender.
3. Stir in flour; add lamb, curry powder, gravy, water, salt. 4. Cover; cook over low heat 10-15 minutes. 5. Serve over the rice or use rice as border around meat mixture.

LAMB SUPREME

6 servings

2 pounds boneless lamb shoulder
2 tablespoons fat
Water to cover
½ teaspoon salt
½ teaspoon dill seeds

½ cup sliced fresh mushrooms
1 cup commercial sour cream
½ teaspoon vinegar
3 tablespoons flour

1. Cut lamb into cubes; brown in hot fat in heavy fry pan.
2. Add water to cover, salt, dill seeds; cover. 3. Simmer over low heat 1½ hours or until meat is tender. 4. Remove meat; add mushrooms, cream, vinegar to liquid in pan; cook 15 minutes. 5. Add flour to liquid; stir; add meat; heat through.

ROAST LEG OF LAMB À LA CRIOLIA
8 servings

4–5 pound leg of lamb
  1 clove garlic, peeled, chopped
¼ teaspoon ground pepper

1 teaspoon oregano
1½ tablespoons olive oil
4–5 teaspoons salt

1. Remove skin, excess fat from lamb; wipe meat with damp cloth. 2. Place meat, fat side up, on rack in Alcoa Wrap lined shallow roasting pan. 3. Carefully make superficial criss-cross gashes on top of roast. 4. Place chopped garlic, pepper, oregano in small bowl; crush together with wooden spoon. 5. Add olive oil, salt; blend well. 6. Rub seasoning into meat; cover with foil; place in refrigerator overnight. 7. Remove meat from refrigerator ½ hour before cooking. 8. Drain off any liquid that may have seeped from meat; pour over meat. 9. Roast uncovered at 325° F. allowing 35-40 minutes per pound, or until meat thermometer registers 182° F. 10. Use pan drippings to make gravy.

LAMCHI AND BOONCHI
4 servings

  Juice of 2 large lemons
¼ cup olive oil
  2 tablespoons grated onion
  1 tablespoon chili powder
  2 teaspoons curry powder
  2 teaspoons ground ginger
  2 teaspoons turmeric
  1 clove garlic, mashed to pulp
  1 tablespoon salt

2 pounds lamb, cut into 1½-inch cubes
8 slices bacon, cut in half
1 large green pepper, cut in 1x1-inch pieces
4 medium onions, cut in quarters
6 slices pineapple, cut in half
4 medium tomatoes, cut in quarters

1. Combine lemon juice, olive oil, grated onion, chili powder, curry powder, ginger, turmeric, garlic, salt; blend thoroughly. 2. Add lamb cubes; cover with Alcoa Wrap; marinate overnight. 3. Wrap half slices bacon around green pepper pieces. 4. Place marinated meat onto four 12-14-inch skewers, alternating with pieces of onion, bacon-wrapped green pepper, half pineapple slices, tomato quarters. 5. Place lamchi on rack of foil-lined broiler pan; place 3 inches below heat; broil

15-20 minutes, turning frequently to brown on all sides.
6. Serve with Sauce.

Sauce:

6 teaspoons prepared mustard
2 tablespoons peanut butter
1 teaspoon turmeric
2 tablespoons soy sauce

2 tablespoons Worcestershire
sauce
Few drops Tabasco sauce

1. Combine mustard, peanut butter; make paste. 2. Add
turmeric, soy sauce, Worcestershire sauce, Tabasco sauce;
blend thoroughly. 3. Serve with Lamchi.
*Good to know: Build a dinner around this with Fluffy Rice, But-
tered Green Beans, Bread Sticks, Lemon Chiffon Pie, Coffee.*

GLAZES FOR LAMB

Curry-Pineapple Glaze
1 teaspoon curry powder

1 flat can crushed pineapple
(1 cup)

Combine all ingredients; blend well; spoon over lamb.

Herb-Butter Glaze
6 tablespoons butter or
margarine, softened
½ teaspoon garlic salt

1½ teaspoons salt
¼ teaspoon coarse-ground pepper
1 tablespoon lemon juice

Combine all ingredients; blend well; spoon over lamb.

Honey-Mustard Glaze
¼ cup prepared mustard
¼ cup honey

½ teaspoon salt
⅛ teaspoon pepper

Combine all ingredients; blend well; spoon over lamb.

Orange Marmalade Glaze
½ cup orange marmalade
⅓ cup lemon juice

1 teaspoon rosemary leaves
¼ cup finely chopped parsley

Combine all ingredients; blend well; spoon over lamb.

Best Ways with Pork

Smoked or fresh, pork is an ever-welcome treat, a hearty and delicious meat around which to center many a meal. Try these old favorites and new ways with delicious roasts, hams, chops, spareribs—you'll want to try one for dinner this very night!

BUYING GUIDE FOR PORK

	Characteristics	Cut	Weight	Number of servings
Pork, fresh	Color, light greyish pink; lean, firm, fine grained; well marbled with fat; fat white, firm, free from fibers; bones slightly pink.	Spareribs Loin Roast Fresh Ham Chops, thick Sausages	1½ lbs. 4 lbs. 12 lbs. 1 lb. 1 lb.	2 7–8 20–24 2 8–16 sausages
Pork, smoked	Color, rich pink; lean, fine grained, well marbled with fat; a good layer of fat on outside; bone small.	Shoulder Picnic Ham Whole Ham Ham Slice Bacon	6 lbs. 12 lbs. 1 lb. 1 lb.	9–10 20–24 2–3 20–24 slices

TEMPERATURE-TIME CHART FOR ROAST FRESH PORK
325° F. Oven Temperature

Cut	Weight Pounds	Approximate Minutes Per Pound	Meat Thermometer Reading When Roast Is Done
Boston Butt	3–6	50–55	185° F.
Fresh Ham	3–6	45–50	185° F.
	6–8	40–45	185° F.
Loin	3–6	35–40	185° F.
	6–8	35–38	
Picnic Shoulder	3–6	40	185° F.
	6–8	35	185° F.
Crown of Pork (no filling)	6–7	40–45	185° F.

ROAST FRESH PORK

1. Wipe meat with damp cloth. 2. Rub with cut side of clove of garlic. 3. Sprinkle with salt, pepper. 4. Line shallow open roasting pan with Alcoa Wrap. 5. Place roast, fat side up, on rack in pan. 6. If using meat thermometer, insert into thickest part; make sure it does not rest on bone, fat, gristle. 7. Do not flour; add no water; do not baste; do not cover. 8. Roast according to chart.

CROWN ROAST OF PORK

1. Have butcher shape two or more sections into "crown." 2. Cover ends of bones with cubes of bread, salt pork, or pieces of foil; remove these before serving. 3. Sprinkle with salt, pepper. 4. Line shallow open roasting pan with Alcoa

Wrap by shaping piece of foil over outside of pan, then fitting it into pan.   5. Place on rack in pan.   6. Fill center with bread stuffing if desired.   7. Roast uncovered according to chart.   8. To serve; if bread stuffing is not used, fill center with mashed potatoes, mashed sweet potatoes or buttered vegetables.   9. Allow 2-3 ribs per person.

PORK CHOPS ALEXANDER
6 servings

1 cup dried apricots	¼ teaspoon thyme
2 cups warm water	6 loin pork chops, ¾ inch thick
½ cup flour	3 tablespoons fat
½ teaspoon salt	¼ cup maple syrup
¼ teaspoon pepper	

1. Cook apricots in water until tender; drain.   2. Combine flour, salt, pepper, thyme; dust over both sides of chops.   3. Brown chops on both sides in hot fat in heavy fry pan.   4. Combine apricots, maple syrup; pour over chops.   5. Cover; cook 1 hour over low heat until chops are tender.

BAKED STUFFED PORK CHOPS
4 servings

1 cup diced apples	2 tablespoons butter or
¼ cup seedless raisins	margarine
¾ cup soft bread crumbs	3 tablespoons hot water
¾ teaspoon salt	4 rib chops, 1½ inches thick
1½ tablespoons sugar	with pocket
1 tablespoon minced onion	Salt, pepper
	½ cup water

1. Mix together apples, raisins, bread crumbs, salt, sugar.   2. Sauté onion in butter 5 minutes; add to bread mixture.   3. Add hot water; blend.   4. Sprinkle salt, pepper on inside of pockets.   5. Fill pockets with stuffing; fasten with toothpicks or poultry pins.   6. Brown chops well on both sides.   7. Place in Alcoa Wrap lined casserole or 8 x 8 x 2-inch pan.   8. Add water to drippings in fry pan; stir to loosen brown sediment; pour around chops.   9. Cover casserole or use Alcoa Wrap on pan.   10. Bake 1 hour at 375° F.; uncover last 15 minutes.

COUNTY KERRY PORK CHOPS
4 servings

4 pork chops, ½ inch thick
2 tablespoons fat
¼ cup diced onion
1 cup condensed cream of
  celery soup
½ cup milk

3 medium potatoes, peeled,
  sliced
1 pound cabbage, shredded
¼ cup flour
1½ teaspoons salt
⅛ teaspoon pepper

1. Brown chops in hot fat in heavy fry pan; remove. 2. Add onion, soup, milk to fat in pan; blend; set aside. 3. Starting with potatoes, put alternate layers of potatoes, cabbage, into a 2-quart Alcoa Wrap lined casserole or 8 x 8 x 2-inch pan; sprinkle each layer with flour, salt, pepper; pour soup sauce over each layer. 4. Place chops on top; cover casserole or use Alcoa Wrap to cover pan. 5. Bake 1¼ hours at 350° F.

PORK CHOPS WITH ORANGE SAUCE
6 servings

6 loin pork chops, ¾ inch thick
1 tablespoon butter or
  margarine
1 medium onion, diced
1 tablespoon flour
2 bouillon cubes
1 cup hot water

½ teaspoon minced parsley
1 drop oil of peppermint
1 teaspoon dry mustard
2 tablespoons lemon juice
½ cup orange juice
1 teaspoon salt
⅛ teaspoon pepper

1. Heat aluminum fry pan over medium high heat until a piece of white paper placed in bottom turns golden brown. 2. Add chops; brown on both sides; remove from pan. 3. Melt butter; add onion; sauté 5 minutes. 4. Stir in flour; dissolve bouillon cubes in hot water; add slowly, stirring constantly; cook 5 minutes. 5. Add parsley, peppermint oil, mustard, lemon and orange juice, salt, pepper; blend thoroughly. 6. Place chops in liquid; cover; cook over low heat 25-35 minutes or until meat is tender.

SWEET-SOUR PORK

4 servings

1½ pounds leftover pork, sliced
2 tablespoons butter or
  margarine
½ cup water
⅓ cup vinegar
¼ cup brown sugar

2 tablespoons cornstarch
½ teaspoon salt
1 No. 2 can pineapple chunks
1 medium green pepper, thinly
  sliced
2 medium onions, thinly sliced

1. Brown meat lightly in melted fat. 2. Combine water, vinegar, sugar, cornstarch, salt, 1 cup pineapple juice drained from chunks. 3. Cook in saucepan until clear, slightly thickened. 4. Pour sauce over meat; cover; cook 30 minutes. 5. Add pineapple chunks, green pepper, onion; cook 2 minutes longer. 6. Serve with fried rice.

SWEET 'N' SOUR SAUSAGE

4–6 servings

1 pound loose sausage meat
1 cup pineapple tidbits, drained
1 cup green pepper strips, about 2
  inches long
1 cup thinly sliced onion
½ cup vinegar

⅔ cup syrup from pineapple tidbits
½ cup brown sugar
2 teaspoons soy sauce
2 small tomatoes, cut in wedges
2 tablespoons cornstarch
2 tablespoons cold water

1. Shape sausage into 1-inch balls; place in cold fry pan.
2. Brown meat balls on all sides; spoon off excess grease.
3. Add pineapple, green pepper, onion; brown lightly. 4. Combine vinegar, syrup, brown sugar, soy sauce; pour over meat

mixture; add tomatoes; cover. **5.** Reduce heat to low. Cook 20-30 minutes or until no trace of pink remains in center of meat balls. **6.** Dissolve cornstarch in water; add to sauce; cook until thickened—about 5 minutes. **7.** Serve over rice.

SPARERIBS AND SAUERKRAUT

4 servings

3 pounds spareribs	2 pounds sauerkraut
¼ teaspoon salt	1 large onion, sliced
⅛ teaspoon pepper	½ cup water

1. Cut ribs into serving size pieces; brown on both sides in fry pan; season with salt, pepper. **2.** Put sauerkraut into large casserole. **3.** Add onion slices, ribs. **4.** Pour water in fry pan; stir to loosen sediment; pour over ribs; cover. **5.** Bake 1½ hours at 350° F.

DRESSED-UP SPARERIBS

4 servings

2 pounds spareribs	1 tablespoon water
Salt, pepper	½ teaspoon salt
1½ cups soft bread crumbs	⅛ teaspoon pepper
1 medium onion, minced	2 tablespoons fat
2 tablespoons minced parsley	1 cup hot water
1 tablespoon melted butter or margarine	

1. Rub ribs with salt, pepper. **2.** Combine bread crumbs, onion, parsley, butter, water, salt, pepper; mix. **3.** Spread over half of ribs; place other half on top; fasten together with skewers or sew together with cord. **4.** Place on rack in Alcoa Wrap lined roasting pan. **5.** Add hot water; cover.

6. Roast 1½ hours at 350° F., remove cover; roast 30 minutes longer or until meat is browned.

CINNAMON-APPLE ROLL-UPS
6 servings

Cinnamon Apples

1½ cups water
¾ cup sugar

½ cup cinnamon candies (2 2-ounce jars)
6 cooking apples, cored, peeled

1. Combine water, sugar, cinnamon candies in saucepan; blend; bring to boil. 2. Add apples when candies have melted; cook over low heat, turning frequently, until tender. 3. Remove apples from hot liquid; save liquid.

Filling
2 pounds pork sausage links

1. Pan fry sausages until well done and browned.

Pancakes

2 cups prepared pancake mix
½ teaspoon dry mustard
¼ teaspoon ground cloves

1 egg
2 cups milk
2 tablespoons melted shortening

1. Combine pancake mix, dry mustard, cloves. 2. Add egg, milk, shortening; stir only to blend. 3. Bake on hot griddle; turn only once. 4. Place two cooked sausages across each pancake; roll up. 5. Arrange on platter or serving plates with apples. 6. Serve with hot liquid from apples.

TEMPERATURE-TIME CHART FOR BAKING SMOKED HAMS

325° F. Oven Temperature

Weight of Ham	Approximate Minutes Per Pound	Meat Thermometer Reading When Ham Is Done
UNCOOKED		
Bone In		
5– 8 pounds half ham (butt or shank)	26–28	160° F.
8–10 pounds whole ham	25–26	160° F.
10–12 pounds whole ham	23–24	160° F.
12–15 pounds whole ham	21–22	160° F.
15–18 pounds whole ham	20	160° F.
Picnic Shoulder	30–35	170° F.
Bone Out		
Half Ham	28	160° F.
Whole Ham	23	160° F.
Boneless Shank End	32–34	160° F.
COOKED, ready to eat Whole or Half	15–20	

BAKED HAM

If packer's wrapper or label contains directions for cooking, they should be followed. If you do not have such directions, use these:

1. Remove outside wrapper but do not remove rind. 2. Line shallow open roasting pan with Alcoa Wrap by shaping piece of foil over outside of pan, then fitting it into pan. 3. Place meat fat side up on rack in pan. 4. If using a meat thermometer, insert through paper into thickest part of meat, being sure bulb does not touch bone, gristle or fat. 5. Add no

water; do not baste during roasting period; do not cover. **6.** Bake according to chart. **7.** About 45 minutes before baking time is completed, remove ham from oven. **8.** Remove rind with sharp knife or kitchen scissors. **9.** Cut or score fat surface into squares or diamonds. **10.** Stick whole cloves in center of each. **11.** Glaze according to directions: To Glaze Baked Ham.

Good to know: Uncooked Smoked Hams . . . 1. Require no soaking or parboiling . . . 2. Cook in much less time . . . 3. Must be kept in refrigerator before and after cooking . . . 4. Are available, whole with bone in. These are known as "regular" and have the skin left on. The wrapper is usually marked "Cook Before Eating" . . . 5. Are available, whole with bone out. These have been boned, rolled and tied or put into a transparent casing which is removed after baking.

Good to know: Cooked Smoked Hams . . . 1. Require no soaking or parboiling . . . 2. Need only to be heated for serving or may be served "as is" . . . 3. Are available, whole with bone in. These are labeled "Ready to Eat, Cooked or Fully Cooked" . . . 4. Are available, whole with bone out. These have been boned, rolled, tied or pressed and are labeled "Ready to Eat" . . . 5. Canned Hams are also of the "Ready to Eat" variety.

SAVORY BAKED HAM

1. Place ham in center of sheet of heavy duty Alcoa Wrap; wrap completely, using tight double folds over top and on ends. **2.** Place wrapped ham on rack in shallow pan. **3.** To bake, use minutes per pound directions on label or those in chart for Smoked Hams using a 425° F. oven. **4.** One half hour before ham is done, remove from oven, reduce oven temperature to 325° F. **5.** Open foil; push down around ham; score fat surface into diamonds; top with desired glaze; return ham to oven for remaining ½ hour.

BAKED HAM FLAMBÉ

1 8–10 pound ham
1 cup brown sugar, firmly packed
2 teaspoons dry mustard
1 teaspoon ground ginger
1 cup Sherry wine

1 tablespoon cornstarch
8 orange slices
8 small lemon slices
4 maraschino cherries, cut in half
¼ cup brandy

1. Place ham in center of sheet of heavy duty Alcoa Wrap. 2. Combine brown sugar, dry mustard, ginger; add Sherry; blend thoroughly. 3. Pour ½ cup wine mixture over ham; wrap ham completely in foil using double folds over top and on ends. 4. Place wrapped ham on rack in shallow pan. 5. Bake ham according to directions given in Savory Baked Ham recipe. 6. While ham is baking, finish preparation of Sherry Glaze and citrus flowers: In a saucepan, mix a little of remaining wine mixture with cornstarch to make smooth paste; add rest of wine mixture; blend thoroughly. 7. Bring mixture to a boil over medium heat; simmer gently until thick (about 5 minutes), stirring constantly. 8. Cut triangular notches around edges of orange, lemon slices; place in Sherry Glaze along with cherry halves. 9. One-half hour before ham is done, remove from oven; reduce oven temperature to 325° F. 10. Open foil; push down around ham; score fat surface into diamonds. 11. Remove fruit from Sherry Glaze; pour glaze over ham; return ham to oven; continue baking ½ hour, basting frequently. 12. To serve: Transfer ham to foil-lined platter; arrange citrus flowers on top of ham (orange slice, lemon slice, cherry half); heat brandy in small pan. Place garnished ham on dining table; ignite brandy in pan; pour flaming brandy over ham.

BURGUNDY GLAZED HAM

1 8–10 pound ham	¾ cup Burgundy wine
1 can (15 oz.) pitted dark sweet cherries	2 tablespoons wine vinegar
¾ cup liquid from cherries	¼ cup light corn syrup
2 tablespoons cornstarch	2 tablespoons lemon juice

1. Bake ham according to directions given in Savory Baked Ham in recipe. 2. To glaze: Drain cherries, reserving ¾ cup liquid. 3. In saucepan, mix a little cherry liquid with cornstarch to make smooth paste; add remaining cherry liquid, Burgundy, vinegar, corn syrup; blend thoroughly. 4. Bring mixture to a boil over medium heat; add lemon juice; simmer gently until thick (about 5 minutes), stirring constantly. 5. One half hour before ham is done, remove from oven; reduce oven temperature to 325° F. 6. Open foil; push down around ham; score fat surface into diamonds; pour ½ cup Burgundy glaze over ham; return ham to oven; continue baking ½ hour, basting frequently. 7. Add cherries to remaining Burgundy glaze; heat; serve with ham.

Serving tip: Heat ¼ cup brandy in pan; ignite; pour flaming brandy over ham.

STUFFED HAM STEAK
4–5 servings

2 ham steaks, ¼ inch thick Whole cloves	1½ cups bread cubes
½ cup finely chopped onion	2 tablespoons chopped parsley
¾ cup finely chopped celery	1 teaspoon salt
2 tablespoons butter or margarine	⅛ teaspoon cinnamon
	1 egg, slightly beaten

1. Slash fat around ham steaks; stud with whole cloves; set aside. 2. Sauté onion, celery in butter 10 minutes. 3. Add bread cubes, parsley, salt, cinnamon, egg; toss lightly. 4. Place one ham steak in center of large double-thick square of Alcoa Wrap; cover steak with stuffing mixture. 5. Top with second ham steak; if necessary, hold in place with toothpicks.

6. Bring torn edges together over meat; fold, then fold again bringing fold down close to meat. Fold ends over and over pressing in close to meat. **7.** Place on cooky sheet or in shallow pan. **8.** Bake 25 minutes at 450° F.; open foil; bake 10 minutes longer.

CRANBERRY HAM ROLLS

4 servings

¼ cup minced onion
¼ cup minced celery
¼ cup butter or margarine
2 cups cooked rice
¼ teaspoon salt

⅛ teaspoon pepper
8 thin slices left over ham
1 can whole cranberry sauce
½ cup brown sugar, firmly packed
2 tablespoons lemon juice

1. Sauté onion, celery in butter until tender. **2.** Add rice, salt, pepper; blend. **3.** Spread mixture over ham slices; roll up; fasten with toothpicks. **4.** Place two ham rolls in center of double-thick square of Alcoa Wrap; shape foil around rolls to make a shallow boat. Place boats on baking sheet. **5.** Put cranberry sauce in a bowl; mash lightly with fork; add brown sugar, lemon juice; blend. **6.** Spoon cranberry mixture over ham rolls in boats. **7.** Bake 20 minutes at 350° F.

ELEGANT HAM ROLLS

8 servings

Sauce

2 tablespoons butter or
margarine

¼ cup light brown sugar, firmly
packed
2 tablespoons water

1. Melt butter in saucepan. **2.** Add brown sugar, water; mix well; cook over low heat 3 minutes. Set aside.

Ham Rolls

2 tablespoons butter or
margarine
¼ cup minced onion
¼ cup minced celery
2 cups cooked rice

⅓ cup seedless raisins
¼ teaspoon salt
⅛ teaspoon nutmeg
8 ⅛-inch slices baked ham

1. Melt butter in fry pan. **2.** Add onion, celery; cook until tender. **3.** Add rice, raisins, salt, nutmeg; mix. **4.** Spread about 2 tablespoons rice mixture on each ham slice; roll up; fasten with toothpicks. **5.** Place ham rolls in fry pan. **6.** Pour sauce over ham rolls; cover. **7.** Cook over medium heat 10 minutes.

STUFFED GREEN PEPPERS
6 servings

6 large green peppers
1 cup boiling water
1½ teaspoons salt
3 cups diced or coarsely ground cooked ham
1½ cups cooked rice
¼ teaspoon pepper

¼ cup butter or margarine
1 cup sliced onions
4 peppercorns
6 whole cloves
1 cup condensed tomato soup, undiluted
2½ cups canned tomatoes

1. Wash peppers; cut thin slices from stem end; remove all seeds. **2.** Cook peppers in boiling salted water in Dutch oven 5 minutes. **3.** Drain; reserve liquid. **4.** Combine ham, rice, pepper. **5.** Fill drained green peppers with this mixture. **6.** Melt butter in Dutch oven; add onion; sauté until golden brown. **7.** Tie peppercorns, cloves in small piece of cheesecloth. **8.** Add tomato soup, canned tomatoes, spice bag, liquid in which peppers were boiled to onions; mix. **9.** Stand peppers upright in sauce. **10.** Cover; simmer over low heat 30 minutes.

GLAZED HAM BALLS
8 servings

1 pound ground ham
1 pound ground pork
⅔ cup cracker crumbs
2 eggs, beaten
1¼ cups evaporated milk
¼ teaspoon salt

¼ teaspoon thyme
⅓ cup minced onion
1 cup brown sugar, firmly packed
1 teaspoon dry mustard
3 tablespoons vinegar

1. Combine ham, pork, cracker crumbs, eggs, evaporated milk, salt, thyme, onion; blend thoroughly. **2.** Make 16 portions using #16 ice cream scoop; place in Alcoa Wrap lined 9 x 13-inch pan. **3.** Combine brown sugar, mustard, vinegar in saucepan; cook on medium high heat until boiling; pour over ham balls. **4.** Bake uncovered 1 hour at 350° F.

Good to know: Ham balls may be wrapped in foil and frozen for future use.

HAWAIIAN HAM LOAF

8 servings

1½ pounds smoked ham, ground	2 tablespoons prepared mustard
1 pound lean fresh pork, ground	½ cup brown sugar
1 cup fine cracker crumbs	6 slices pineapple
2 eggs, slightly beaten	6 maraschino cherries
1½ cups milk	

1. Combine ham, pork, crumbs, eggs, milk, mustard. **2.** Grease bottom, sides of heavy fry pan with butter or margarine. **3.** Pat brown sugar on bottom. **4.** Arrange pineapple slices on sugar. **5.** Put cherry in center of each slice. **6.** Pat meat mixture on top of pineapple. **7.** Cover; place over medium low heat 10 minutes; reduce heat to low; cook 1 hour. **8.** Remove from heat; tilt cover; drain off all liquid. **9.** Place meat platter over loaf; invert ham; lift off.

PLANKED HAM PUFF

4 servings

1 cup diced, cooked ham	1 12-ounce package frozen French
1 cup mashed potatoes	cut green beans
Salt, pepper	2 tablespoons butter or margarine
2 egg yolks, beaten	1 4-ounce can mushroom buttons,
2 egg whites, stiffly beaten	sliced
1 cup grated American cheese	

1. Combine ham, mashed potatoes, salt, pepper; blend well. **2.** Add egg yolks; fold in beaten egg whites. **3.** Completely cover large meat platter with sheet of Alcoa Wrap. **4.** Pile ham mixture in center of platter; sprinkle with grated cheese. **5.** Bake 30 minutes at 325° F. **6.** Cook green beans as directed on package. **7.** Sauté mushrooms in butter. **8.** Surround ham puff with green beans; garnish with sautéed mushrooms; serve at once.

ACROSS-THE-BORDER BACON ROAST

6 servings

1½ pounds Canadian bacon
   Whole cloves .
⅓ cup brown sugar

1½ tablespoons prepared mustard
1 cup canned pineapple juice

1. Remove casing from Canadian bacon. 2. Score fat side
with sharp knife; stud with cloves. 3. Combine sugar, mustard
to make paste; spread over meat. 4. Place in Alcoa Wrap
lined shallow baking pan; pour pineapple juice around sides.
5. Bake 1 hour or 35 minutes per pound at 350° F.

VIRGINIA OR KENTUCKY STYLE HAM

These hams have a special type of cure. Their surface is ex-
tremely dark and firm. They need special cooking to develop
their fine flavor.

1. Scrub thoroughly with soapsuds and brush. 2. Wash well
in hot water to remove all soap, using a knife to scrape off
mold. 3. Soak 12-36 hours (depending on age) in cold water
to cover; drain. 4. Place on rack in deep regular roaster.
5. Add warm water to cover ⅓ of ham. 6. Bake *uncovered* in
moderate oven 350° F., allowing about 18 minutes per pound.
7. Turn once when ham is half done. 8. When done, tiny bone
at end can be pulled out easily. 9. Allow to cool slightly; remove skin but use it as cover to keep ham moist. 10. Serve

hot or cold; slice thin. 11. If desired, after scrubbing and soaking, ham may be simmered until tender allowing 30 minutes per pound. Then cool in cooking liquid, skin and glaze according to directions: To Glaze Baked Ham.

TO BAKE OLD TYPE SMOKED HAM

These are the hams that are heavy cured, heavy smoked.
1. Soak overnight or for several hours in cold water to cover.
2. Drain; add fresh water to cover. 3. Cover; simmer until tender, allowing 25-30 minutes per pound. 4. Drain; remove skin; score fat and glaze according to directions: To Glaze Baked Ham.

TO GLAZE BAKED HAM

1. Cook ham according to recipe. 2. Remove rind; score or cut fat into squares or diamonds. 3. Insert whole clove into center of each diamond. 4. Spread or baste with one of the following:

¾ cup canned crushed pineapple combined with ¾ cup brown sugar
Pat brown sugar over ham; drizzle on honey or molasses

1 cup brown sugar mixed with juice and grated rind of 1 orange

1 cup currant jelly or canned whole cranberry sauce, beaten with fork

1 cup orange, or orange grapefruit marmalade, beaten with fork

1 cup brown sugar combined with 1 cup juice from spiced or pickled peaches

1 cup puréed applesauce, apricots or peaches

1 cup brown sugar mixed with 1 teaspoon dry mustard, 2 tablespoons vinegar, fruit juice or cider or 1 teaspoon horseradish

1 cup brown sugar combined with ¼ cup fine soft bread crumbs

Pat brown sugar over ham; place drained pineapple slices on top and maraschino cherry in center of each slice. Fruit may be fastened to ham with toothpicks and removed before serving. Use pineapple juice for basting.

Pat brown sugar over ham. Arrange canned sliced peaches on ham to resemble Black Eyed Daisies. Make centers with small clusters of whole cloves. Use juice for basting.

Canned pineapple juice, cider, canned fruit nectar, corn syrup, maple syrup, Muscatel or Tokay wine may be used for basting.

REVBENSSPJALL
(Roast Spareribs)

4 servings

1 tablespoon salt
¼ teaspoon pepper
¼ teaspoon ginger

4 pounds lean spareribs
2 tablespoons shortening

1. Mix salt, pepper, ginger together; sprinkle over spareribs.
2. Fry spareribs in shortening until browned. 3. Place each serving on a double-thick square of Alcoa Wrap. 4. Fold torn edges together in tight double fold on top of meat; fold ends up using tight double folds. 5. Place on rack in shallow pan. 6. Bake 1 hour at 425° F.

HAM CONES, HAWAIIAN

10 servings

3 cups ground cooked ham
1 tablespoon grated onion
1 tablespoon chopped parsley
2 teaspoons dry mustard
¼ cup brown sugar

2 tablespoons pineapple syrup
1 egg, slightly beaten
½ cup crushed cornflakes
10 drained pineapple slices (1 No. 2 can)

1. Combine ham, onion, parsley, mustard, sugar, syrup, egg; mix well. 2. Shape into 10 cone-shaped patties; roll in crushed cornflakes. 3. Place on baking sheet; quick-freeze for 1 hour; wrap each cone in heavy duty Alcoa Wrap; freeze. 4. When ready to use, unwrap cones; place a drained pineapple slice on foil under each ham cone; bring edges of foil up around side of pineapple slice to form cup. 5. Place on baking sheet; bake 45 minutes at 375° F. 6. Serve in foil cups.

JULSKINKA
(Christmas Ham)

10–12 pound smoked ham
2 bay leaves
15 whole allspice
1 egg white, beaten slightly
2 tablespoons prepared mustard

1 tablespoon sugar
¼ cup dry bread crumbs
2 cups sifted confectioners sugar
1 egg white

1. Place ham with bay leaves, whole allspice on double-thick sheet of Alcoa Wrap. 2. Fold torn edges together in tight double fold on top of meat; fold ends up using tight double folds. 3. Place on rack in shallow pan. 4. Roast 15-18 minutes per pound at 425° F. 5. Open foil 30 minutes before ham is done. 6. Combine egg white, mustard, sugar; brush over ham. 7. Sprinkle with dry bread crumbs. 8. Reduce oven to 325° F.; return ham to oven; bake 30 minutes longer. 9. Chill. 10. Combine confectioners sugar, egg white; mix well. 11. Decorate ham by piping sugar mixture through pastry tube.

Best Ways with Veal

Veal is such an accommodating meat—it takes kindly to all sorts of flavors, so many methods of cooking! How long since you've served your family a veal roast, a tasty veal Parmesan, dressed-up veal chops? Doesn't just listing those old standbys make your mouth water? Then see what happens when you read the recipes for new ways with veal!

BUYING GUIDE FOR VEAL

Characteristics	Cut	Weight	Number of Servings
Color, light greyish pink; lean, firm, fine grained, well marked with fat; fat white, firm, free from fiber; bones slightly pink.	Chops, thick	2	1 lb.
	Steaks	2–3	1 lb.
	Leg Roast	6–8	4 lbs.
	Shoulder Roast	3–4	2 lbs.

TEMPERATURE-TIME CHART FOR ROAST VEAL
325° F. Oven Temperature

Cut	Approximate Minutes Per Pound 3–6 Pounds	Approximate Minutes Per Pound 6–8 Pounds	Meat Thermometer Reading When Roast Is Done
Leg, Round, Rump	35–40	30	180° F.
Loin	35	30	180° F.
Shoulder			
Bone In	40	35	180° F.
Boned	45	40	180° F.

ROAST VEAL

1. Wipe meat with damp cloth to remove any loose small pieces of bone. 2. Rub meat, if desired, with cut side of clove of garlic. 3. Line shallow open roasting pan with Alcoa Wrap by shaping foil over outside of pan then fitting into pan. 4. Place meat, fat side up on rack in pan. 5. Lay several strips bacon or salt pork over roast to provide additional fat and flavor. 6. If using a meat thermometer, insert it into center of thickest part of roast, being certain bulb does not rest on bone, fat or gristle. 7. Sprinkle with salt, pepper. 8. Do not flour; add no water; do not baste; do not cover during roasting period. 9. Roast according to chart.

ROAST STUFFED LOIN OF VEAL   *8 servings*

3½ pounds loin of veal, with pocket
2 cups fine bread crumbs
1 small onion, minced
½ cup diced celery
2 tablespoons butter or margarine
¼ cup hot water
¼ cup grated American cheese
1 teaspoon salt
¼ teaspoon pepper
4 strips bacon

1. Wipe meat with damp cloth. 2. To make stuffing, combine crumbs, onion, celery; moisten with butter melted in water; add cheese, salt, pepper. 3. Place stuffing in pocket; sew or fasten with skewers. 4. Line shallow open roasting pan by shaping piece of Alcoa Wrap around outside of pan, then fitting into pan. 5. Place meat on rack in pan; add no water; do not cover. 6. Place bacon strips over veal. 7. Roast 2 hours at 325° F.

BRAISED VEAL CHOPS

4 servings

¼ cup flour
½ teaspoon salt
⅛ teaspoon pepper
4 loin or rib veal chops, ¾ inch thick
2 tablespoons fat

1¼ cups water, tomato juice or Sauterne wine
2 tablespoons flour
3 tablespoons cold water
Salt
Pepper

1. Combine flour, salt, pepper; coat chops. 2. Melt fat in heavy fry pan. 3. Add chops; sauté until well browned on both sides. 4. Add liquid; cover; simmer 45-50 minutes or until meat is tender. 5. Remove chops to hot platter; remove pan from heat. 6. Combine flour, cold water to make paste; add ¼ cup liquid from pan to paste. 7. Stir paste into remaining liquid; return to heat; cook, stirring constantly until gravy bubbles. 8. Add seasoning to taste; pour over chops.

Variations: 1. Use half sour cream, half water for liquid: 2. Add sautéed mushrooms to the gravy. 3. Sprinkle chopped parsley or chives over chops.

SPANISH CHOPS

4 servings

3 tablespoons flour
1 teaspoon salt
¼ teaspoon pepper
6 loin or rib veal chops
5 tablespoons fat, drippings
1 cup sliced, peeled onions
1 cup canned tomatoes

½ cup water
1 tablespoon chopped parsley
1 bay leaf
1 teaspoon salt
½ teaspoon pepper
2 tablespoons cornstarch
½ cup cold water

1. Combine flour, salt, pepper; coat chops. 2. Melt fat in heavy fry pan; add chops; brown thoroughly on both sides; remove to warm platter. 3. Sauté onions in fat 5 minutes; place chops on top of onions. 4. Add tomatoes, water, parsley, bay leaf, salt, pepper. 5. Cover; simmer one hour. 6. Remove chops to platter. 7. Mix cornstarch, water to smooth paste; add a little liquid from pan; add paste to remaining liquid; cook until thickened; pour over chops.

VEAL SCALLOPINI

4 servings

6 thin slices veal shank
6 tablespoons flour
4 tablespoons butter or margarine
3 medium onions, sliced thin
1 clove garlic, minced
2 bouillon cubes

1 cup boiling water
1 teaspoon dry mustard
3 teaspoons paprika
3 tablespoons minced parsley
4 tablespoons butter or margarine
1 cup commercial sour cream

1. Dust veal with flour.   2. Melt 4 tablespoons butter in heavy fry pan; add onions, garlic; cook until yellow.   3. Add bouillon cubes, water; stir until cubes dissolve; add mustard, paprika, parsley; stir; pour into bowl; set aside.   4. Melt 4 additional tablespoons butter in fry pan; add floured meat; cook until browned on both sides.   5. Pour onion mixture over meat; cover; cook over low heat 30 minutes.   6. Stir in cream; bring to boil; remove from heat.

BREADED VEAL CUTLET

4 servings

2 pounds veal cutlet, ½ inch thick
1 cup dry crumbs
½ teaspoon salt
⅛ teaspoon pepper

1 egg, beaten
¼ cup milk
4 tablespoons butter or margarine

1. Cut veal into serving pieces.   2. Combine crumbs, salt, pepper.   3. Combine egg, milk.   4. Dip veal into crumbs, then into egg mixture and into crumbs again.   5. Place breaded veal in refrigerator 30 minutes.   6. When ready to use, melt fat in heavy fry pan.   7. Add meat; cook slowly about 15 minutes on each side until browned.

Variations: 1. Pour can of tomato sauce over meat after browning; cover; simmer 15 minutes.   2. Pour can of undiluted mushroom, celery or chicken soup over meat after browning; cover; simmer 15 minutes.   3. Pour one pint sour cream over meat after browning; cover; simmer 5 minutes.   4. Brush veal with French dressing before dipping into crumb-egg mixture.   5. Rub veal with cut side of clove of garlic before breading.

SAVORY VEAL CUTLETS

6 servings

2 tablespoons fat
3 onions, sliced
¼ cup flour
1 teaspoon salt

½ teaspoon paprika
1 veal cutlet (1½ inches thick,
   about 2 pounds)
1 cup commercial sour cream

1. Heat fat in fry pan; add onions; brown.   2. Combine flour,
salt, paprika in paper bag.   3. Cut veal into serving pieces;
flour pieces by shaking in bag.   4. Remove onions from pan
when brown; brown veal in same pan.   5. Add onions, sour
cream; cover.   6. Simmer 1 hour or until tender.

SESAME VEAL

3-4 servings

2 tablespoons flour
½ teaspoon salt
¼ teaspoon poultry seasoning
½ teaspoon paprika
⅛ teaspoon pepper
1 pound veal steak, cut into
   serving pieces
2 tablespoons fat

½ cup soft bread crumbs
1 tablespoon butter or margarine,
   melted
¼ cup grated Parmesan cheese
2 tablespoons sesame seeds,
   toasted
½ cup hot water

1. Combine flour, salt, poultry seasoning, paprika, pepper.
2. Coat veal in flour mixture.   3. Melt fat in fry pan.   4. Add
veal; brown on all sides.   5. Place meat in Alcoa Wrap lined
baking pan.   6. Combine bread crumbs, melted butter, Parmesan cheese, sesame seeds; spoon over veal.   7. Pour water
around veal.   8. Bake 45-50 minutes at 350° F.   9. Serve
sauce from pan over veal.

VEAL PAPRIKA
8 servings

4 pounds veal shoulder, boned, rolled, tied
2 tablespoons butter or margarine, melted
1 tablespoon paprika
¼ cup flour
1 teaspoon salt

2 tablespoons shortening
1 medium onion, minced (about ½ cup)
¾ cup finely diced celery
¼ cup water
2 tablespoons flour
½ cup commercial sour cream

1. Wipe meat with damp cloth; brown on all sides in fry pan.
2. Combine butter, paprika, flour, salt to make paste; spread over browned meat. 3. Place meat on double-thick sheet of Alcoa Wrap; fold down edges together in tight double fold on top of meat; double fold ends. 4. Place on rack in shallow pan; roast one hour at 425° F. 5. Melt shortening in fry pan; add onion; cook until lightly browned; add celery, water; cook 8-10 minutes. 6. After veal has cooked one hour, remove from oven; open foil; pour celery-onion mixture over top; re-seal foil, return to oven; roast 45 minutes; remove; open foil. 7. Stir flour into sour cream; combine with juices in foil; spoon over veal; re-seal foil; roast 15 minutes longer.

VEAL WITH MUSHROOMS IN RICE RING
6 servings

2 pounds cubed veal
½ cup flour
4 tablespoons butter or margarine
1¼ cups boiling water

1 tablespoon Worcestershire sauce
1 cup diced canned mushrooms
1 teaspoon salt
⅛ teaspoon pepper

1. Coat veal with flour. 2. Melt butter in heavy fry pan; add meat; brown on all sides. 3. Add water, Worcestershire sauce, mushrooms, salt, pepper; mix. 4. Cover; cook over low heat 35-40 minutes. 5. Fill buttered ring mold with cooked rice, patting it firmly. 6. Turn mold onto platter; put meat mixture into center. 7. Garnish rice with minced parsley.

VEAL FRICASSEE

4 servings

2 pounds cubed veal, rump
¼ cup flour
2 tablespoons fat
½ cup hot water
½ cup diced onion

½ cup diced celery
1 cup cubed raw potatoes
1 cup sliced raw carrots
1½ teaspoons salt
¼ teaspoon pepper

1. Roll veal in flour; brown in Dutch oven or heavy fry pan; add remaining ingredients. 2. Cover; cook over low heat 30-35 minutes. 3. If necessary, add more water during cooking; thicken gravy if desired.

GINGERY VEAL

6 servings

3 tablespoons shortening
4 tablespoons flour
2 cups milk
½ teaspoon salt
⅛ teaspoon pepper
½ teaspoon nutmeg
¼ teaspoon ginger

2 cups cooked diced veal
1 cup quartered stuffed olives
½ cup canned mushrooms
2 tablespoons dry bread crumbs
4 tablespoons grated American or Parmesan cheese

1. Melt shortening in sauce pan; remove from heat; add flour; blend. 2. Add milk; cook over low heat, stirring constantly until thickened. 3. Add salt, pepper, nutmeg, ginger; stir until blended. 4. Combine veal, olives, mushrooms; place in Alcoa Wrap lined casserole or 8 x 8 x 2-inch cake pan. 5. Pour creamed mixture over meat. 6. Sprinkle with crumbs, cheese. 7. Bake 35-40 minutes at 375° F.

SCHEITERHAUFEN
6 servings

(Pancakes with Veal and Vegetables)

Pancakes
2½ cups sifted all purpose flour
5 teaspoons baking powder
¼ cup sugar
1½ teaspoons salt

2 eggs, beaten
2½ cups milk
6 tablespoons melted butter or
   margarine

Filling
1 small head cauliflower (about
   1 pound)
1 8½-ounce can peas, drained
1 cup cooked rice
2 3-ounce cans sliced mushrooms,
   drained

½ pound ground veal or leftover
   veal cut into bite-size pieces
1 quart commercial sour cream
1 egg yolk, beaten

1. Combine flour, baking powder, sugar, salt; add eggs, milk, melted butter; mix until flour is dampened, but still lumpy; set aside. 2. Separate cauliflower into flowerettes; cook in boiling, salted water until tender; drain; chop coarsely; add peas, one cup sour cream; mix lightly. 3. Combine rice, mushrooms; add one cup sour cream; mix. 4. Brown ground veal; add ½ cup sour cream; mix. 5. In 10-inch fry pan, bake 4 large pancakes (large enough to cover entire bottom); remove to absorbent paper. 6. Place one pancake in lightly greased

10-inch fry pan; cover with peas, cauliflower mixture; place second pancake on top; cover with rice-mushroom mixture; add third pancake; cover with veal-sour cream mixture; place fourth pancake on top.   **7.** Combine remaining 1½ cups sour cream, egg yolks; spread over fourth pancake.   **8.** Bake 50-55 minutes at 350° F.

WIENER SCHNITZEL
(Braised Veal)

4 servings

1 pound veal cutlet, cut ½ inch thick	4 cups crushed cornflakes
½ cup all purpose flour	2 tablespoons butter or margarine
1 teaspoon salt	½ cup blanched, toasted almonds
2 eggs, beaten	

1. Cut veal into 4 serving pieces.   **2.** Combine flour, salt; sprinkle half of flour mixture over veal slices; pound into meat using rim of saucer.   **3.** Turn meat; pound remaining flour into second side.   **4.** Dip meat into beaten egg, then into crushed cornflakes.   **5.** Melt butter in heavy fry pan; brown veal on both sides; cover; simmer until tender, about 30 minutes. **6.** To serve: sprinkle toasted almonds over each piece.

Best Ways with Variety Meats

Kitchen stepchildren—that's what liver, heart, brains, sweetbreads and the other variety meats too often turn out to be. Make a resolution: serve at least one variety-meat meal a week, based on these flavor-wonder recipes. You'll earn a family vote of thanks.

SWEETBREADS

1. Wash in cold water; let stand in cold water 20 minutes; drain. 2. Plunge into 2 quarts boiling water to which 2 tablespoons vinegar, 2 teaspoons salt have been added. 3. Cover; simmer 30 minutes. 4. Lift out; plunge again into cold water. 5. Drain; remove fat, connecting tissues, fine membrane; dry. 6. Split into halves lengthwise if very thick. 7. To serve, either broil or combine with medium white sauce. Serve on toast if broiled or in patty shells if creamed.

To broil Sweetbreads:

a. Brush with melted butter.
b. Sprinkle with salt, pepper.
c. Line broiler pan with Alcoa Wrap; place sweetbreads on rack.
d. Broil until golden brown, 5-7 minutes per side.

Good to know: *Medium white sauce may be varied by adding 1½ teaspoons white wine, Sherry or lemon juice with a little minced parsley.*

BROILED KIDNEYS

1. Wash kidneys; split; remove fat, tubes with scissors.
2. Brush with melted butter or French Dressing.   3. Sprinkle with salt, pepper.   4. Line broiler pan with foil; place kidneys on rack.   5. Broil 5-7 minutes on each side.   6. Serve on toast with melted butter to which a little lemon juice has been added.

FRESH TONGUE
6 servings

1 3–5 pound tongue	¼ cup chopped onion
4 cups cold water	½ cup sliced carrots
1½ teaspoons salt	¼ cup vinegar
½ cup diced celery	¼ cup sugar

1. Wash tongue; place in Dutch oven; add remaining ingredients.   2. Cover; bring to boil; simmer over low heat until tender, allowing about 50 minutes per pound.   3. Let tongue cool in cooking liquid.   4. Remove skin; trim off thick end where small bones are apparent. *To serve cold:* Chill; slice thin. *To serve hot:* reheat; serve with Horseradish Sauce, Barbecue Sauce, Spanish Sauce or Mustard Sauce.

BARBECUED BEEF LIVER
4 servings

1 pound beef liver	1 teaspoon sugar
Salt, pepper	⅛ teaspoon pepper
1 cup sliced onions	1 teaspoon prepared mustard
2 tablespoons butter or margarine	⅛ teaspoon chili powder
1 tablespoon vinegar	¼ cup ketchup
1 tablespoon Worcestershire sauce	1 tablespoon water

1. Cut liver into ¼ inch slices; cut each slice in half crosswise.
2. Arrange half the slices in bottom of covered baking pan, lined with Alcoa Wrap.   3. Sprinkle lightly with salt, pepper.
4. Sauté onions in butter until lightly browned; place half of them over liver.   5. Combine remaining ingredients.   6. Spoon half of sauce over liver and onions.   7. Arrange another layer

of liver and onions; cover pan.　**8.** Bake 25 minutes at 325° F.
9. Uncover; pour remaining sauce over liver.　**10.** Bake uncovered 10 minutes.

BROILED CALVES LIVER

4 servings

8 slices liver, ½ inch thick　　　Pepper
　Salt　　　　　　　　　　　　4 tablespoons melted butter

1. Wipe liver with damp cloth; pat dry.　**2.** Sprinkle with salt, pepper; brush with melted butter.　**3.** Line broiler pan with Alcoa Wrap; place liver on rack.　**4.** Broil about 5 minutes each side.
Good to know: Bacon strips may be broiled along with liver.

SIMMERED BRAINS

1. Wash beef, veal, lamb or pork brains in cold water.　**2.** Soak ½ hour in salted water, allowing 1 tablespoon salt per quart water.　**3.** Remove membrane.　**4.** Place in pan; add water to cover, 1 teaspoon salt, 1 tablespoon lemon juice or vinegar for each quart water.　**5.** Cover; simmer over low heat 15-20 minutes.　**6.** Drain; drop into cold water; drain again.
Taste Tip: Serve with Mushroom, Tomato or Butter Sauce.
Good to know: Count on 4 servings from one pound of brains.
Sautéed Brains: **1.** Prepare Simmered Brains.　**2.** Dip into beaten egg, then in fine dry crumbs or corn meal.　**3.** Sauté in butter in fry pan until brown.

TRIPE

4 servings

1 pound fresh honeycomb tripe　　2 tablespoons water
　Water to cover　　　　　　　　　Dry bread crumbs
½ teaspoon salt　　　　　　　　　4 tablespoons fat
1 egg, beaten

1. Wash tripe; place in Dutch oven or saucepan; cover with water; add salt.　**2.** Cover; simmer over low heat 1 hour.
3. Drain; cut into serving pieces.　**4.** Combine egg, water.

5. Dip tripe into egg mixture, then into crumbs.   **6.** Sauté in melted fat until nicely browned on both sides.

BRAISED OXTAILS

4 servings

2 oxtails, cut into 2-inch lengths	½ teaspoon minced garlic
1 cup minced onion	2 teaspoons salt
3 tablespoons fat	⅛ teaspoon pepper
2 cups hot water	1 tablespoon sugar
1 tablespoon vinegar	

1. Wipe oxtails with damp cloth.   **2.** Place under broiler; brown on all sides.   **3.** Sauté onion in fat in Dutch oven until tender.   **4.** Add meat, remaining ingredients.   **5.** Cover; simmer over low heat 3½-4 hours until meat is tender, adding more boiling water if necessary.   **6.** Thicken liquid in pan for gravy.

LIVER LOAF

6 servings

1 pound liver (veal, beef or pork)	1 egg, beaten
¼ pound bacon, fried, crumbled	1 cup dry bread crumbs
¼ cup onion, minced	Salt, pepper
1 tablespoon chopped celery	Hard-cooked eggs for garnish
1 tablespoon chopped parsley	

1. Cover liver with boiling water; let stand 10 minutes; drain; dry.   **2.** Grind liver.   **3.** Combine liver with bacon, onion, celery, parsley, egg, bread crumbs, salt, pepper; mix thoroughly.   **4.** Pack into 9 x 5 x 3-inch loaf pan lined with lightly greased strips of Alcoa Wrap; allow strips of foil to extend up over edges of pan.   **5.** Bake 1 hour at 350° F.   **6.** Grasp edges of foil; remove loaf to platter; push foil down around bottom of loaf.   **7.** Garnish with hard-cooked eggs.

BEEF KIDNEY STEW

4 servings

1 beef kidney	⅛ teaspoon pepper
6 cups boiling water	⅛ teaspoon paprika
2 tablespoons minced onion	3 tablespoons butter or margarine
6 tablespoons flour	1 minced hard cooked egg
2 teaspoons salt	

1. Cut kidney crosswise into ¼ inch slices. 2. Remove all fat, gristle; cut into small pieces. 3. Soak in cold water ½ hour; drain. 4. Add boiling water, onion; simmer uncovered 1 hour. 5. Cover; simmer ½ hour longer or until tender and only 3 cups liquid remain; cool. 6. Mix flour with 6 tablespoons cooled liquid to make paste. 7. Heat kidney mixture; add flour paste gradually, stirring constantly; cook until thickened. 8. Add salt, pepper, paprika, butter, egg. 9. Serve on toast or with hashed browned potatoes.

SPICED TONGUE

6 servings

1 4–5 pound smoked tongue	3 bay leaves
4 cups hot water	18 whole cloves
⅓ cup vinegar	¾ cup sliced onion
2 teaspoons salt	1 tablespoon grated lemon rind
3 tablespoons sugar	

1. Soak tongue overnight in cold water; drain. 2. Place in Dutch oven; add remaining ingredients. 3. Cover; bring to

boil; simmer until tender, allowing about 50 minutes per pound.   **4.** Let tongue cool in cooking liquid.   **5.** Remove skin; trim thick end where small bones are apparent.   **6.** Serve as in Fresh Tongue.

LIVER PATTIES
4 servings

1 pound ground beef, pork or lamb liver	1 teaspoon salt
1 onion, grated	⅛ teaspoon pepper
	4 tablespoons fat

1. Combine liver, onion, salt, pepper; mix thoroughly; shape into 12 small patties.   **2.** Melt fat in fry pan.   **3.** Add patties; sauté over low heat until browned on both sides and cooked.

LIVER AND ONIONS

1. Roll slices of liver in seasoned flour.   **2.** Sauté in butter until brown on both sides.   **3.** Sauté thinly sliced onion rings in another fry pan until golden brown.   **4.** Place liver on platter; turn onion rings into pan in which liver was cooked. Add 2 tablespoons hot water; stir to loosen sediment in pan; mix; pour over liver.

Fabulous Fowl

Everybody loves poultry, from the youngest member of the family to the oldest. That's why every cook who takes pride in her kitchen needs to have a wide variety of poultry-cooking ways at her fingertips. Here's all you need to make you as proud as a poultry cook has any right to be!

BUYING GUIDE FOR POULTRY

	Characteristics	Cut	Weight	Number of Servings
Chicken Capon Turkey	Skin smooth, unbroken, moist; legs smooth, soft; fat distributed evenly; breast bone pliable.	Broilers	¼–½ bird	1
		Fryers	¾ pound	1
		Pieces	¾ pound	1
		Roasting Chicken, Capon	⅔–¾ pound	1
		Stewing Chicken	⅓–⅔ pound	1
		Whole Turkey	½–¾ pound	1
Cornish Hen		Whole Hen	½–1 hen	1–2
Duck	Breast firm, thick, tender; breastbone and bill pliable.	Whole Duck	¾–1 pound	1

POULTRY

Chicken, Capon, Turkey and Duck may be roasted by either the Tent Method or the Alcoa Wrap Method. Goose should be done by Tent Method.

Good to know: *When consulting the Time-Temperature Charts that follow keep in mind that meat and bone structure of fowl, particularly chickens and turkeys, vary greatly because of new raising and feeding methods. For this reason, times given are approximate, and should serve only as a guide.*

Start to test for doneness about one-half hour before bird is supposed to be done. Fowl is done when leg will move up and down freely. Another test is to press the thickest part of the drumstick between the fingers—meat should be soft. Protect fingers with piece of paper towel.

TENT METHOD

This method is like the conventional open roasting method. The only essential difference is that a piece of Alcoa Wrap replaces the fat-soaked cloth normally used over the fowl. The foil protects better than old-style cloth, is less messy to handle, prevents spattering of oven walls, and the fowl will come out deliciously moist and tender. Add a bonus—the roasting pan comes out of the oven almost as clean as it went in!

1. Line shallow open roasting pan by shaping piece of Alcoa Wrap over outside of pan, then fitting into pan.
2. Prepare fowl according to recipe.
3. Place fowl breast side up on rack in pan. If using a V-type rack, place breast down, turning bird when ¾ done.
4. Fold piece of Alcoa Wrap, 4-5 inches longer than fowl, in half lengthwise to form Tent.
5. Place Tent over fowl, pressing one end lightly around drumsticks, other around neck opening.
6. Add no water. Occasional basting of chicken and turkey with drippings in pan is desirable, especially in dry areas; it improves flavor.
7. If wrapper has a printed time-temperature chart, use those directions. Otherwise use following charts as guides.

TENT METHOD FOR CHICKEN, CAPON, DUCK, GOOSE

Time Guide
Oven Temperature 325° F.

Purchased Weight	Approximate Total Time* Stuffed	Approximate Total Time Unstuffed
CHICKEN		
3 pounds	2½ hours	2¼ hours
6 pounds	4　hours	3½ hours
CAPON		
6 pounds	4　hours	3½ hours
8 pounds	4½ hours	3¾ hours
DUCK		
3 pounds	2¼ hours	2　hours
6 pounds	3¾ hours	3¼ hours
GOOSE		
8 pounds	4　hours	3¼ hours
11 pounds	4½ hours	3½ hours

*Five minutes per pound has been added for stuffed bird.

TENT METHOD FOR ROAST TURKEY

Time Guide
Oven Temperature 325° F.

Purchased Weight	Approximate Total Time* Stuffed	Approximate Total Time** Unstuffed
8–10 pounds	3½–4¼ hours	3 –3½ hours
10–12 pounds	4¼–4¾ hours	3½–4 hours
12–14 pounds	4¾–5½ hours	4 –4½ hours
14–16 pounds	5½–6 hours	4½–5 hours
16–18 pounds	6 –6¾ hours	5 –5½ hours
18–20 pounds	6¾–7½ hours	5½–6 hours
20–24 pounds	7½–8¾ hours	6 –7 hours

*Five minutes per pound has been added for stuffed bird.
**Total time has been based on oven-ready weight of turkey which is purchased weight of turkey minus neck and giblets packed inside bird. The oven-ready weight is from 1 to 3 pounds less than the purchased weight, depending on size of bird.

ALCOA WRAP METHOD

This method resembles the covered roasting still preferred by many homemakers. The fowl is cooked by both heat and steam, keeping it plump and juicy. The skin will be moist and tender. This method is especially recommended for older birds.

1. Prepare fowl according to recipe.
2. Place on sheet of Alcoa Wrap. If foil is not wide enough, fold two pieces together lengthwise, using a double fold.
3. Bring torn edges together over fowl; fold down twice to press foil close against fowl. Fold ends over and over, pressing close to fowl.

4. Place on rack in shallow pan. Add no water; do not cover.
5. Disregard any printed directions that may have accompanied the fowl. Use following charts as guides.
6. 15-20 minutes before cooking time is completed, open foil; push it down away from fowl so skin will brown.

ALCOA WRAP METHOD FOR CHICKEN, CAPON, DUCK

Time Guide
Oven Temperature 425° F.

Purchased Weight	Approximate Total Time* Stuffed	Approximate Total Time Unstuffed
CHICKEN		
3 pounds	1½ hours	1¼ hours
6 pounds	2¼ hours	1¾ hours
CAPON		
6 pounds	2½ hours	2 hours
8 pounds	3¼ hours	2½ hours
DUCK		
3 pounds	1½ hours	1¼ hours
6 pounds	2½ hours	2 hours

*Five minutes per pound has been added for stuffed bird.

ALCOA WRAP METHOD FOR ROAST TURKEY

Time Guide
Oven Temperature 425° F.

Purchased Weight	Approximate Total Time* Stuffed	Approximate Total Time** Unstuffed
8–10 pounds	3 –3½ hours	2½–2¾ hours
10–12 pounds	3½–3¾ hours	2¾–3 hours
12–14 pounds	3¾–4¼ hours	3 –3¼ hours
14–16 pounds	4¼–4¾ hours	3¼–3½ hours
16–18 pounds	4¾–5 hours	3½–3¾ hours
18–20 pounds	5 –5½ hours	3¾–4 hours
20–24 pounds	5½–6¾ hours	4 –5 hours

*Five minutes per pound has been added for stuffed bird.

**Total time has been based on oven-ready weight of turkey which is purchased weight of turkey minus neck and giblets packed inside bird. The oven-ready weight is from 1 to 3 pounds less than the purchased weight, depending on size of bird.

ROAST STUFFED CHICKEN OR CAPON

1. Wash, clean, dry chicken.   2. Rub inside with salt, about ⅛ teaspoon per pound.   3. Fill cavity, neck opening with desired stuffing; pack lightly as stuffing swells during cooking. 4. Close cavity with skewers or poultry pins; lace with cord. Pull neck skin back over stuffing; fasten with skewers or poultry pins to back of bird.   5. Using long cord, tie ends of legs together; bring cord from legs down around tail, drawing it just tight enough to hold legs down and yet not too close to body. When chicken is two thirds done, cut cord around legs.

6. Bend tip ends of wings backward so they are held against back of bird. **7.** Grease bird thoroughly with soft butter or margarine; sprinkle with salt, pepper. **8.** Follow directions for either Tent Method or Alcoa Wrap Method of Roasting. **9.** When bird is done, remove skewers or pins, cord. **10.** Make gravy from juices in pan. **11.** If bird is allowed to set 5 minutes after removal from oven, it will be easier to carve. **12.** To store leftover chicken or capon: Remove remaining stuffing. Wrap stuffing and carcass separately in Alcoa Wrap. Refrigerate.

GIBLETS

1. Wash heart, liver, gizzard, neck. **2.** Cook heart, gizzard, neck in water to cover; season with salt, pepper, a small bay leaf, a little diced onion, celery, carrot. **3.** Simmer covered until gizzard is fork tender; add liver 10-20 minutes before giblets are done. Chicken giblets . . . 1-1½ hours; Turkey giblets . . . 2-3 hours. **4.** Giblets may be diced and added to gravy or used in the stuffing. Use broth in making gravy.

ROAST STUFFED TURKEY

1. Prepare, stuff, truss turkey as for Roast Chicken or Capon. **2.** Grease turkey thoroughly with soft butter or margarine; sprinkle with salt, pepper. **3.** Follow directions for either Tent Method or Alcoa Wrap Method of Roasting. **4.** When turkey is two-thirds done, cut cord or band of skin at drumsticks. **5.** When turkey is done remove cord, pins or skewers. **6.** Make gravy from juices in pan. **7.** If turkey is allowed to set 5-10 minutes after removal from oven, it will be easier to carve. **8.** To store leftover turkey: Remove all stuffing from neck opening and body. Remove meat from bones. Wrap stuffing and meat separately in Alcoa Wrap. Refrigerate.

ROAST HALF TURKEY

1. Wash, clean turkey. 2. Rub inside with salt, ⅛ teaspoon per pound. 3. Fasten skin to breast meat on keel bone edge to prevent shrinkage of skin. 4. Tie leg to tail; pin or tie wing flat against breast. 5. Place turkey, cut side down, on rack in shallow Alcoa Wrap lined roasting pan. 6. Brush bird with melted fat. 7. Place piece of Alcoa Wrap, tent fashion, over top of turkey allowing it to remain loose so heat can circulate around under it. 8. Add no water; do not cover; do not baste. 9. Roast 25-30 minutes per pound at 325° F. 10. Prepare Bread Stuffing. 11. When bird is half done, remove from rack. 12. Cut a double-thick piece of Alcoa Wrap into an oval about the size of turkey. 13. Grease; lay on rack; make mound of stuffing. 14. Place turkey, skin side up, over stuffing. 15. Return to oven; complete roasting. 16. Additional stuffing may be baked in Alcoa Wrap.

ROAST GOOSE

1. Clean, wash, dry goose. 2. Rub cavity with salt, allowing ⅛ teaspoon salt per pound. 3. To reduce fat: place goose on rack in shallow Alcoa Wrap lined open roasting pan, in 375° F. oven for 15-20 minutes or until fat runs; dip out fat; repeat until fat ceases to drip; then stuff. 4. Stuff with Celery Stuffing, Apple Raisin Stuffing or place 1 quartered apple, 1 peeled onion, 2 stalks celery in cavity; remove after roasting. 5. Prick fat on back, around tail and skin around wings and legs with fork. 6. Follow directions for Tent Method of Roasting. 7. If goose is very fat, remove excess fat from pan during roasting.

ROAST DUCK

4 servings

1 4–5 pound drawn duck	½ cup minced celery
½ teaspoon salt	1 teaspoon salt
4 cups bread crumbs	⅛ teaspoon pepper
¼ cup minced onion	1 tablespoon sage
¼ cup minced green pepper	

1. Wash, clean, dry duck.   2. Rub inside with salt.   3. Combine remaining ingredients to make stuffing.   4. Stuff cavity, neck; tie legs together.   5. Place breast side up on rack in Alcoa Wrap lined shallow pan.   6. Do not grease; add no water; do not cover.   7. Roast according to Tent Method of Roasting. These times are approximate; differences in ducks may necessitate increasing or decreasing time.   8. Do not prick skin with fork; this allows juices to escape.   9. If duck is very fat, remove excess fat from pan during roasting.

Variations: 1. Instead of stuffing duck, place 1 quartered apple, 1 quartered onion, 2 stalks celery in cavity; remove after roasting.

2. Five minutes before roasting time is completed, spoon Orange Sauce over duck.

BROILED CHICKEN

1. Line broiler pan with Alcoa Wrap.   2. Pre-heat broiler— with broiler pan in position 10 minutes or as manufacturer directs.   3. Wash, clean, split 1¼-2 pound young chicken. 4. Place on broiler rack 3-3½ inches from heat, skin side down. 5. Brush well with melted butter or other fat.   6. Broil slowly so chicken just begins to brown at end of 10-12 minutes. 7. Turn; brush with melted butter every 10 minutes as browning increases.   8. Broil until tender and evenly browned— about 30-45 minutes, depending upon size.   9. Chicken is done when meat of drumstick is tender and it has lost all pink color.   10. Chicken may be served in halves if small, in quarters if larger.

BROILED SQUAB

1. Clean, wash, dry, split squab. 2. Season with salt, pepper.
3. Broil as in Broiled Chicken, until tender, about 30-45 minutes. 4. Allow 1 squab per person.

MAGGIE'S CHICKEN MORNAY
4 servings

Part One

4 breasts of chicken	⅛ teaspoon ginger
½ cup flour	½ cup butter or margarine
1 teaspoon salt	1 cup water
⅛ teaspoon pepper	

Part Two

4 tablespoons butter or margarine	½ cup milk
4 tablespoons flour	1 cup liquid from fry pan
1 teaspoon salt	1 cup grated American Cheese
½ cup cream	1 cup diced canned mushrooms

Part One
1. Coat chicken breasts with flour combined with salt, pepper, ginger. 2. Brown on all sides in butter in heavy fry pan.
3. Cover; cook over low heat 30-45 minutes or until fork tender; a little water may be added if necessary. 4. Place breasts in Alcoa Wrap lined shallow baking pan. 5. Add water to drippings in fry pan; stir to loosen any sediment in pan.

Part Two
1. Melt butter in saucepan; remove from heat. 2. Add flour, salt; blend thoroughly. 3. Add cream; blend. 4. Add milk, liquid from fry pan. 5. Return to low heat; cook, stirring constantly until thickened. 6. Add ½ cup cheese; stir until melted. 7. Add mushrooms. 8. Pour sauce over chicken.
9. Sprinkle remaining grated cheese over top. 10. Bake 25-30 minutes at 350° F. until cheese is melted, just lightly browned.
11. Sprinkle with paprika; serve at once.

CHICKEN BROCCOLI

4 servings

4 tablespoons butter or margarine
4 tablespoons flour
2 cups milk
1 cup grated sharp cheese

4 chicken breasts, cooked, boned
1 10-ounce package frozen broccoli, cooked until just tender
Parmesan cheese

1. Melt butter in saucepan; stir in flour. 2. Add milk; cook over low heat, stirring constantly until thickened. 3. Add cheese; cook until melted. 4. Place cooked broccoli in Alcoa Wrap lined shallow 1-quart casserole or divide among 4 individual foil casseroles. 5. Place chicken breasts on top of broccoli. 6. Pour cheese sauce over chicken. 7. Sprinkle with Parmesan cheese; place 4-5 inches under pre-heated broiler until nicely browned.

SPICED MUSHROOMS WITH CHICKEN

6 servings

1 pound fresh mushrooms
4 tablespoons butter or margarine
4 tablespoons flour
4 tablespoons ketchup
4 tablespoons chili sauce

2 tablespoons Worcestershire sauce
1 cup evaporated milk
1 cup chicken broth
1 cup finely diced cooked chicken

1. Wash, quarter mushrooms; drain. 2. Melt butter in fry pan; brown mushrooms. 3. Add flour; blend. 4. Add ketchup, chili sauce, Worcestershire sauce, milk, chicken broth; blend. 5. Cook over low heat, stirring constantly until slightly thickened. 6. Add chicken just before serving. 7. Serve over toast or waffles.

CURRIED CHICKEN INDIAN STYLE

4 servings

2½ cups water
1 cup raw rice
1 teaspoon salt
5 tablespoons butter or margarine
½ cup minced onion
6 tablespoons flour
2½ teaspoons curry powder

1¼ teaspoons salt
1½ teaspoons sugar
¼ teaspoon ground ginger
1 chicken bouillon cube
1 cup boiling water
2 cups milk
4 cups diced cooked chicken
1 teaspoon lemon juice

1. Bring the 2½ cups water to boil in saucepan. 2. Add rice, salt; cover; cook over low heat until all water is absorbed, rice tender, about 20-25 minutes. 3. Melt butter in fry pan; add onion; simmer over low heat 5 minutes; remove from heat. 4. Stir in flour, curry powder, salt, sugar, ginger. 5. Dissolve bouillon cube in boiling water; add with milk to flour mixture. 6. Cook over very low heat stirring constantly until thickened, smooth. 7. Add chicken, lemon juice; heat. 8. To serve: Pile rice in center of shallow bowl, chop plate or meat platter. Pour chicken mixture over rice.

COUNTRY CHICKEN

4 servings

1 3-pound chicken, cut into serving pieces
⅓ cup flour
2 teaspoons salt
½ cup butter or margarine

1 pound fresh mushrooms, sliced
2 10½-ounce cans chicken rice soup
1 cup hot water

1. Roll chicken in combined flour, salt. 2. Melt butter in fry pan; add chicken; brown thoroughly on all sides. 3. Remove chicken from fat; add mushrooms; simmer over medium heat 5 minutes. 4. Return chicken to pan; add soup, water. 5. Cover; cook over low heat 1-1½ hours or until fork tender. 6. Remove chicken from pan to hot serving platter. 7. Thicken chicken gravy with flour-water paste; pour over chicken; garnish with parsley.

Good to know: Medium-thin paste for thickening gravies (about 1 part water to 2 parts flour) can be made in quantity and kept tightly covered in the refrigerator.

FRENCH ROAST CHICKEN

4 servings

1 5-pound roasting chicken	3 tablespoons milk
1 pound fresh mushrooms	½ teaspoon thyme
3 tablespoons butter or margarine	½ teaspoon salt
3 slices bacon, diced	¼ teaspoon pepper
3 carrots, sliced	⅓ cup chopped parsley
¼ pound boiled ham, shredded	2 tablespoons butter or margarine,
2 medium onions, chopped	softened
2 stalks celery, chopped	6 small white onions
1 cup soft bread crumbs	½ teaspoon tarragon

1. Clean chicken; wash; dry inside and out. 2. Remove caps from mushrooms; set aside; slice stems. 3. Melt butter in large fry pan; add bacon; cook 3 minutes. 4. Add mushroom stems, carrots, ham, onions, celery; fry 5 minutes; cover; simmer 5 minutes. 5. Soak bread crumbs in milk; add to vegetable mixture. 6. Add thyme, salt, pepper, half the parsley. 7. Stuff chicken with this mixture; truss; sew. 8. Rub butter over chicken. 9. Place in center of large piece of Alcoa Wrap. 10. Lay mushroom caps, onions around chicken; sprinkle remaining parsley, tarragon over all. 11. Fold foil tightly around chicken; place on rack in shallow pan. 12. Bake 1 hour at 400° F. 13. Reduce heat to 350° F.; open foil; roast 45 minutes longer, or until brown.

FRIED CHICKEN

1. Wash, dry chicken; rub skin lightly with cut side of clove of garlic. 2. Cut chicken into desired serving pieces. 3. Coat each piece with flour combined with salt, pepper, dash of ginger. 4. Brown thoroughly on all sides in fat (part butter or margarine, part shortening) in heavy fry pan. 5. Sprinkle all pieces generously with paprika. 6. Add 1 cup boiling water. 7. Cover; cook over low heat 30-60 minutes or until fork tender.

FRENCH FRIED CHICKEN

1 3-pound young chicken	1 teaspoon salt
1 cup boiling water	2 cups all purpose flour
2 stalks celery, diced	3 teaspoons baking powder
1 carrot, sliced	½ teaspoon salt
1 small onion, sliced	2 eggs, beaten
2 sprigs parsley	1½ cups milk

1. Wash, clean chicken; cut into desired serving pieces. 2. Place in saucepot; add water, celery, carrots, onion, parsley, salt. 3. Cover; simmer 30-45 minutes until tender. 4. Allow to cool in liquid; remove; dry each piece thoroughly with towel. 5. To make batter; sift flour, baking powder, salt together; combine eggs, milk; add liquid to dry ingredients; beat until smooth. 6. Dip each piece of chicken into batter. 7. Melt 1 pound fat in Dutch oven or French fryer; heat to 375° F. 8. Drop chicken into fat, cooking until golden brown; do only 2-3 pieces at a time.

CHICKEN 'N' DUMPLINGS   6 servings

1 5–6 pound stewing chicken	1 small onion, sliced
3 cups water	2 stalks celery, cut
1 sliced carrot	

1. Wash, clean chicken; cut into desired serving pieces. 2. Place water in large saucepot or Dutch oven. 3. Add carrot, onion, celery; bring to boil. 4. Add chicken; bring to boil. 5. Cover; reduce heat to low. 6. Simmer 2-2½ hours or until fork tender. 7. Remove chicken; strain liquid; add milk, cream or water to make 2 cups. 8. Return chicken to pot. 9. Prepare drop dumplings. 10. Drop on top of chicken. 11. Cover; cook 12-15 minutes; do not remove cover until end of cooking time.

CHICKEN CACCIATORE

6 servings

1 3½-pound chicken
½ cup fat
1 onion, sliced

2½ cups canned tomatoes
½ teaspoon salt
⅛ teaspoon pepper

1. Wash, clean chicken; cut into serving pieces. 2. Brown on all sides in melted fat in Dutch oven. 3. Add onion, tomatoes, salt, pepper. 4. Cover; reduce heat to low. 5. Cook 45-50 minutes or until chicken is fork tender. 6. Serve with spaghetti.

CHICKEN FRICASSEE

6 servings

1 4½–5 pound chicken
½ cup flour
2 teaspoons salt
⅛ teaspoon pepper
4 tablespoons fat

4 cups boiling water
1 large onion, peeled, quartered
Few celery tops
1 teaspoon salt

1. Wash, clean chicken; cut into desired pieces. 2. Combine flour, salt, pepper in paper bag. 3. Add chicken; shake until coated. 4. Melt fat in Dutch oven. 5. Add chicken; brown thoroughly on all sides. 6. Add water, onion, celery tops, salt. 7. Cover; simmer over low heat until fork tender; allow about 1-1½ hours for roaster, 3-4 hours for older fowl; add more water if necessary. 8. Remove chicken; thicken gravy.

CHICKEN PIE

6 servings

1 4-pound chicken
  Boiling water
1 tablespoon salt
2 stalks celery
1 bay leaf
1 medium onion, sliced
3 cups cooked diced potatoes
2 cups cooked diced carrots
1 cup cooked or canned peas

7 tablespoons butter or fat from chicken
7 tablespoons flour
1 teaspoon salt
⅛ teaspoon pepper
1 cup milk or cream
2 cups chicken broth
  Dash nutmeg
½ teaspoon Worcestershire sauce
  Pinch tarragon

1. Wash, clean chicken; cut into desired serving pieces.
2. Place in Dutch oven or saucepot. 3. Add boiling water to cover chicken half way. 4. Add salt, celery, bay leaf, onion. 5. Cover; simmer until fork tender; allow 1-1½ hours for roaster; 3-4 hours for older fowl; additional water may be added if necessary. 6. Remove chicken; allow to cool. 7. Strain broth; add water to make 2 cups; skim off fat as it cools. 8. Remove skin from chicken; cut meat into 1-inch cubes. 9. Arrange chicken, potatoes, carrots, peas in Alcoa Wrap lined casserole or shallow baking pan. 10. Melt fat in saucepan; remove from heat. 11. Stir in flour, salt, pepper. 12. Add milk, chicken broth, nutmeg, Worcestershire sauce, tarragon. 13. Cook over low heat, stirring constantly until thickened. 14. Pour over chicken-vegetable mixture. 15. Top with baking powder biscuits or flaky pie crust. 16. Brush with milk. 17. Bake 20-25 minutes at 425° F.

Variations: 1. Leftover chicken may be used.

2. Part chicken, part ham may be used.

3. Heap fluffy mashed white or sweet potatoes on top instead of biscuits or pie crust.

CHICKEN PAPRIKA

4 servings

1 2½–3 pound chicken
3 tablespoons butter or margarine
1 cup chopped onion
2 teaspoons paprika
2 chicken bouillon cubes

2 cups boiling water
1 teaspoon salt
1 teaspoon flour
1 cup commercial sour cream

1. Wash, clean chicken; cut into desired serving pieces. 2. Melt butter in Dutch oven. 3. Add onions; sauté until browned. 4. Add paprika, bouillon cubes dissolved in boiling water; salt. 5. Bring to boil; add chicken. 6. Cover; cook over low heat about 1 hour or until chicken is tender. 7. Stir flour into sour cream. 8. Pour slowly into liquid in pot; stir; spoon over chicken. 9. Cover; cook five minutes longer.

GOLDEN CHICKEN '49

2 servings

1 2-pound broiler or fryer, cut
   into serving pieces
¾ teaspoon salt
¼ cup butter or margarine
3 tablespoons flour
¼ cup sugar

¾ teaspoon salt
¼ teaspoon dry mustard
¼ teaspoon cinnamon
1½ cups orange juice
1 whole orange

1. Sprinkle chicken with salt. 2. Melt butter in fry pan; add chicken; brown on all sides; remove chicken. 3. Add flour, sugar, salt, dry mustard, cinnamon to drippings; stir to smooth paste. 4. Gradually add orange juice; cook; stirring constantly until mixture boils; add chicken; cover; simmer over low heat 35 minutes. 5. Grate 1 tablespoon orange rind; cut membrane from orange; cut out sections. 6. When chicken is tender, sprinkle orange rind and sections over chicken; cook 5 minutes longer.

BAKED CHICKEN

8 servings

2 cups dry bread crumbs
Poultry seasoning
Salt, pepper

8 serving pieces of chicken
(breasts, thighs, legs)
½ cup butter or margarine, melted
½ cup butter or margarine

1. Combine bread crumbs, poultry seasoning, salt, pepper.
2. Dip pieces of chicken in the melted butter; roll in crumb mixture. 3. Line 9 x 13-inch baking pan with Alcoa Wrap; place chicken in pan. 4. Dot with remaining butter; cover with foil. 5. Bake 45 minutes at 400° F.; remove foil cover; bake an additional 30-45 minutes.

CHICKEN 'N' BACON STICKS

2 servings

2 tablespoons butter or margarine
4 tablespoons flour
½ teaspoon salt
¼ teaspoon pepper
2 chicken bouillon cubes
1 cup water, boiling
2 cups diced cooked chicken

2 tablespoons chopped celery
1 tablespoon chopped onion
Coarse dry bread crumbs
1 egg
1 tablespoon water
4 slices bacon, halved

1. Melt butter in saucepan; remove from heat; stir in flour, salt, pepper. 2. Dissolve bouillon cubes in boiling water; add gradually to mixture. 3. Cook, stirring constantly, until sauce thickens and boils—1 minute; remove; stir in chicken, celery, onion. Chill. 4. Shape chilled mixture into 8 sticks; dip in bread crumbs, then in egg beaten with water, again in bread crumbs. 5. Place on baking sheet; quick-freeze for 1 hour; wrap individually in Alcoa Wrap. Return to freezer. 6. When ready to serve, remove from freezer; roll foil down around sides of sticks; top with half slice of bacon; place on baking sheet. 7. Bake 30 minutes at 400° F.

CHICKEN LIVERS SAUTÉ

3-4 servings

½ pound chicken livers
¼ cup butter or margarine
1 cup commercial sour cream

½ teaspoon salt
⅛ teaspoon pepper

1. Clean, cut livers into halves.   2. Sauté in butter in fry pan until lightly browned.   3. Add sour cream, salt, pepper; blend. 4. Serve over cooked rice or on toast.
Variation: Mushrooms, a few slices green pepper or onion may be cooked with livers.

BAKED SALAD BOATS

4 servings

1½ cups coarse-cut cooked
   chicken or turkey
1½ cups sliced celery
½ cup chopped walnuts
   Dash pepper

2 teaspoons minced onion
2 tablespoons lemon juice
¾ cup mayonnaise
1 cup crushed potato chips

1. Combine all ingredients except potato chips; toss lightly. 2. Shape 4 boats from double-thick squares of Alcoa Wrap, about 4 x 3 x 1-inches.   3. Fill boats with salad mixture; top with crushed potato chips; place on baking sheet.   4. Bake 15-20 minutes at 450° F.   5. Serve in foil boats,

ROAST SQUABS

2 servings

2 1-pound squabs

Wild Rice Stuffing

1. Wash, clean squabs; dry thoroughly.   2. Rub inside with salt.   3. Fill cavities with Wild Rice Stuffing, close cavities with skewers or poultry pins, lace with cord.   4. Tie feet together; bend tips of wings backward so they are held against back of squab.   5. Grease squabs thoroughly with soft butter or margarine; sprinkle with salt, pepper.   6. Place squabs on sheet of Alcoa Wrap; bring torn edges together above hens; fold down in tight double folds; fold ends up in tight double folds.   7. Place on rack in shallow pan; add no

water; do not cover.   **8.** Roast 1¼ hours at 425° F.   **9.** Ten minutes before squabs are done, open foil; push it down away from squabs so they will brown.

Good to know: When roasting squabs unstuffed, reduce time 15-20 minutes.

ALMOND CHICKEN

4 servings

¼ cup chopped onion
½ cup chopped cucumber
½ cup chopped carrots
1 8-ounce can water chestnuts, chopped
1 4-ounce can mushrooms, stems and pieces drained

1 8-ounce can bamboo shoots, drained
2 cups boiling water
2 cups uncooked, diced chicken
1 tablespoon olive oil
1 teaspoon salt
½ cup whole almonds or walnuts
1 tablespoon olive oil

1. Combine onion, cucumber, carrots, water chestnuts, mushrooms, bamboo shoots in bowl; pour over boiling water; allow to stand 10 minutes; drain.   **2.** Sauté chicken over low heat in olive oil 10-15 minutes; add drained vegetables, salt; blend; cook 5 minutes longer.   **3.** Sauté almonds or walnuts in olive oil.   **4.** To serve: place chicken mixture in serving dish; top with sautéed almonds.

CORNISH HEN IN FOIL

1 serving

1 Cornish hen (about 1 pound)
Wild Rice Stuffing

Melted butter or margarine
Salt

1. Clean, wash, dry cornish hen.   **2.** Stuff hen with Wild Rice Stuffing.   **3.** Tie legs to tail.   **4.** Brush with melted butter; sprinkle with salt.   **5.** Place in center of a sheet of Alcoa Wrap; wrap tightly using double folds over top and at each end.   **6.** Place on rack in shallow pan.   **7.** Roast 1 hour 15 minutes at 425° F.; for last 15 minutes, open foil for browning.

APPLE RAISIN STUFFING

1 cup minced onion
3 cups diced, pared, cored apples
1 cup seedless raisins
3 tablespoons granulated sugar

¾ cup melted butter or
   margarine
1½ teaspoons salt
7½ cups day-old bread crumbs
⅛ teaspoon pepper

1. Combine all ingredients. 2. Sufficient stuffing for 10-pound fowl.

OYSTER STUFFING

1 cup stewing oysters, chopped
4 cups stale bread cubes
2 teaspoons salt
⅛ teaspoon pepper
⅛ teaspoon sage

3 tablespoons butter or margarine
1 onion, minced
2 tablespoons minced parsley
¾ cup minced celery

1. Place chopped oysters in fry pan; cover; sauté 5 minutes; drain. 2. Combine bread cubes, salt, pepper, sage; add oysters. 3. Melt butter in fry pan; add onion, parsley, celery. 4. Sauté until tender; add to bread mixture; blend. 5. Sufficient stuffing for a 4-pound fowl.

CELERY STUFFING

6 cups finely diced celery
3 cups boiling water
¾ cup minced onion
¾ cup butter or margarine

3 teaspoons poultry seasoning
4 teaspoons salt
1 teaspoon pepper
6 quarts day-old bread cubes

1. Simmer celery in boiling water 15-20 minutes or until tender; drain, reserving 1 cup of liquid. 2. Sauté onion in butter over low heat until tender. 3. Combine seasonings, bread cubes; add celery, the 1 cup celery liquid, onion-butter mixture. 4. Blend thoroughly. 5. Sufficient stuffing for a 15-pound turkey.

CHESTNUT STUFFING

½ pound chestnuts
1 tablespoon butter or margarine
½ pound sausage meat
¼ cup minced onion

½ cup hot water
1 teaspoon dried sage
1½ teaspoons salt
⅛ teaspoon pepper
2 cups soft bread cubes

1. Wash chestnuts; make long slit through shell on both sides.
2. Bake 15 minutes at 500° F. 3. Remove shells; skin; boil in salted water 20 minutes; drain; chop fine. 4. Melt butter; add sausage, onion; sauté until sausage is cooked. 5. Add remaining ingredients, chestnuts; toss together lightly. 6. Sufficient stuffing for a 4 pound fowl.

BREAD STUFFING

½ cup butter or margarine
¼ cup minced onion
¼ cup diced celery
16 slices bread
Milk

¾ teaspoon salt
½ teaspoon poultry seasoning
1 tablespoon minced parsley
⅛ teaspoon pepper

1. Melt butter in large fry pan; add onion, celery; sauté until tender 2. Cut crusts from bread; toast bread. 3. Dip bread into milk, then squeeze out; crumble into butter mixture. 4. Add salt, poultry seasoning, parsley, pepper; stir until mixed. 5. Cook over low heat 3 minutes, stirring frequently; cool. 6. Sufficient stuffing for a 4 pound fowl.

WILD RICE STUFFING #1

¾ cup wild rice, washed
2½ cups boiling water
2 tablespoons butter or margarine
2 tablespoons chopped celery

1 tablespoon chopped onion
1 tablespoon chopped green pepper
½ teaspoon sage
Salt, pepper

1. Cook wild rice in boiling water 15 minutes; drain. 2. Melt butter, add celery, onion, green pepper, sage, salt, pepper;

cook over low heat 5 minutes.   **3.** Add wild rice to seasoning mixture; blend.   **4.** Sufficient stuffing for 2 Cornish hens.

WILD RICE STUFFING #2

1 cup minced onion
½ cup minced celery
¼ cup butter or margarine
1 cup seedless grapes, cut in fourths

¼ cup Sherry wine
1 teaspoon salt
2 cups cooked wild rice*

1. Sauté onion, celery in butter until tender (about 5 minutes).
2. Add grapes, Sherry, salt, wild rice; blend well.   **3.** Yield: about 4 cups stuffing or enough for 4 Cornish hens.

*Good to know: To cook Wild Rice

1 cup water
1 teaspoon salt

½ cup wild rice, raw

1. Bring water to boil; add salt, wild rice; cover.   **2.** Cook 40-45 minutes over low heat.   **3.** Yield: 2 cups wild rice.

COQ AU VIN
(Chicken with Mushroom Sauce)

4 servings

½ pound bacon (about 10 slices)
½ cup sliced onion
1 2-pound frying chicken, quartered
1 cup syrup from canned fruit (peaches, pears, apricots, etc.)
1 teaspoon salt
⅛ teaspoon pepper
Dash garlic salt
Dash thyme
1 bay leaf
1 teaspoon grated lemon rind
1 4-ounce can chopped mushrooms
Pinch saffron, optional
1 cup Burgundy wine

1. Fry bacon until golden brown; remove to absorbent paper; place in warming oven. 2. Sauté onion rings in bacon fat; place in warming oven with bacon. 3. Brown chicken on all sides in hot bacon fat. 4. Combine fruit syrup, salt, pepper, garlic salt, thyme, bay leaf, lemon rind; simmer 10 minutes; pour over browned chicken; cover. 5. Cook 20 minutes over low heat; add mushrooms, saffron, wine; cook 15 minutes longer. 6. To serve: Lay bacon strips on warmed platter; place chicken on top; cover with onion rings; pour sauce over all.

CHICKEN INDIAN STYLE

4 servings

¼ cup butter or margarine
1 medium onion, minced
1 apple, peeled, chopped
⅓ cup all purpose flour
1 tablespoon curry powder
1½ teaspoons salt
⅛ teaspoon pepper
¼ teaspoon ginger
1 cup chicken broth
1 cup milk
½ cup heavy cream
¼ cup lemon juice
3 cups coarsely cut cooked chicken
4 cups hot cooked rice

1. Melt butter in top part of double boiler directly over heat. 2. Add onion, apple; cook until tender. 3. Blend in flour, curry powder, salt, pepper, ginger. 4. Gradually add broth, milk, cream; place over hot water, stirring constantly until mixture is thickened. 5. Cover; cook 10 minutes longer. 6. Add lemon juice, chicken; heat well. 7. Serve over rice.

CHICKEN RICE

4 servings

1 2-pound chicken, cut into pieces
¼ cup olive oil
Salt, pepper
2 4-ounce cans tomato sauce
1 medium onion, chopped

1 medium green pepper, chopped
2 bay leaves
1 clove garlic, minced
2 cups uncooked regular rice
4 chicken bouillon cubes
4 cups boiling water

1. Brown chicken in olive oil in Dutch oven. 2. Sprinkle with salt, pepper. 3. Pour tomato sauce over chicken. 4. Add onion, green pepper, bay leaves, garlic; cover; simmer 15 minutes. 5. Add rice. 6. Dissolve bouillon cubes in boiling water; pour over rice. 7. Cover; simmer 40-45 minutes, stirring several times during cooking.

PANO ESTOFADO

8 servings

7 cloves garlic, peeled
¾ teaspoon ground pepper
5 teaspoons oregano
10 teaspoons salt
2 tablespoons vinegar
8½ pound turkey, cut into serving pieces
12 dry prunes, pitted

10 small whole onions, peeled
4 bay leaves
12 green olives, pitted
2 tablespoons capers
1 tablespoon liquid from jar of capers
½ cup white wine
¾ cup sugar

1. Grind garlic, pepper, oregano, salt together; add vinegar; rub into turkey pieces. 2. Place turkey, giblets in Dutch oven; place prunes, onions, bay leaves, olives, capers, caper juice on top of turkey pieces. 3. Cover; place in refrigerator overnight. 4. Next day, cook over medium heat 10 minutes; reduce heat to low; cook 2 hours. 5. Add wine, sugar; simmer 1 hour longer.

Elegant Eggs

A so-so cook serves eggs for breakfast, period. But a good cook—that's you—knows that the egg can come to lunch, too, and to dinner, and double for snacks, and turn up in fancy dress for parties.

EGG SALAD TOMATO CUPS

6 servings

6 large tomatoes
8 hard-cooked eggs, chopped
¼ cup minced celery
2 tablespoons minced green
  pepper
1 tablespoon minced onion

1 teaspoon salt
¼ cup lemon juice
2 teaspoons prepared mustard
¼ cup mayonnaise
⅓ cup bread crumbs
1 tablespoon butter or margarine,
  melted

1. Cut stem end from tomatoes, scoop out pulp; turn upside down to drain. 2. Combine eggs, celery, green pepper, onion, salt, lemon juice, mustard, mayonnaise; mix. 3. Fill tomatoes with egg mixture. 4. Toss crumbs in melted butter; sprinkle over tops of tomatoes. 5. Place each tomato on a square of Alcoa Wrap; bring up foil to form a cup; place cups in baking pan. 6. Bake 30 minutes at 350° F.

SCRAMBLED EGGS DELUXE

4 servings

3 tablespoons butter or margarine
8 eggs, beaten
½ cup milk

Salt, pepper
4 slices Swiss cheese
1 tablespoon fine bread crumbs

1. Melt 2 tablespoons butter in fry pan. 2. Combine eggs, milk; blend thoroughly. 3. Pour egg mixture into fry pan; cook, stirring constantly, until eggs are partially set. 4. Season with salt, pepper. 5. Shape 4 individual casseroles from double-thick squares of Alcoa Wrap. 6. Place egg mixture in casseroles; top with cheese slices; dot with remaining 1

tablespoon butter; sprinkle with bread crumbs. **7.** Place on baking sheet; bake 12-15 minutes at 375° F. or until top is lightly browned.

SAVORY SCRAMBLED EGGS
6 servings

¼ cup butter or margarine	Salt, pepper
12 eggs, beaten	2 3-oz. packages cream cheese,
⅔ cup milk	cut in ½-inch squares

1. Melt butter in fry pan. **2.** Combine eggs, milk, seasonings; pour into fry pan. **3.** Cook slowly, stirring constantly until eggs begin to thicken. **4.** Add cream cheese cut in squares. **5.** Continue cooking, stirring until cheese is blended and eggs are firm but moist.

BENEDICT-STYLE EGGS
6 servings

½ cup minced onion	⅓ cup milk
2 tablespoons butter or margarine	6 eggs
1 can condensed cream of mush-	3 English muffins, split
room soup, undiluted	6 thin slices cooked ham

1. In large fry pan cook onions in butter until tender. **2.** Blend in soup, milk; heat to boiling. **3.** Lower heat; break eggs into sauce; cook covered about 10 minutes, or until eggs are of desired doneness. **4.** Split muffins; toast under broiler; butter. **5.** Top toasted muffin half with ham slice, then egg. **6.** Spoon sauce remaining in pan over eggs, if desired.

FRENCH OMELET IN FOIL
4 servings

2 tablespoons butter or margarine, melted	1 tablespoon cold water
8 eggs	1 teaspoon salt
	Dash pepper

1. Line large fry pan with heavy duty Alcoa Wrap, extending foil up sides of pan, allowing enough to grasp easily. **2.** Brush foil generously with melted butter. **3.** Place fry pan over low heat. **4.** Combine eggs, water, salt, pepper; beat until just blended. **5.** Pour eggs into pre-heated foil lined fry pan. **6.** As mixture starts to set at edge, lift this portion gently with spatula and move the foil so that uncooked portions flow to bottom.   **7.** When eggs are set and surface is still moist, increase heat to brown bottom quickly.   **8.** Lift omelet from fry pan with extended foil; fold one side over the other; flip onto platter.

BASQUE EGGS AND POTATOES
4-5 servings

3 medium potatoes, cooked, peeled	⅛ teaspoon pepper
¼ cup butter or margarine	4 eggs, beaten
1 medium onion, sliced thin	¼ cup minced green onions or chives
¼ teaspoon salt	2 tablespoons minced parsley

1. Slice cooked potatoes ¼ inch thick.   **2.** Melt butter in fry pan over medium heat.   **3.** Add potatoes, onion slices; brown on one side, turn.   **4.** Sprinkle with salt, pepper; brown on other side.   **5.** Pour eggs over top; sprinkle with minced onions, parsley.   **6.** Turn heat to very low; cover; cook 7-10 minutes until eggs set.

"FRENCHY" EGG SALAD LOAF
6 servings

1 15-inch loaf French bread	1 egg, beaten
8 hard-cooked eggs, chopped	1 clove garlic, minced
⅓ cup diced, stuffed olives	Salt, pepper
1½ cups diced celery	¼ teaspoon oregano
½ cup mayonnaise	3 tablespoons butter or margarine, melted
¼ cup milk	

1. Cut lengthwise slice from top of French bread; reserve. **2.** Scoop out enough crumbs from loaf to make 2 cups.   **3.** Cut almost through to bottom of loaf to make 6 thick slices; replace top slice; cut to match; remove top slices.   **4.** Place hollowed out loaf of bread on 18- x 18-inch square of heavy duty Alcoa Wrap.   **5.** To bread crumbs add eggs, olives, celery, mayonnaise, milk, egg, garlic, salt, pepper, oregano; mix well. **6.** Fill loaf with egg salad mixture.   **7.** Add top bread slices; brush with butter.   **8.** Fold torn edges of foil together in tight double fold on top of loaf of bread; fold ends up using tight double folds.   **9.** Place on baking sheet.   **10.** Bake 35-40 minutes at 425° F.   **11.** To serve, pull foil down around loaf; cut all the way through the bread.

The Well-Dressed Fish

Fish cooked in Alcoa Wrap keep their figures—no falling apart, no loss of delicate flavor, no drying out. Here are the foil-best ways with fish, plus a bonus of other wonderful taste-best fish recipes for year-around eating pleasure.

POACHED FISH

1. Put 2 cups boiling water in fry pan; add 1½ teaspoons salt, 1 slice lemon, 1 slice onion, 2 sprigs parsley, ¼ teaspoon pepper, 1 bay leaf; boil 5 minutes. 2. Reduce heat to low; add fish; cover; simmer gently 10 minutes or until fish flakes easily with a fork. If fish is thick, turn once during cooking.

PAN FRIED FISH

1. Scale; split; clean fish; wipe dry. 2. Melt 2 tablespoons shortening in fry pan over medium heat. 3. Place fish in pan; skin side up. 4. Reduce heat to medium low. 5. Fry 15-20 minutes or until golden brown and tender.

Good to know: *This method is used for all small whole fish such as bass, pickerel, bluefish, red snapper, whitefish, trout and mackerel.*

BROILED FISH

1. Place sheet of Alcoa Wrap on broiler pan. 2. Place fillets or fish halves on foil, skin side down. 3. Brush with melted butter; sprinkle with lemon juice, salt, pepper, paprika. 4. Broil 3-5 inches from heat 10-15 minutes, or until fish has browned and will flake readily when tested with a fork.

BAKED SALMON WITH HERB BUTTER
8 servings

2 to 2½ pounds salmon fillet
4 tablespoons butter or margarine
1 clove garlic, minced or mashed
1 small onion, finely chopped
3 tablespoons minced parsley

3 tablespoons lemon juice
½ teaspoon sweet basil
1 teaspoon salt
½ teaspoon pepper

1. Place salmon fillet on double-thick square of Alcoa Wrap; place in shallow baking pan. 2. Combine butter, garlic, onion, parsley, lemon juice, basil, salt, pepper; blend. 3. Spread over salmon. 4. Bake 25-30 minutes at 300° F. or until fish flakes with a fork. 5. Lift fish with foil onto platter to serve.

STUFFED FLOUNDER WITH TOMATO SAUCE
6 servings

½ package prepared stuffing mix
¼ cup butter or margarine, melted
2 tablespoons water

2 pounds fillet of flounder
1 can condensed cream of tomato soup, undiluted
1 No. 303 can tomatoes

1. Toss stuffing with butter, water until well mixed. 2. Cut each flounder fillet in half; spread each half with stuffing; roll up as for jelly roll; secure with toothpicks. 3. Combine soup, tomatoes; pour into fry pan; lay stuffed flounder rolls on top; cover. 4. Cook 15 minutes over medium heat.

LEMON FLOUNDER
6 servings

2 pounds fillet of flounder
2 tablespoons butter or margarine

½ package prepared stuffing mix
6 slices lemon

1. Cut flounder in 4-inch squares. 2. Prepare stuffing according to package directions. 3. Melt butter in fry pan; add flounder; spread stuffing on each square. 4. Lay lemon slices on top of flounder; cover; cook 5 minutes over low heat.

TUNA-CHEESE PIE

6 servings

Pastry

½ cup shredded sharp Cheddar
cheese

2 sticks pie crust mix
4–5 tablespoons water

1. Add cheese to pie crust mix. 2. Add water; mix. 3. Roll half of pastry to 12-inch circle; fit into 9-inch foil pie pan; chill. 4. Roll other half of pastry to 10-inch circle; cut into ¾-inch strips; reserve for lattice topping.

Filling

2 tablespoons butter or margarine
¼ cup finely chopped green
pepper
¼ cup finely chopped onion
1 10 ½-ounce can cream of
celery soup, undiluted

½ cup shredded sharp Cheddar
cheese
2 6½- or 7-ounce cans chunk
style tuna, drained
¼ cup chopped pimiento

1. Melt butter; add green pepper, onion; cook until tender. 2. Add soup, cheese; stir until blended. 3. Add tuna, pimiento; toss lightly. 4. Cool mixture. 5. Pour into pie shell. 6. Make lattice top on pie; flute edges of pastry. 7. Bake 30 minutes at 400° F.

Good to know: This pie may be cooled, wrapped in Alcoa Wrap, and stored in freezer for about 3 weeks. To bake frozen pie, unwrap; bake 40-45 minutes at 400° F.

FILLET OF HADDOCK MORNAY

4 servings

1 large onion, sliced
2 tablespoons butter or margarine
1 package frozen chopped
spinach, thawed
½ teaspoon salt
⅛ teaspoon pepper
⅛ teaspoon thyme

1 pound fresh or frozen haddock
fillets, thawed
⅓ cup flour
1 teaspoon paprika
1 teaspoon salt
¼ cup butter or margarine

1. Sauté onion in 2 tablespoons butter until tender, lightly browned. 2. Add spinach, salt, pepper, thyme; stir; cover; cook over low heat 7-8 minutes. 3. Line 8 x 8 x 2-inch baking pan with Alcoa Wrap; crimp edges of foil around rim of pan.

4. Place mixture in bottom of foil lined pan. 5. Wash fish fillets; pat dry; cut into halves. 6. Combine flour, paprika, salt in paper bag. 7. Drop fillet pieces into bag; shake to completely flour each piece. 8. Sauté fish in butter until golden brown; place on top of spinach. 9. Cover fish with Mornay Sauce; sprinkle with paprika. 10. Bake 12-15 minutes at 450° F.; place under broiler 2-3 minutes until top is slightly browned.

Mornay Sauce

¼ cup butter or margarine	½ cup grated Parmesan or Swiss
1 tablespoon minced onion	cheese
¼ cup flour	¾ teaspoon salt
1½ cups warm milk	¼ teaspoon pepper
	¼ teaspoon thyme

1. Melt butter; add onion, flour; blend until smooth. 2. Add milk slowly; cook over low heat, stirring constantly until bubbly and thickened. 3. Blend in grated cheese, salt, pepper, thyme.

BAKED SALMON LOAF
4 servings

1 1-pound can salmon	¼ teaspoon monosodium
2 cups fresh bread crumbs	glutamate
1 egg, beaten	2 tablespoons lemon juice
½ cup milk	3 tablespoons melted butter or
2 tablespoons minced parsley	margarine
2 tablespoons minced onion	Green pepper or red pimiento
½ teaspoon salt	strips
¼ teaspoon Tabasco sauce	

1. Combine in large bowl all ingredients except 1 tablespoon of the butter and the green pepper or pimiento strips; toss together lightly. 2. Tear off 36-inch sheet of Alcoa Wrap; fold to make double thickness; grease one side with remaining 1 tablespoon butter. 3. Place salmon mixture in center of sheet; shape into a loaf. 4. Place green pepper or pimiento strips on top of loaf. 5. Bring two edges of Alcoa Wrap together over loaf; make double fold; make double fold on each end.
6. Place on baking sheet. 7. Bake 1 hour at 375° F.

FISH CUPS WITH MUSHROOMS

3 servings

½ cup mushrooms, sliced
2 tablespoons butter or
margarine
1 teaspoon salt
⅛ teaspoon pepper
1½ cups soft bread crumbs

½ cup milk
¾ pound fish fillets, cut into 1-
inch strips
2 tablespoons butter or
margarine

1. Sauté mushrooms in butter. 2. Add salt, pepper, bread crumbs, milk; blend thoroughly. 3. Line 6 greased muffin cups with fillet strips. 4. Fill centers with mushroom stuffing. 5. Cover muffin pan with sheet of Alcoa Wrap, tucking edges under for tight seal. 6. Bake 20 minutes at 350° F.; remove foil cover; dot with butter; continue baking for an additional 20 minutes.

Convenience Cooking: Prepare Fish Cups with Mushrooms the night before or the morning before serving. Refrigerate unbaked cups. When ready to serve, bake as directed, adding 5 minutes to the first baking period.

BAKED SALMON WITH SOUR CREAM

2 servings

1 14-ounce package frozen
salmon steaks
Salt, pepper

½ cup commercial sour cream
4 thin lemon slices
2 tablespoons minced parsley

1. Thaw salmon steaks. 2. Shape 2 individual casseroles from double-thick squares of Alcoa Wrap. 3. Place salmon steaks in casseroles; sprinkle with salt, pepper. 4. Cover with sour cream, lemon slices; sprinkle with parsley. 5. Bake 40 minutes at 350° F. 6. Serve in foil casseroles.

Convenience Cooking: Prepare Salmon with Sour Cream the night before or the morning before serving. Refrigerate unbaked casseroles. When ready to serve, bake as directed, allowing 5 additional minutes for baking.

FISH ON-A-SILVER-SEA

6 servings

1 2½ pound whole whitefish
1½ cups soft bread cubes
½ teaspoon salt
1 small onion, minced
¼ cup chopped celery

1 tablespoon lemon juice
⅓ cup melted butter or margarine, melted
1 tablespoon chopped parsley

1. Clean fish; remove scales, bones, head, tail; pat dry; sprinkle inside with salt. 2. Mix bread cubes, salt, onion, celery, lemon juice, butter, parsley. 3. Pack lightly into fish. 4. Sew up opening or fasten with toothpicks; brush skin of fish with melted butter. 5. Line shallow baking pan with Alcoa Wrap; place fish on foil. 6. Bake 1 hour at 375° F. 7. To serve: Pick up corners of foil; lift fish on foil to heated serving platter; push foil down around the fish; garnish with lemon wedges, parsley.

STUFFED STRIPED BASS

6 servings

Oyster Stuffing

1 cup stewing oysters, chopped
3 cups stale bread cubes
2 teaspoons salt
⅛ teaspoon pepper
⅛ teaspoon sage

3 tablespoons butter or margarine
1 onion, minced
2 tablespoons minced parsley
½ cup minced celery

1. Place chopped oysters in fry pan; cover; sauté 5 minutes; drain. 2. Combine bread cubes, salt, pepper, sage; add oysters. 3. Melt butter in fry pan; add onion, parsley, celery. 4. Sauté until tender; add to bread mixture; blend.

1 striped bass (about 6 pounds), split, boned
Oyster Stuffing

¼ cup butter or margarine, melted
Salt, pepper

1. Place half of fish, skin side down, in center of a lightly greased sheet of heavy duty Alcoa Wrap; spread with Oyster Stuffing; place other half, skin side up, on stuffing.   2. Fasten both sides with skewers.   3. Brush with melted butter; sprinkle with salt, pepper.   4. Bring up sides of foil over fish in tight double folds; fold up ends.   5. Place on baking sheet; bake 1 hour at 400° F.   6. Open foil; push down around fish; brush with melted butter.   7. Return to oven for additional 30 minutes, or until fish is golden brown; brush occasionally with melted butter.

PAELLA   6 servings

⅔ cup olive oil
4 cloves garlic, mashed
1 cup minced onions
½ cup chopped sweet red pepper
2 bay leaves
  Dash saffron
1 cup diced chicken, uncooked
½ cup diced lobster, cooked
1 cup flaked pompano or red snapper, cooked

½ cup chopped shrimp, cooked
¾ cup chopped clams, cooked
1 cup regular rice, uncooked
1½ cups boiling water
1 cup green peas, uncooked
2 teaspoons salt
  Dash pepper
½ cup Sherry wine

1. Sauté in ⅓ cup olive oil, the garlic, onions, red pepper, bay leaves, saffron; add chicken; cook 15-20 minutes.   2. Add lobster, pompano, shrimp, clams.   3. Add rice to remaining ⅓ cup olive oil; fry until lightly brown.   4. Combine fish mixture, rice, water, peas, salt, pepper; simmer 15 minutes or until rice is cooked.   5. Place in 350° F. oven, 20 minutes or until dry.   6. Remove from oven; let stand 10 minutes; add Sherry. 7. Garnish with hard cooked egg slices, strips sweet red pepper.

Good to know: The rest of a menu starring Paella can be simple: Asparagus Spears, Head Lettuce Salad, French Bread, Half Cantaloupe, Coffee.

Superb Seafood

*Sea creatures who started life in shells often find them-
selves coming to the table in a new kind of dress—one
fashioned of foil—and all the better for it! Try these
new ways with oysters, crab, lobsters and the rest of the
deep-sea denizens, all fascinatingly flavored to bring out
their rich and appetizing best.*

COOKED SHRIMP

1. Shell, de-vein raw shrimp. **2.** Drop shrimp into boiling
salted water to cover to which a small sliced onion, 3 slices
lemon, 1 stalk celery, a bay leaf and ⅛ teaspoon pepper have
been added. **3.** Simmer covered 10-15 minutes or until shrimp
is tender and pink.

SAVORY SEAFOOD IN FOIL-BAKED POTATOES

4 servings

4 large baking potatoes	1 tablespoon chopped chives
½ pint commercial sour cream	½ teaspoon seasoned salt
½ cup crab meat or 1 package	Dash pepper
frozen shrimp, cooked, cleaned	4 tablespoons butter or margarine

1. Wash, dry potatoes; wrap in Alcoa Wrap; bake 1 hour at
400° F. **2.** Combine sour cream, crab meat or shrimp, chives,
seasoned salt, pepper; blend well. **3.** Split hot potatoes; add
1 tablespoon butter, ¼ of the seafood sauce to each; serve.

LOBSTER CREOLE

8 servings

1 medium onion, chopped
1 green pepper, chopped
1 clove garlic, minced
¼ cup olive oil
1 medium tomato, quartered
¾ teaspoon salt

⅛ teaspoon pepper
1 8-ounce can tomato sauce
1 pound cooked lobster meat, diced
¼ cup white wine

1. Sauté onions, green pepper, garlic in olive oil until tender.
2. Add tomato; cook until soft. 3. Add salt, pepper, tomato sauce, lobster; simmer 15 minutes. 4. Add wine; cook 2-3 minutes longer. 5. Serve in Alcoa Wrap lined casserole.

JAMES' CRAB MEAT PIE

4-6 servings

Flaky Pastry for one-crust pie
¼ cup chopped parsley
1 teaspoon grated onion
1 cup flaked crab meat

5 eggs
1½ cups light cream
½ teaspoon salt

1. Line a 9-inch pie pan with pastry. 2. Combine parsley, onion; sprinkle over bottom of shell. 3. Spread crab meat over parsley, onion. 4. Combine eggs, cream, salt; beat well, but not frothy; pour into shell. 5. Bake 35 minutes at 425° F. or until set. 6. Cool slightly; cut into wedges.

MARY'S SHRIMP IN BREAD CUPS

6 servings

1 pound fresh shrimp
5 tablespoons butter or margarine
5 tablespoons flour
1½ cups milk
1 teaspoon salt
⅛ teaspoon pepper
2 tablespoons ketchup
1 teaspoon minced onion

1 teaspoon prepared mustard
2 teaspoons Worcestershire sauce
⅛ teaspoon celery salt
1 tablespoon lemon juice
Dash paprika
6 slices bread
2 tablespoons softened butter or margarine

1. Cook shrimp; remove shells, vein. 2. Melt butter in saucepan over low heat; add flour; stir until blended. 3. Add milk gradually; cook until thickened, stirring constantly. 4. Add

salt, pepper, ketchup, onion, mustard, Worcestershire sauce, celery salt, lemon juice, paprika; stir until well blended. 5. Add shrimp; stir gently until shrimp are heated through. 6. Trim crusts from bread slices; spread with butter. 7. Tear off 6-inch lengths of Alcoa Wrap; fold double; shape 6 cups like muffin cups. 8. Place one slice of buttered bread in each cup; push down into shape of cup. 9. Place under broiler until bread is toasted a golden brown. 10. To serve: fill each cup with shrimp mixture; garnish with parsley.

CLAM SOUFFLÉ WITH SAUCE VERTE   6 servings

2 cups minced clams (2 10-ounce cans)
2 cups soft bread crumbs
1 cup liquid from clams
1 tablespoon butter or margarine, melted
½ cup milk
½ teaspoon salt
⅛ teaspoon pepper
4 egg yolks, well beaten
4 egg whites stiffly beaten

1. Combine minced clams, bread crumbs, clam liquid; let stand 10 minutes. 2. Add butter, milk, salt, pepper, egg yolks to clam mixture; mix well. 3. Fold in egg whites. 4. Line 9 x 5 x 3-inch loaf pan with Alcoa Wrap; pour mixture into pan. 5. Bake 40-50 minutes at 350° F. 6. Serve at once with Sauce Verte.

Sauce Verte

3 tablespoons butter or margarine
3 tablespoons flour
¼ teaspoon salt
⅛ teaspoon pepper
1 cup milk
¼ teaspoon celery salt
1 teaspoon onion juice
1 tablespoon lemon juice
¾ cup cooked spinach, finely chopped

1. Melt butter; add flour, salt, pepper; blend to form smooth paste. 2. Add milk gradually, stirring constantly until thick. 3. Add celery salt, onion juice, lemon juice, spinach; blend. 4. Serve hot over Clam Soufflé.

SHRIMP CREOLE

6-8 servings

¼ cup salad oil
1 cup thinly sliced onions
1 cup thinly sliced celery
1 cup green pepper strips, about 2 inches long
3½ cups canned tomatoes
1 8-ounce can tomato sauce
2 bay leaves

1 tablespoon salt
1 tablespoon sugar
1 tablespoon chili powder
⅛ teaspoon Tabasco sauce
1 pound cooked, cleaned shrimp (3½–4 cups)
2 tablespoons flour
⅓ cup water

1. Heat oil in fry pan; sauté onions, celery, green pepper until tender but not brown—about 5 minutes.   2. Add tomatoes, tomato sauce, bay leaves, salt, sugar, chili powder, Tabasco sauce, shrimp; mix well; cover.   3. Simmer 30 minutes. 4. Combine flour, water; add to mixture in fry pan; cook until thickened—about 5 minutes.   5. Serve over rice.

SOUTHERN CRAB CAKES

6 servings

2 6½-ounce cans crab meat, drained, boned, flaked
1 teaspoon salt
¾ teaspoon dry mustard
¼ teaspoon pepper
2 eggs, slightly beaten
1½ teaspoons Worcestershire sauce
2 teaspoons mayonnaise

¼ cup butter or margarine, melted
1½ teaspoons snipped parsley
1 cup dry bread crumbs
1 egg, slightly beaten
2 tablespoons water
½ cup dry bread crumbs
4–6 tablespoons butter or margarine

1. Mix crab meat, salt, mustard, pepper, the 2 eggs, Worcestershire sauce, mayonnaise, the ¼ cup melted butter, parsley, bread crumbs; toss together lightly; chill 1 hour.   2. Shape into 6 medium-sized flat patties.   3. Dip patties into egg and water which have been mixed together, then into remaining ½ cup bread crumbs.   4. Melt the remaining butter in fry pan; add cakes; fry until golden brown on both sides—about 15 minutes—adding more butter if necessary.

SHRIMPS EN COQUILLE

4 servings

1 cut clove garlic
2 tablespoons butter or margarine
2 tablespoons flour
1 cup light cream
½ cup ketchup
1 tablespoon Worcestershire sauce
½ teaspoon salt
⅛ teaspoon pepper
Dash paprika
1 pound cleaned, cooked shrimp
4 baked patty shells

1. Rub fry pan with cut clove of garlic; melt butter; stir in flour to make smooth paste; add cream gradually. 2. Cook over low heat, stirring constantly until smooth, thickened. 3. Add ketchup, Worcestershire sauce, salt, pepper, paprika, shrimp. 4. Cook 2 minutes longer, stirring constantly; serve in baked patty shells.

FRENCH FRIED OYSTERS

6 servings

1 pint fresh oysters
½ cup sifted flour
½ teaspoon salt
½ teaspoon paprika
1 egg, slightly beaten
1 tablespoon water
1 cup fine dry bread or cracker crumbs

1. Drain oysters well. 2. Combine flour, salt, paprika; combine egg, water. 3. Roll oysters in flour mixture; dip in egg mixture; roll in crumbs. 4. Heat fat in French Fryer to 375° F. or until hot enough to brown a cube of bread in 40 seconds.

5. Fry oysters to a deep golden brown—about 2 minutes.
6. Remove from fat; drain on absorbent paper.

PARTY SHRIMP NEWBURG
20 servings

15 pounds raw shrimp
1½ cups butter or margarine
¼ teaspoon nutmeg
¼ teaspoon paprika

2 dozen egg yolks
3 pints heavy cream
½ cup cooking Sherry
  wine

1. Cook shrimp; clean.   2. Melt butter in top of double boiler; add shrimp; cook 3 minutes over direct heat.   3. Add seasonings; place over lower part of double boiler.   4. Beat egg yolks slightly; add cream; mix well.   5. Gradually add egg mixture to shrimp; stir until thickened.   6. Just before serving, stir in Sherry wine.

CURRIED LOBSTER
2 servings

2 tablespoons butter or
  margarine
1 tablespoon flour
½ teaspoon curry powder
1 teaspoon salt
¼ teaspoon sugar

⅛ teaspoon red pepper
1¾ cups milk
1 cup flaked, cooked lobster
2 teaspoons grated onion
2 teaspoons lemon juice
3 radishes, sliced

1. Melt butter over low heat; add dry ingredients; blend until smooth.   2. Add milk; cook, stirring constantly until thickened.
3. Add remaining ingredients; simmer 20 minutes.

CHINESE FRIED SHRIMP
3 servings

1 teaspoon salt
2 teaspoons cornstarch
½ pound shrimp, cooked, cleaned
¼ cup butter or margarine

1 tablespoon Sherry wine
1 cup cooked peas
½ teaspoon sugar

1. Sprinkle salt, cornstarch over shrimp; toss until well coated.
2. Melt butter in fry pan; add shrimp; cook until lightly browned.   3. Add Sherry, cooked peas, sugar, heat; serve.

Good to know: If a chafing dish is used instead of a fry pan, this turns into a fine make-at-the-table party dish.

SHRIMP IN CHEESE SAUCE

4-6 servings

2 tablespoons butter or margarine
2 tablespoons flour
¼ teaspoon salt
⅛ teaspoon pepper
1 cup milk
1 teaspoon Worcestershire sauce

½ cup shredded sharp process cheese
1½ pounds shrimp, cooked, cleaned
1 10-ounce package frozen peas, cooked, drained
1 teaspoon lemon juice

1. Melt butter in saucepan; remove from heat. 2. Add flour, salt, pepper; blend; add milk. 3. Cook over low heat, stirring constantly until thickened. 4. Add Worcestershire sauce, cheese; stir until melted. 5. Add shrimp, peas, lemon juice; stir. 6. Heat thoroughly before serving. 7. Serve in pastry shells or bread baskets.

OYSTERS KILPATRICK

6 servings

1 dozen large oysters or 1 12-ounce can frozen oysters, thawed
1½ teaspoons lemon juice
Dash pepper

¼ cup tomato paste
½ cup grated sharp cheese
1 strip bacon, cut into 6 pieces
Dash paprika

1. Cut out 6 circles from double-thick squares of Alcoa Wrap using saucer for pattern; turn up edges ½ inch around circles to form casseroles. 2. Wash, drain oysters; place in foil casseroles. 3. Sprinkle ¼ teaspoon lemon juice, dash pepper over each casserole. 4. Spread tomato paste on oysters; cover with 1 tablespoon grated cheese; lay piece of bacon on cheese; place 1 more teaspoon grated cheese on bacon; top with dash of paprika. 5. Place casseroles on baking sheet; bake 10 minutes at 500° F.

Dreams in a Dish

Everybody loves casserole dishes, and there are so many exciting kinds that you could serve one every day of the year with never a repeat. But, you say, there's always that crusty, torture-to-scrub pan facing you when the meal's over? Not any more—not when you've learned the wonder-working magic of aluminum foil casserole cookery!

CASSEROLES

Casserole dishes are real budget stretchers, an excellent way to use the last bit of Sunday's roast. They are the answer to what to have for dinner on a busy day, in that many can be prepared ahead and stored in the refrigerator until dinner time. A casserole dish is perfect for the hostess who must double as cook and waitress too.

The container used can add a gala touch even to family meals especially if you have fashioned your own from Alcoa Wrap.

Strong, sturdy and flexible, it can be formed into any shape you desire all the way from simple individual casseroles to a more elaborate fish or lobster baking container. And there is no clean up! Simply use and toss away.

Here are a few suggestions on how to make Alcoa Wrap casseroles.

How to Make Individual or Large Round Casseroles:

1. Mold double-thick sheet of Alcoa Wrap over the bottom of: glass or custard cup for individual casseroles; 2- or 3-quart mixing bowl for large casserole.
2. Remove; crimp edges of foil for added strength.
3. Place on baking sheet before putting into oven.

How to Make Foil Casserole with Bread Basket Server:

1. Shape double-thick sheet of Alcoa Wrap over outside of bread basket (about 7 inches in diameter, 3 inches deep).
2. Remove; place inside, pressing firmly into place.
3. Crush edges down to form collar, handles along rim.
4. Use foil casserole for baking; place in bread basket for serving.

How to Make Individual Crab or Seafood Shell:

1. Tear off 7 x 18-inch piece heavy duty foil.
2. Fold in half lengthwise.
3. By folding and crimping bring the two longer sides in toward center to shape a cup 2½ inches wide by 3¾ inches long, about ¾ inch deep.
4. Bring two ends together; crimp so that at least 1 inch sticks out to simulate crab legs.

How to Make Individual Lobster Mold:

1. Tear off 16 x 18-inch piece heavy duty foil.
2. Fold in half lengthwise.
3. Lay on side two 4-ounce juice glasses which have been stacked together. (Closed end of glass 4 inches from one end of foil.)

4. Mold foil ⅔ of the way up sides and ends of glasses to make body.
5. Crimp in any excess on sides to make ½-inch edge.
6. Mold excess foil at closed end of glass into a fantail.
7. Excess foil at other end of glasses should measure approximately 6 inches.
8. From this excess foil cut two claws allowing 2 inches in center for feelers.
9. From center portion make 2 strips which are crimped and turned to form feelers.
10. Remove the glasses from body cavity and fill with baked lobster.

How to Line Casserole:
1. Shape sheet of Alcoa Wrap over outside of casserole.
2. Remove; place inside, pressing firmly into place.
3. Crush edges down to form a collar along rim.

STUFFED MUSHROOMS   6 servings

1 pound large fresh mushrooms	⅛ teaspoon pepper
¼ cup butter or margarine	1 tablespoon ketchup
1 cup soft bread crumbs	1 tablespoon lemon juice
1 cup canned crab meat flaked	3 strips bacon
1 teaspoon salt	½ cup light cream

1. Wash mushrooms; remove stems; chop stems fine. 2. Melt butter in heavy fry pan; add chopped stems; cook 5 minutes over low heat. 3. Stir in bread crumbs, crab meat; cook 2 minutes. 4. Remove from heat; add salt, pepper, ketchup, lemon juice; stir until well blended. 5. Stuff mushroom caps with mixture. 6. Line a 9-inch square cake pan with Alcoa Wrap. Allow the foil to extend down over sides of pan to be crinkled or shaped attractively. 7. Place stuffed mushroom caps in pan. 8. Cut each strip of bacon into quarters; place two quarters criss-cross fashion on top of stuffing; fasten with toothpicks. 9. Pour cream around mushrooms. 10. Bake 25 minutes at 400° F. 11. Remove from oven; serve at once.

SUNSHINE BROCCOLI

6 servings

2 10½ ounce packages frozen
  broccoli spears, cooked, drained

Cheese Sauce:

¼ cup butter or margarine
¼ cup flour
½ teaspoon salt

1 cup milk
½ pound sharp Cheddar cheese,
  shredded (about 2 cups)

1. Melt butter; blend in flour, salt. 2. Add milk gradually; cook, stirring constantly until thick, smooth. 3. Add cheese; stir until melted. 4. Remove from heat.

Stuffed Eggs:

6 warm, hard-cooked eggs
2 tablespoons mayonnaise
1 tablespoon vinegar

½ teaspoon dry mustard
Salt, pepper

1. Cut eggs in half lengthwise. 2. Remove yolks; mash. 3. Add mayonnaise, vinegar, dry mustard, salt, pepper; mix well. 4. Stuff egg halves with mixture.

To Assemble:

1. Shape six oval or oblong individual casseroles from double-thick squares of Alcoa Wrap. 2. Divide broccoli spears among casseroles. 3. Place 2 halves stuffed eggs on top of broccoli. 4. Pour cheese sauce over eggs. 5. Place casseroles on baking sheet; bake 15 minutes at 375° F.

OLIVE CHEESE CUSTARD

4 servings

5 slices bread
2 tablespoons butter or
  margarine
  Salt, pepper
½ cup sliced stuffed olives

1 cup shredded Cheddar cheese
3 eggs
¼ teaspoon dry mustard
2⅓ cups milk

1. Spread both sides of slices of bread with butter; cut into cubes. 2. Place layer of bread cubes in 1½ quart casserole

lined with Alcoa Wrap; sprinkle lightly with salt, pepper. 3. Cover with layer of olives; then cheese. 4. Repeat steps 2, 3 until all ingredients have been used. 5. Beat eggs; add dry mustard, milk; blend thoroughly. 6. Pour over mixture in casserole. 7. Bake 40-45 minutes at 300° F.

Good to know: For Mushroom Cheese Custard, omit olives; use instead ½ cup sautéed sliced mushrooms.

SWISS CHEESE PIE

6 servings

½ recipe your favorite pastry
1 tablespoon softened butter or margarine
3 eggs, beaten
1½ cups heavy cream
½ teaspoon salt
⅛ teaspoon sugar
⅛ teaspoon pepper
Dash nutmeg
Dash cayenne pepper
1 cup grated Swiss cheese (¼ pound)

1. Prepare ½ recipe pastry; roll it out; fit into 9-inch pie pan; chill. 2. Spread softened butter over surface of unbaked pie shell. 3. Combine eggs, cream, salt, sugar, pepper, nutmeg, cayenne; blend well. 4. Sprinkle grated cheese over bottom of pie shell; pour in cream mixture. 5. Bake 15 minutes at 425° F.; reduce heat to 300° F.; bake additional 15-20 minutes.

CHEESE SOUFFLÉ

5-6 servings

¼ cup butter or margarine
¼ cup flour
1½ cups milk

1 teaspoon salt
Dash cayenne
½ pound Cheddar cheese, grated
6 eggs, separated

1. Melt butter; add flour; blend thoroughly. 2. Add milk gradually; blend well. 3. Cook, stirring constantly until sauce is thick, smooth. 4. Add salt, cayenne, cheese; stir until cheese melts. 5. Remove from heat. 6. Beat egg yolks until thick, lemon-colored; gradually stir into sauce. 7. Beat egg whites until stiff but not dry; slowly fold into sauce. 8. Tear off 12 x 36-inch piece of Alcoa Wrap; fold in half lengthwise; bring fold around 2-quart casserole, molding it to sides; fold down edges together in tight double fold to make 3-inch collar extending above casserole. 9. Pour mixture into the un-greased casserole. 10. Bake 1¼ hours at 300° F. 11. Remove foil collar gently; serve immediately.

NOODLE PUDDING

8 servings

¼ pound wide noodles, uncooked
3 egg yolks
¾ cup sugar
½ pound farmer's cheese (or cottage cheese)

1 pint commercial sour cream
½ teaspoon salt
¼ cup raisins
1 teaspoon vanilla
3 egg whites

1. Cook noodles 15 minutes in boiling salted water; drain; do not rinse. 2. Combine egg yolks, sugar; blend thoroughly. 3. Add cheese, sour cream, salt, raisins, vanilla, noodles; blend well. 4. Beat egg whites until stiff but not dry; fold into noodle mixture. 5. Line bottom and sides of 9 x 13 x 2-inch bake pan with sheet of heavy duty Alcoa Wrap, allowing foil to extend over top of pan; crimp foil around edges. 6. Pour noodle mixture in pan; spread evenly. 7. Bake uncovered 50-60 minutes at 350° F. or until knife comes out clean.

Good to know: Pudding may be baked ahead of time; cooled slightly; covered with foil; refrigerated. When ready to serve, heat covered pudding 30 minutes at 400° F.

COTTAGE CHEESE HERBED ONIONS
6 servings

2 pounds whole small onions
4 tablespoons butter or margarine
4 tablespoons flour
½ cup milk
½ teaspoon salt
Dash pepper

¾ teaspoon marjoram
1½ cups cottage cheese, cream style
1½ cups buttered fresh bread crumbs

1. Cook peeled whole onions in boiling salted water 20 minutes, or until tender; drain. 2. Shape 6 individual casseroles from double-thick squares of Alcoa Wrap; place onions in casseroles. 3. Melt butter; blend in flour; add milk; cook until thick, stirring constantly. 4. Quickly blend in salt, pepper, marjoram, cheese; spread evenly over onions; sprinkle with crumbs. 5. Place casseroles on baking sheet; bake 25 minutes at 375° F.

CHICKEN DIVAN
6 servings

2 pounds asparagus
1 10½-ounce can condensed cream of chicken soup, undiluted
¼ teaspoon nutmeg
1 teaspoon Worcestershire sauce

1 cup grated Parmesan cheese
1 cup sliced cooked chicken or turkey
½ cup heavy cream, whipped
¾ cup mayonnaise or Hollandaise sauce

1. Make 6 individual foil casseroles by molding double-thick squares of Alcoa Wrap around outside of individual casserole dish. 2. Cook asparagus in boiling salted water until tender; drain; place in Alcoa Wrap casseroles. 3. Combine soup, nutmeg, Worcestershire sauce; pour half of mixture over asparagus; sprinkle with ⅓ cup of the cheese. 4. Top with chicken; pour over remaining soup mixture; sprinkle with ⅓ cup cheese. 5. Bake 25 minutes at 400° F. 6. Fold whipped cream into mayonnaise or Hollandaise sauce; spread over chicken; sprinkle with remaining ⅓ cup cheese. 7. Broil 2-3 minutes or until golden brown.

Taste Tip: Casseroles may be lined with toast rounds to add crispness.

ROCKINGHAM CHICKEN PIE

6 servings

2 cups diced cooked chicken
1 cup cooked peas
½ cup diced, cooked celery
2 cups chicken gravy or medium cream sauce

1 teaspoon salt
1 tablespoon chopped parsley
Relish Crust Biscuits

1. Combine chicken, peas, celery, gravy, salt, parsley; blend well. 2. Shape 6 individual casseroles from double thick squares of Alcoa Wrap. 3. Pour chicken mixture into foil casseroles; top with Relish Crust Biscuits; place foil casseroles on baking sheet. 4. Bake 20-25 min. at 425° F., or until biscuits are golden brown.

Relish Crust Biscuits

2 cups biscuit mix
⅛ teaspoon paprika
1 tablespoon chopped parsley
2 tablespoons shredded raw carrot

1 tablespoon chopped green pepper
⅔ cup milk

1. Combine biscuit mix, paprika, parsley, carrot, green pepper; blend well. 2. Make a well in biscuit mix; add milk; stir lightly. 3. Turn onto floured board; knead several times. 4. Roll dough to ½-inch thickness; cut into six rounds or diamonds; place over hot chicken mixture in casseroles.

SALMON CASSEROLE WITH LEMON CUCUMBER SAUCE
4-5 servings

1½ cups water
1½ cups packaged pre-cooked rice
2 tablespoons instant minced onion
¼ cup cold water
1 pound can salmon, drained, flaked

2 teaspoons salt
¼ teaspoon pepper
2 egg whites
1 egg, whole
2 tablespoons butter or margarine, melted

1. Bring water to boil in saucepan; add rice; cover; remove from heat; let stand 5 minutes. 2. Combine onion, cold water; let stand five minutes. 3. Combine rice, onion, salmon, salt, pepper. 4. Beat egg whites, egg; add to salmon mixture; blend well. 5. Press into 1½ quart Alcoa Wrap lined casserole; brush top with melted butter. 6. Bake 30 minutes at 375° F. 7. Garnish with lemon wedges, parsley; serve with Lemon Cucumber Sauce.

Lemon Cucumber Sauce

2 egg yolks
¼ cup lemon juice
½ cup butter or margarine

½ cup well-drained, grated cucumber

1. Beat egg yolks slightly in small saucepan. 2. Add lemon juice, ¼ cup butter; stir over low heat until blended. 3. Add remaining ¼ cup butter; continue cooking, stirring constantly, until thickened, smooth. 4. Stir in grated cucumber.

SUPERB HALIBUT

6 servings

1½ pounds halibut fillets or 2 packages frozen halibut, semi-thawed
1 cup water
¼ cup dry white wine
¼ cup lemon juice
2 tablespoons butter or margarine
2 tablespoons flour
1 cup milk

¼ teaspoon salt
⅛ teaspoon pepper
1 10-ounce package frozen chopped spinach, cooked, drained
¼ cup finely chopped onion
¾ cup grated sharp cheese
2 eggs, slightly beaten
1 tablespoon butter or margarine

1. Place fish in large fry pan; add water, wine, lemon juice; cover; simmer 5 minutes. 2. Remove fish, set aside; cook liquid until ¾ cup broth remains. 3. Melt butter; stir in flour; add milk; cook, stirring constantly until mixture is thickened; add salt, pepper. 4. Pour fish broth gradually into white sauce. 5. Add spinach, onion, ¼ cup grated cheese; cook 5 minutes. 6. Stir in beaten eggs, quickly. 7. Place fish in 2-quart Alcoa Wrap lined casserole. 8. Pour sauce over fish; sprinkle with remaining ½ cup grated cheese; dot with butter. 9. Bake uncovered 10-12 minutes at 400° F.

FISH BAKE SUPREME

4 servings

6 ounces thin spaghetti, uncooked
½ cup butter or margarine, melted
¼ cup chopped parsley
1 tablespoon lemon juice
1 teaspoon grated onion

⅓ cup chutney, cut fine
½ teaspoon salt
¼ teaspoon pepper
¾ pound fish fillets, thawed

1. Cook spaghetti in boiling salted water until tender; drain. 2. Combine butter, parsley, lemon juice, onion, chutney, salt, pepper. 3. Add about two-thirds butter mixture to spaghetti. 4. Divide mixture into four 1½ cup individual casseroles shaped from Alcoa Wrap. 5. Arrange fish fillets on top. 6. Pour remaining butter mixture over fish; place foil casseroles on baking sheet. 7. Cover each casserole with foil; bake 30 minutes at 350° F.; remove cover; bake about 5 minutes longer.

MILE-HIGH TUNA SOUFFLÉ

5-6 servings

½ cup butter or margarine
½ cup flour
2 teaspoons salt
½ teaspoon paprika
   Dash cayenne

2 cups milk
8 egg yolks
2 6½- or 7-ounce cans chunk-style tuna, drained
8 egg whites

1. Melt butter in top of double boiler placed over boiling water. 2. Remove from boiling water; add flour, salt, paprika, cayenne; blend thoroughly. 3. Add milk gradually; blend well. 4. Return to boiling water; cook, stirring constantly until sauce is thick, smooth. 5. Remove from heat. 6. Beat egg yolks until thick, lemon-colored; gradually stir into sauce. 7. Add tuna; mix thoroughly. 8. Beat egg whites until stiff but not dry; slowly fold in sauce. 9. Tear off 12 x 36-inch piece of Alcoa Wrap; fold in half lengthwise; bring foil around 2-quart casserole, molding it to sides; fold torn edges together in tight double fold to make 3-inch collar extending above casserole. 10. Pour mixture into the ungreased casserole. 11. Bake 1¼ hours at 300° F. 12. Remove foil collar gently. 13. Serve immediately.

Variations: 2 cups crab meat, shrimp, or clams, drained, chopped, may be substituted for tuna.

TUNA TETRAZZINI

6 servings

1 tablespoon butter or margarine
¼ cup chopped onion
1 10½ ounce can condensed cream of mushroom soup, undiluted
1 6-ounce can (⅔ cup) evaporated milk or ⅔ cup light cream
⅓ cup grated sharp Cheddar cheese

1 6½- 7-ounce can tuna, drained
1 3-ounce can sliced mushrooms, drained
½ cup chopped ripe olives
2 teaspoons lemon juice
¼ cup chopped pimiento
¼ teaspoon garlic salt
¼ cup grated Parmesan cheese
½ teaspoon paprika

1. Melt butter in saucepan. 2. Add onions; sauté until tender. 3. Add soup, milk, sharp cheese; heat, stirring constantly. 4. Add tuna, mushrooms, olives, lemon juice, pimiento, garlic salt. 5. Shape 2-quart casserole from double thick square of

Alcoa Wrap. 6. Pour mixture into foil casserole. 7. Sprinkle with grated cheese, paprika. 8. Place casserole on baking sheet. 9. Bake 20-25 minutes at 375° F.

TUNA PUFF CUPS

8 servings

4 eggs, slightly beaten
2 cups milk
2 cups fresh bread crumbs
1 6½-ounce can tuna, flaked
1 teaspoon salt

1 tablespoon prepared mustard
1 tablespoon minced onion
1 10½-ounce can condensed cream
    of mushroom soup, undiluted
2 tablespoons butter or margarine

1. Combine eggs, milk, crumbs, tuna, salt, mustard, onion. 2. Shape 8 individual cups from double thick squares of Alcoa Wrap. 3. Pour tuna mixture into cups. 4. Place cups in shallow baking pan; add warm water to depth of ¾ to 1 inch. 5. Bake, uncovered, 35 minutes at 400° F. 6. Before puffs are done, heat soup; add butter. 7. Serve puffs in foil cups with hot soup sauce.

Convenience Cooking: Prepare Tuna Puff Cups early in the day. Refrigerate unbaked cups. When ready to serve, bake as directed, allowing 5 additional minutes for baking.

HAM ROLL-UPS

6 servings

2 10-ounce packages frozen
    asparagus spears
6 slices boiled ham
1 pint commercial sour cream
½ medium sized onion, finely
    grated
¾ teaspoon salt

⅛ teaspoon pepper
¼ teaspoon dry mustard
½ clove garlic, minced
2 tablespoons butter or margarine,
    melted
2 slices bread, cut in ½-inch
    cubes

1. Cook asparagus as directed on package; drain. 2. Roll 3-4 spears of asparagus in each ham slice; place with fold side down in Alcoa Wrap lined casserole. 3. Mix together sour cream, onion, salt, pepper, mustard, garlic; spoon over ham rolls. 4. Pour melted butter over bread cubes; toss lightly; arrange on top of casserole. 5. Bake uncovered 20 minutes at 375° F.

BEEF BALL CASSEROLES

8 servings

2 pounds ground beef
1 teaspoon salt
½ teaspoon pepper
1 cup finely chopped onion
2 eggs, beaten
24 stuffed olives
¼ cup butter or margarine

¼ cup flour
½ cup water
1 pint commercial sour cream
1 teaspoon lemon juice
½ teaspoon chopped parsley
¼ teaspoon salt
¼ teaspoon paprika

1. Combine ground beef, salt, pepper, chopped onion, eggs; blend well. 2. Form mixture into 24 1½ inch balls with an olive in center of each. 3. Brown meat balls in butter. 4. Shape 8 individual casseroles from double thick Alcoa Wrap. 5. Place 3 browned meat balls in each casserole. 6. Pour off fat in fry pan; reserve ¼ cup. 7. Blend flour with the ¼ cup fat in fry pan. 8. Add water, sour cream, lemon juice, parsley, salt, paprika; cook until thickened, stirring constantly. 9. Pour sauce over meat balls in foil casseroles. 10. Place casseroles on baking sheet; bake 10 minutes at 350° F.

Good to know: Beef casseroles can be prepared ahead of time and refrigerated; allow 5 additional minutes to heat chilled casseroles.

VEAL CASSEROLE WITH CURRY BISCUITS   6 servings

¼ cup butter or margarine
¼ cup chopped onion
¼ cup minced green pepper
¼ cup flour

2 chicken bouillon cubes
2 cups hot water
3 cups cubed cooked veal
¼ cup chopped pimiento

1. Melt butter in fry pan.   2. Add onion, green pepper; cook until tender.   3. Blend in flour; add chicken bouillon cubes dissolved in water; cook until thickened.   4. Add veal, pimiento; mix thoroughly.   5. Place in Alcoa Wrap lined 1-quart casserole; bake uncovered 10 minutes at 425° F.   6. Remove from oven; top with biscuits; bake 10 minutes longer.

Curry Biscuits

2 cups sifted all purpose flour
3 teaspoons baking powder
½ teaspoon salt

½ teaspoon curry powder
¼ cup shortening
⅔ cup milk (approximate)

1. Sift flour, baking powder, salt, curry powder together.
2. Cut in shortening until mixture resembles corn meal.
3. Make a well in center of mixture; add almost all milk; stir until soft dough is formed, adding remaining milk if necessary.   4. Knead dough gently on lightly floured board about 30 seconds.   5. Pat out to ½-inch thickness; cut into small biscuits; place on top of casserole.

PERFECT CASSEROLE   4 servings

1 pound ground beef
¼ cup commercial sour cream
1½ tablespoons dried onion soup
  (mix well before measuring)
1 egg, slightly beaten
¾ cup soft bread crumbs
3 tablespoons flour
½ teaspoon paprika

2 tablespoons butter or
  margarine
½ cup canned sliced mushrooms
  with liquid
¾ cup condensed cream of
  chicken soup
¾ cup water

1. Mix meat, cream, onion soup, egg, bread crumbs together; shape into 8 balls.   2. Roll meat balls in flour blended with

paprika; brown slowly on all sides in fat. 3. Combine mush-rooms with liquid, cream of chicken soup, water; pour over balls. 4. Cover; simmer over low heat 20 minutes. 5. Pour into Alcoa Wrap lined casserole. 6. Top with Butter Crumb Dumplings. 7. Bake uncovered 20-25 minutes at 400° F.

Butter Crumb Dumplings

1 cup sifted all purpose flour
2 teaspoons baking powder
2 teaspoons poppy seeds
½ teaspoon celery salt
½ teaspoon poultry seasoning
1 teaspoon dried onion flakes

1 tablespoon salad oil
½ cup milk
2 tablespoons butter or margarine, melted
1 cup soft bread crumbs

1. Combine flour, baking powder, poppy seeds, celery salt, poultry seasoning, onion flakes. 2. Combine oil, milk; add to flour mixture; beat until smooth. 3. Stir melted butter into crumbs; spread out on sheet of Alcoa Wrap. 4. Drop dough by tablespoons in 8 equal portions into buttered crumbs; roll around to coat with crumbs. 5. Place on top of Perfect Casserole; bake as directed.

SOUTHERN CASSEROLE

6 servings

2 tablespoons fat
½ cup fresh or canned mushrooms
2 tablespoons flour
1 cup meat stock
½ pound Brussels sprouts
3 cups chopped cooked ham
5 cooked sweet potatoes, peeled

½ cup top milk or cream
2 tablespoons melted butter or margarine
2 tablespoons brown sugar
Salt
Dash nutmeg

1. Melt fat in fry pan; add mushrooms; brown lightly over medium heat. 2. Sprinkle flour over mixture; blend well. 3. Add stock slowly, stirring constantly; cook until thick, smooth. 4. Cook Brussels sprouts 15 minutes in small amount of water; drain. 5. In 2-quart Alcoa Wrap lined casserole, place ham, Brussels sprouts, mushroom mixture. 6. Bake un-covered 30 minutes at 350° F. 7. Mash sweet potatoes; add milk or cream, butter, brown sugar, salt, nutmeg; beat until

light, fluffy. **8.** Remove casserole from oven; spread sweet potato mixture over top baked ingredients. **9.** Return to oven; bake 25-30 minutes at 425° F. or until potatoes are browned.

DEVILED MUSHROOMS

4 servings

1 pint fresh mushrooms
Salt, pepper
2 teaspoons lemon juice
1 hard-cooked egg yolk
1 raw egg yolk, beaten

½ cup bread crumbs
1 tablespoon butter or margarine, softened
Dash of Tabasco sauce

1. Wash mushrooms; drain; dry; remove stems. **2.** Shape a 1½ quart casserole from double thick square of Alcoa Wrap. **3.** Place mushroom caps, stems in casserole. **4.** Season with salt, pepper, lemon juice. **5.** Mash hard-cooked egg yolk; add raw egg yolk, bread crumbs, softened butter, Tabasco sauce; blend well. **6.** Sprinkle egg-bread crumb mixture on top of mushrooms. **7.** Place casserole on baking sheet; bake 25-30 minutes at 350° F.

CHOW STRING BEANS WITH SOUR CREAM

6 servings

2 10-ounce packages frozen cut green beans
¼ cup vegetable oil
3 tablespoons chopped onion
1 teaspoon flour
1 tablespoon water
½ teaspoon salt

⅛ teaspoon pepper
¼ teaspoon grated lemon peel
1½ tablespoons chopped parsley
½ cup commercial sour cream
2 tablespoons cornflake crumbs
¼ cup grated Cheddar cheese

1. Thaw green beans. **2.** Heat oil in fry pan using high heat; add green beans, onions; cook, stirring constantly about 1 minute; cover; cook additional 1 minute. (Note: beans should be bright green with crisp, crunchy texture.) **3.** Stir in flour; add water, salt, pepper, lemon peel, parsley, sour cream; blend thoroughly. **4.** Line 1½ quart casserole with Alcoa Wrap, crimping foil around edges. **5.** Pour bean mixture into casserole; sprinkle with cornflake crumbs; top with grated cheese. **6.** Bake 30 minutes at 350° F.

Good to know: Casserole may be prepared ahead of time; covered with foil; refrigerated, then baked right before serving time. (Increase baking time to 40 minutes.)

SHRIMP CASSEROLE HARPIN
6 *servings*

2 pounds large fresh shrimp
1 tablespoon lemon juice
3 tablespoons salad oil
¾ cup raw regular or processed rice
2 tablespoons butter or margarine
¼ cup minced green pepper
¼ cup minced onion
1 teaspoon salt
⅛ teaspoon pepper
⅛ teaspoon mace
Dash cayenne pepper
1 can condensed tomato soup, undiluted
1 cup heavy cream
½ cup slivered almonds
½ cup Sherry wine
Paprika

1. Shell, clean, cook shrimp in boiling salted water 5 minutes; drain. 2. Place in 2-quart Alcoa Wrap lined casserole; sprinkle with lemon juice, oil. 3. Cook rice as package directs; drain. 4. Melt butter; add green pepper, onion; sauté five minutes; add rice, salt, pepper, mace, cayenne pepper, tomato soup, cream, ¼ cup of the slivered almonds, Sherry wine; pour over shrimp. 5. Top with remaining almonds; sprinkle with paprika. 6. Bake uncovered approximately 55 minutes at 350° F. or until bubbly.

EGGPLANT PARMESAN

4-6 servings

1 medium eggplant
1 cup dry bread crumbs
1 egg, beaten
2 tablespoons water
3 tablespoons olive oil
Salt, pepper

1 onion, sliced
2½ cups canned tomatoes
1 tablespoon sugar
¾ cup grated Parmesan cheese

1. Peel, slice eggplant. 2. Dip slices into crumbs, egg combined with water, then crumbs again. 3. Fry slices in olive oil until lightly browned. 4. Place eggplant in Alcoa Wrap lined baking pan; sprinkle with salt, pepper. 5. Toss onion slices in fry pan; add to eggplant. 6. Combine tomatoes, sugar; pour over eggplant. 7. Sprinkle cheese over top. 8. Bake 20-25 minutes at 375° F.

DEVILED OYSTERS

6 servings

3 tablespoons butter or margarine
1 medium onion, finely chopped
1 quart oysters, drained, chopped
1 tablespoon chopped parsley
⅛ teaspoon pepper
1 tablespoon Worcestershire sauce
1 teaspoon dry mustard

2 eggs, beaten
½ cup dry bread crumbs.

Topping:
1 tablespoon melted butter or margarine
¼ cup dry bread crumbs

1. Melt butter in fry pan. 2. Add onions; sauté until tender. 3. Add oysters, parsley, pepper, Worcestershire sauce, dry

mustard; simmer 2 minutes.   **4.** Blend oyster mixture gradually into beaten eggs.   **5.** Add bread crumbs; mix lightly.   **6.** Shape casserole from double thick square of Alcoa Wrap around 1-quart bowl.   **7.** Pour mixture into greased foil casserole.   **8.** Combine melted butter, dry bread crumbs; sprinkle over oyster mixture.   **9.** Place foil casserole on baking sheet.   **10.** Bake 15 minutes at 425° F.

OYSTERS ROCKEFELLER

3 servings

1 pint fresh or frozen oysters, thawed
1 package frozen chopped spinach, cooked
⅓ cup finely chopped onion
¼ teaspoon celery salt
¼ teaspoon salt
Dash Tabasco sauce
3 tablespoons butter or margarine
¼ cup dry bread crumbs

1. Drain oysters; pat dry between paper towels.   **2.** Shape three individual casseroles from double thick squares of Alcoa Wrap.   **3.** Place oysters in foil casseroles.   **4.** Combine spinach, onion, celery salt, salt, Tabasco sauce, butter; cook 5 minutes; add bread crumbs.   **5.** Spread spinach mixture over oysters; place casseroles on baking sheet.   **6.** Bake 20 minutes at 425° F.   **7.** Serve in foil casseroles.

VEGETABLE BUYING GUIDE

Vegetable	Characteristics of Good Quality	Number of Servings	Amount to Buy
Asparagus	Stalks straight, crisp, green; tips moist, compact, unbroken	2 4 6	⅔ pound; 8-10 stalks 1⅓ pounds; 16-20 stalks 2 pounds; 24-30 stalks
Beans, Green or Yellow	Pods crisp, bright color, well filled	2 4 6	½ pound 1 pound 1½ pounds
Beans, Lima	Pods clean, unspotted, green, well filled	2 4 6	1-1½ pounds in pod 2-3 pounds in pod 4 pounds in pod
Beets	Young, tops fresh, unwilted; mature; smooth velvety skin	2 4 6	½ pound; 2-4 beets 1 pound; 4-8 beets 1½ pounds; 6-12 beets
Broccoli	Buds dark green, compact; stems short, crisp	2 4 6	⅔ pound 1⅓ pounds 2 pounds
Brussels Sprouts	Head, round, solid, compact, green	2 4 6	½ pound 1 pound 1½ pounds; 1 quart
Cabbage	Head solid, heavy; leaves fresh	2 4 6	½ pound 1 pound 1½ pounds
Carrots	Firm, uniform shape; bright color; fresh tops	2 4 6	⅔ pound 1⅓ pounds 2 pounds
Cauliflower	Head white, well filled; leaves fresh, green	2 4 6	small; 1 pound medium; 1½ pounds large; 2½ pounds
Corn on Cob	Ears well filled; husks green; kernels soft, milky	2 4	2-4 ears 4-8 ears
Greens, Kale, Spinach, Swiss Chard	Leaves fresh, crisp, tender	2 4 6	¾ pound 1½ pounds 2½ pounds
Peas	Pods green, unspotted, velvety, well filled	2 4 6	1 pound 2 pounds 3 pounds
Potatoes	Clean, smooth, firm. Regular shape and size	2 4 6	2 medium; ⅔ pound 4 medium; 1⅓ pounds 6 medium; 2 pounds
Squash, Summer (Cymling, Crookneck, Straightneck, Vegetable marrow)	Young, firm, thin skinned	2 4 6	small; ½ pound medium; 1 pound large; 1½ pounds
Squash, Winter (Hubbard, Acorn)	Thick skinned; heavy for size	2 4	1 acorn; ¼ Hubbard 2 acorns; ½ Hubbard
Turnips and Rutabagas	Roots smooth, firm, heavy; size small to medium	2 4 6	⅔ pound 1⅓ pounds 2 pounds

Vegetables Up To Date

Fresh vegetables, frozen ones, all kinds can profit from being cooked in a snug foil package. There they braise in their own vitamin-rich juices, absorbing butter and seasonings to achieve never-before flavor. The family will want to know, "How did you get them to taste so good?"

HEATING LEFTOVER VEGETABLES

1. At end of meal, wrap leftover vegetables in Alcoa Wrap; store in refrigerator. 2. When ready to use, place unopened packages in a fry pan; add 1½-2 inches water; cover pan. 3. Bring water to boil; reduce heat to low; heat 10-15 minutes. 4. Vegetables will look and taste fresh; there will be no pans to wash.

MUSHROOMS BAKED IN FOIL
3-4 servings

1 pint fresh mushrooms   Salt, pepper

1. Trim stems of mushrooms; remove blemishes; wash; drain; dry. 2. Place mushrooms on double thick sheet of Alcoa Wrap; add salt, pepper. 3. Place sheet of Alcoa Wrap over mushrooms; fold each side over in double fold; seal tightly.

4. Place foil package on baking sheet. **5.** Bake 30 minutes at 350° F.

BAKED POTATO

Medium-size baking potatoes   Butter or margarine

1. Scrub potatoes; dry thoroughly. **2.** Place each potato in center of square of Alcoa Wrap. **3.** Bring up sides of Alcoa Wrap; fold down onto potato in tight double fold; fold over ends, bringing up tightly. **4.** Bake 1 hour at 425° F. **5.** To serve: Open foil to form cup around potato; make criss-cross cut in top of potato; press on each side of cut to open; place pat of butter in opened potato. **6.** Serve in foil package.

FOIL BAKED POTATO VARIATIONS

Follow directions for baking potatoes in foil; open foil to form cup around potato; make a criss-cross cut in top; use one of the following variations for serving.

1. Sour cream with crisp bacon bits.
2. Buttered toasted walnuts.
3. Sesame seeds with sprinkles of browned sausage.
4. Browned chunks of frankfurters.
5. Wedges of sharp Cheddar cheese.
6. Process cheese spread.

7. Sour cream with chopped chives or green onions.
8. Shredded American cheese and sliced olives.
9. Hot condensed mushroom soup diluted with ½ cup milk.
10. Hot shrimp cocktail sauce.

SOUFFLÉED CAULIFLOWER   6 servings

3 10-ounce packages frozen cauliflower
2 eggs, separated
1 10½-ounce can condensed mushroom soup, undiluted
2 tablespoons Sherry wine

1 tablespoon light cream
¼ teaspoon salt
⅛ teaspoon pepper
½ cup grated Cheddar cheese
Paprika

1. Cook cauliflower as directed on package; drain.   2. Arrange in 1½ quart Alcoa Wrap lined casserole.   3. Beat egg yolks slightly; add mushroom soup, Sherry, cream, salt, pepper; beat thoroughly; add cheese.   4. Beat egg whites until stiff; fold into egg yolk mixture.   5. Spoon over cauliflower; sprinkle with paprika.   6. Bake 20 minutes at 425° F.

STUFFED VEGETABLE BOATS   4 servings

2 medium size zucchini
1 tablespoon butter or margarine
1 tablespoon flour
½ cup milk
1 4½-ounce can deviled ham
2 hard cooked eggs, chopped
1 teaspoon finely chopped parsley
1 teaspoon finely chopped chives

1 tablespoon minced onion
¼ cup chopped celery
1 teaspoon salt
¼ teaspoon pepper
¼ teaspoon nutmeg
¾ cup thin whole wheat cracker crumbs (about 40 crackers)

1. Slice zucchini lengthwise through center; scoop out center.
2. Place zucchini pulp in saucepan; cover with cold water; bring to boil; simmer 5 minutes; drain.   3. Melt butter; add flour, milk; cook until thick, smooth.   4. Combine deviled ham, eggs, parsley, chives, onion, celery, salt, pepper, nutmeg, ½ cup crumbs; blend thoroughly.   5. Add cream sauce,

cooked zucchini pulp; blend thoroughly **6.** Fill each zucchini shell with stuffing; sprinkle with remaining crumbs; place in Alcoa Wrap lined shallow baking pan. **7.** Bake 30 minutes at 375° F.

BAKED STUFFED ONIONS

6 servings

6 large onions	1 egg yolk
¾ cup leftover stuffing	Salt, pepper
¾ cup chopped cooked chicken	½ cup buttered cracker crumbs
¾ cup thin white sauce	

1. Remove skins from onions; boil 10 minutes in salted water, uncovered; drain; turn upside down to cool. **2.** Remove centers of onions, leaving shell thick enough to retain shape. **3.** Chop onion removed from center; combine with stuffing, chicken, white sauce, egg yolk, salt, pepper to taste. **4.** Place each onion in center of square of Alcoa Wrap; bring sides of foil up around onion to form cup. **5.** Fill onions with stuffing mixture; sprinkle cracker crumbs on top; place on baking sheet. **6.** Bake 40 minutes at 350° F. **7.** Serve in foil cups.

STUFFED BAKED TOMATOES

6 servings

6 large tomatoes	1 tablespoon chopped parsley
2 tablespoons butter or margarine	Salt, pepper
1¼ cups fine dry rye bread crumbs	2 egg yolks, beaten
1 teaspoon grated onion	2 tablespoons grated Cheddar cheese

1. Cut stem end of tomatoes; scoop out pulp; rub through sieve. **2.** Melt butter; add 1 cup bread crumbs, onion, parsley, salt, pepper; cook 3 minutes. **3.** Remove pan from heat; add tomato pulp, beaten egg yolks. **4.** Fill tomatoes with mixture. **5.** Combine remaining ¼ cup bread crumbs, grated cheese; sprinkle over tops of tomatoes. **6.** Place each tomato on a square of Alcoa Wrap; bring up foil to form cup; place in shallow baking pan. **7.** Bake 30 minutes at 350° F.

STUFFED ARTICHOKES WITH MORNAY SAUCE

4 servings

4 artichokes
2 pounds fresh asparagus tips
3 tablespoons butter or margarine
3 tablespoons flour
½ teaspoon salt

½ cup light cream
1 cup hot artichoke liquid or meat stock
½ cup grated American cheese

1. Wash artichokes; drain; remove loose discolored leaves around base; drop into boiling unsalted water to cover; simmer 15-20 minutes or until just tender. (Retain 1 cup liquid for sauce.) 2. Cut away fuzzy centers or "chokes" of artichokes; discard; set artichokes aside. 3. Wash asparagus tips; drain; place in large fry pan; pour over 1 inch boiling water; cover; simmer about 10 minutes or until tips are just tender; drain; set aside. 4. *To make Mornay Sauce:* melt butter in saucepan; add flour, salt; blend thoroughly. 5. Gradually add cream, artichoke liquid; cook over low heat, stirring constantly, until thickened. 6. Add cheese; stir until melted. 7. Place each artichoke in center of a sheet of Alcoa Wrap; crush foil around artichokes to form cups. 8. Fill centers of artichokes with asparagus tips; pour Mornay Sauce over top. 9. Place foil cups with artichokes on baking sheet. 10. Bake 20-25 minutes at 350° F. or until sauce is bubbly, just lightly browned. 11. Serve in foil cups; garnish with truffles.

SUMMER VEGETABLE MEDLEY

8 servings

2 cloves garlic, cut in half
¼ cup butter, margarine or salad oil
3 medium potatoes, cubed
4 carrots, sliced
2 onions, sliced
2 green peppers, quartered

1 unpared small eggplant, cubed
4 zucchini, sliced
4 summer squash, quartered
1 8-ounce can tomato sauce
1 cup water
Dash Tabasco sauce
Salt, pepper

1. Sauté garlic in butter; remove pieces. 2. Add vegetables; pour over tomato sauce, water, Tabasco. 3. Cover; simmer 20-25 minutes, or until vegetables are tender. 4. Season to taste with salt, pepper.

CARROTS IN SAUCE

6 servings

3 large carrots (about 1 pound)
2 whole cloves
1 bay leaf
2 tablespoons butter or margarine
2 tablespoons flour

1 cup milk
1 teaspoon chopped parsley
½ teaspoon salt
Dash cayenne
1 lemon

1. Wash, scrape carrots; dice. 2. Put in saucepan; cover with boiling water; add cloves, bay leaf; cook until tender. 3. Drain; reserve water. 4. Melt butter in pan; add flour, blend; add milk, 1 cup reserved water from carrots. 5. Cook sauce until thickened; add parsley, salt, cayenne, cooked carrots; reheat about 5 minutes. 6. Serve garnished with lemon.

CREOLE STUFFED PEPPERS

6 servings

6 medium green peppers
2 6½-ounce cans crab meat, drained
2 cups cooked rice
1 cup mayonnaise

2 tablespoons chopped onion
Salt, pepper to taste
Dash Tabasco sauce
2 8-ounce cans tomato sauce

1. Cut tops off peppers; remove seeds, membrane. 2. Precook green peppers in boiling water 5 minutes; drain. 3. Sprinkle inside with salt. 4. Combine crab meat, rice, mayonnaise, onion, salt, pepper, Tabasco sauce. 5. Fill peppers with mixture. 6. Line 8 x 8 x 2-inch pan with sheet of Alcoa Wrap; place peppers upright in pan; pour tomato sauce around peppers. 7. Bake 30 minutes at 350° F. 8. Spoon tomato sauce over peppers before serving.

ASPARAGUS À LA KING

6-8 servings

1 pound fresh asparagus, cut into
   1-inch pieces
¼ cup butter or margarine
¼ cup flour
2 cups milk

½ teaspoon salt
Dash pepper
1 teaspoon leaf oregano
2 cups grated Cheddar cheese
4 hard cooked eggs, diced

1. Cook asparagus until just tender. 2. Melt butter in saucepan; remove from heat. 3. Add flour; stir; add milk. 4. Cook over low heat, stirring constantly until thickened. 5. Add salt, pepper, oregano, cheese; stir until cheese melts. 6. Add eggs, asparagus; blend well. 7. Serve in patty shells or over chow mein noodles.

Good to know: Two 9-ounce packages frozen asparagus may be substituted for fresh asparagus.

BAKED ASPARAGUS WITH BASIL SOUR CREAM

4 servings

¾ pound fresh asparagus spears,
   trimmed
½ cup commercial sour cream
½ cup butter or margarine, melted

2 cups soft bread crumbs (4
   slices)
1 tablespoon sweet basil
½ teaspoon salt

1. Cook asparagus spears until just tender. 2. Place spears in 9 x 9 x 1¾-inch pan lined with Alcoa Wrap; spread sour cream over spears. 3. Combine melted butter, bread crumbs, basil, salt; blend well. 4. Sprinkle over sour cream. 5. Bake 15-20 minutes at 375° F. or until crumb topping is browned.

Good to know: Two 9-ounce packages frozen asparagus spears may be substituted for fresh asparagus.

SPANISH GREEN PEAS

4 servings

2 tablespoons butter or margarine
½ teaspoon onion salt
¼ teaspoon crushed oregano
¼ teaspoon pepper

1 1-pound can green peas,
  drained
2 whole pimientos, chopped
¼ cup ripe olive slices

1. Melt butter in saucepan. 2. Add onion salt, oregano, pepper, simmer 3 minutes. 3. Add peas, pimiento, olives; toss lightly to mix. 4. Cover; simmer about 10 minutes or until peas are hot; shake pan occasionally.

CORN PUDDING

8 servings

1 cup minced green pepper
1 cup minced onion
¼ cup butter or margarine
¼ cup flour
2 teaspoons salt
1 teaspoon paprika
1 teaspoon dry mustard

⅛ teaspoon cayenne pepper
1 cup milk
2 No. 303 cans cream-style corn
2 eggs, slightly beaten
1 cup bread cubes
3 tablespoons butter or margarine

1. Sauté green pepper, onion in butter 5 minutes. 2. Add flour, salt, paprika, dry mustard, pepper; blend. 3. Stir in milk; cook, stirring constantly, until thickened. 4. Combine corn, beaten eggs; slowly add hot milk mixture to egg mixture; blend well. 5. Sauté bread cubes in butter until brown; stir into corn pudding. 6. Pour pudding into 2½-quart Alcoa Wrap lined casserole; bake 1 hour at 350° F.

GOLDEN POTATO WEDGES

2-3 servings

2 medium size baking potatoes,
  peeled
¼ cup butter or margarine, melted

½ cup fine dry bread crumbs
  Salt, pepper
2 tablespoons butter or margarine

1. Slice peeled potatoes in half; cut each half in four long wedges. 2. Dip wedges in melted butter, bread crumbs. 3. Line shallow baking pan with a sheet of Alcoa Wrap.

4. Place potato wedges in pan; sprinkle with salt, pepper; dot with butter. **5.** Bake 35-40 minutes at 400° F. or until golden brown.

RAREBIT STUFFED PEPPERS

6 servings

3 large peppers, cut lengthwise	½ teaspoon Worcestershire sauce
2 tablespoons butter or margarine	½ teaspoon salt
2 tablespoons minced onion	Dash pepper
1 No. 2 can kidney beans, drained	½ pound Cheddar cheese, cubed
2 tablespoons ketchup	

1. Cut peppers in half lengthwise; remove seeds; parboil 5 minutes; drain. **2.** Melt butter; sauté onion until tender; remove from heat. **3.** Add kidney beans, ketchup, Worcestershire sauce, salt, pepper, cheese. **4.** Fill peppers with cheese mixture. **5.** Place each filled pepper half on a square of Alcoa Wrap; bring up foil around pepper to form a cup; place in shallow baking pan. **6.** Bake 30 minutes at 350° F.

COTTAGE POTATOES

3-4 servings

2 medium potatoes, pared, cut into ⅜-inch strips	Pepper
	1 tablespoon chopped parsley
1 tablespoon butter or margarine	¼ cup milk or cream
Salt	Grated Parmesan cheese

1. Place potato strips in center of double thick square of Alcoa Wrap. **2.** Dot with butter; add salt, pepper, parsley, milk; sprinkle Parmesan cheese over the top. **3.** Bring torn edges together over potatoes; fold, then fold again bringing fold down close to potatoes. Fold ends over and over pressing in

close to potatoes.   **4.** Place foil package on baking sheet.
5. Bake 40-45 minutes at 425° F.

DUBLIN CHEESE AND POTATO PIE   *4 servings*

1 cup milk
1 cup grated Cheddar cheese
1 teaspoon Worcestershire sauce
¾ teaspoon salt
¼ teaspoon pepper
1 tablespoon flour

4–5 medium uncooked, peeled potatoes, sliced ⅛-inch thick (3 cups)
2 cups sliced onions
3 tablespoons butter
2 tablespoons dry bread crumbs

1. Combine milk, cheese; cook over boiling water until cheese melts; remove from heat; add Worcestershire sauce.   **2.** Combine salt, pepper, flour; mix well.   **3.** Place layer of sliced potatoes in bottom of 1½-quart Alcoa Wrap lined casserole; sprinkle heaping teaspoon of flour mixture over top; add layer of sliced onions; dot with butter; repeat using remaining ingredients.   **4.** Pour cheese sauce over all; top with bread crumbs.   **5.** Bake 1 hour at 350° F.

PETITS POIS À LA BOURGEOISE   *4 servings*
(*French Green Peas*)

3 slices bacon
2 tablespoons flour
1½ cups chicken stock
½ teaspoon salt
Dash pepper

2 cups shelled green peas or 1 10-ounce package frozen peas
4 sprigs parsley
2 small onions, sliced
½ pimiento, cut in strips

1. Dice bacon slices; fry until crisp in fry pan; remove to absorbent paper to drain.   **2.** Add flour to bacon fat in fry pan; blend until smooth; brown over low heat.   **3.** Add chicken stock, salt, pepper; cook, stirring constantly, until smooth. **4.** Add peas, parsley, onions; cover; cook over low heat until tender, about 20 minutes.   **5.** To serve: Remove parsley sprigs; turn into serving dish; garnish with crisp bacon, pimiento strips.

STUFFED ANDEAN AVOCADO

10 servings

5 avocados
⅓ cup chopped celery
2 tablespoons chopped parsley
1 tablespoon chopped chives
¼ cup chopped green onions
½ cup chopped onions
2½ teaspoons curry powder
½ cup chopped green pepper
½ cup chopped red pepper

⅓ cup chopped carrot, partially cooked
2 medium potatoes, cooked, chopped (2 cups)
1 teaspoon garlic salt
3 tablespoons mayonnaise
3 tablespoons salad oil
1 omelet of 5 eggs, chopped
1½ teaspoons salt

1. Wash avocados; cut in half; remove pits. 2. Combine celery, parsley, chives, onions, curry powder, green pepper, red pepper, carrot, potatoes, garlic salt, mayonnaise, salad oil, chopped omelet, salt; blend thoroughly. 3. Stuff filling into centers of avocado halves; chill. 4. Garnish with tomato slices, stuffed olives, radish roses.

PILUS

6 servings

(*Sweet Potato Balls*)

2 cups mashed sweet potatoes
2 tablespoons flour
2 tablespoons sugar

1 egg, beaten
1½ quarts oil for frying
Confectioners sugar

1. Mix potatoes, flour, sugar, egg together thoroughly. 2. Form balls, 1 inch in diameter. 3. Pour oil into large fry pan; heat to 375° F. 4. Drop potato balls into hot oil; fry to golden brown; drain. 5. Sprinkle with confectioners sugar; serve hot.

Success-Story Salads

A salad can make or break a meal—and sometimes, when it's good enough and hearty enough, a salad can be a meal in itself. Here are all kinds to try on your family, along with a bonus of delicious, exciting-taste dressings.

CHICKEN SALAD SUPREME

6 servings

1 tablespoon unflavored gelatin
¼ cup cold water
1 cup mayonnaise
½ teaspoon salt
2 cups cooked chicken, diced

½ cup chopped celery
1 11-ounce can mandarin orange segments, drained
1 cup heavy cream, whipped

1. Soften gelatin in cold water. 2. Stir in mayonnaise, salt, chicken, celery, orange segments; blend well. 3. Fold in whipped cream. 4. Pour into 1½-quart mold. Refrigerate until firm. 5. Unmold on bed of lettuce; garnish with pimiento strips, sprigs parsley.

JELLIED HAM SALAD
6 servings

2 3-ounce packages lemon-flavored gelatin
2¼ cups boiling water
3 tablespoons vinegar
1 tablespoon Worcestershire sauce
3 cups cooked ham, finely diced

¼ cup mayonnaise
1½ tablespoons prepared horse-radish
½ teaspoon prepared mustard
½ teaspoon pepper
1½ tablespoons chopped pimiento

1. Dissolve gelatin in boiling water. 2. Add vinegar, Worcestershire sauce; blend well; chill until mixture starts to thicken. 3. Combine ham, mayonnaise, horseradish, mustard, pepper, pimiento; add to partially set gelatin; blend lightly. 4. Pour into 1½-quart mold; chill until set. 5. Unmold on bed of lettuce; garnish with pimiento strips, sprigs parsley.

SHRIMP SALAD PLATE
6 servings

Lettuce cups
Shredded lettuce
1½ pounds cooked shrimp
3 tomatoes, cut in wedges
2 10-ounce packages frozen peas, cooked, chilled

6 hard cooked eggs, halved lengthwise
Parsley sprigs
French dressing

1. Take double thick 18-inch square heavy duty Alcoa Wrap. 2. Place 9-inch dinner plate on top of foil. 3. Bring up foil around plate; crimp 1-inch edge around container; remove plate. 4. Repeat procedure until 6 containers are made. 5. Place 2 large lettuce cups in each foil container; place some shredded lettuce in each. 6. Place shrimp in one lettuce cup; garnish each with 3 tomato wedges. 7. Place cooked peas in second lettuce cup; garnish with 2 egg halves. 8. Garnish salad with parsley. 9. Cover each foil container with sheet of Alcoa Wrap. 10. Chill until serving time; serve with French dressing.

STUFFED CUCUMBER SLICES

2 long, narrow cucumbers
1 3-ounce package cream cheese
2 tablespoons milk

2 strips bacon, finely minced, crisp
cooked

1. Cut cucumbers in half crosswise; remove center with apple corer. 2. Combine cream cheese, milk, bacon; blend well. 3. Fill centers with cheese mixture. 4. Wrap in Alcoa Wrap; thoroughly chill. 5. To serve: slice.

Taste Tip: These stuffed cucumber slices make a delicious—and pretty—addition to a relish tray.

MOLDED SHRIMP SALAD

6-8 servings

2 envelopes unflavored gelatin
½ cup cold water
1 10½-ounce can condensed
tomato soup
½ cup water
2 3-ounce packages cream cheese

1 cup mayonnaise
1 cup chopped celery
⅓ cup chopped onion
½ teaspoon salt
3 cups cooked shrimp, cut into
pieces (1 pound cooked)

1. Dissolve gelatin in cold water. 2. Dilute tomato soup with ½ cup water; heat to boiling point. 3. Blend cream cheese until softened; gradually add hot soup. 4. Add gelatin; stir until dissolved. 5. Add mayonnaise, celery, onion, salt, shrimp; blend well. 6. Pour into 1½-quart mold; refrigerate until firm. 7. Unmold on bed of lettuce.

FROZEN FRUIT SALAD

6-10 servings

1 pint commercial sour cream
2 tablespoons lemon juice
¾ cup sugar
⅛ teaspoon salt
1 9-ounce can crushed pineapple, drained
¼ cup chopped maraschino
cherries

¼ cup chopped walnuts
or
2–3 cups of any combination of the
following: blueberries, cherries,
strawberries, grapes, black-
berries, sliced or diced
peaches, plums, nectarines

1. Combine sour cream, lemon juice, sugar, salt; blend well. 2. Add fruit; pour into Alcoa Wrap lined 9 x 9 x 1¾-inch pan or foil lined muffin cups; freeze until firm.

MOLDED CRANBERRY SALAD

12 servings

1 No. 2 can (2½ cups) crushed pineapple
2 3-ounce packages cherry-flavored gelatin
¾ cup sugar
2 cups hot water
½ cup cold water
1–2 tablespoons lemon juice
1 pound raw cranberries, ground
1 small orange, ground (½ cup)
1 cup chopped celery
½ cup broken walnuts

1. Drain pineapple, reserving syrup. 2. Combine gelatin, sugar; dissolve in hot water. 3. Add cold water, lemon juice, pineapple syrup. 4. Chill until partially set. 5. Add pineapple, raw cranberries, orange, celery, walnuts. 6. Pour into 2-quart mold or individual molds. 7. Chill until firm.

CONFETTI RELISH MOLD

14-18 servings

8 beef bouillon cubes
4 3-ounce packages lemon-flavored gelatin
1 quart boiling water
½ cup tarragon vinegar
2 teaspoons salt
1 quart commercial sour cream
2 cups minced, unpared cucumber
1 cup minced green pepper
1 cup thinly sliced radishes
½ cup minced green onions

1. Dissolve bouillon cubes, gelatin in boiling water; add vinegar, salt; chill until partially set. 2. Add sour cream; blend thoroughly. 3. Add cucumber, green pepper, radishes, onions; blend. 4. Pour into 3-quart mold; chill until firm.

CUCUMBER RING MOLD

8 servings

2 tablespoons unflavored gelatin
½ cup cold water
½ cup hot water
4 cups cottage cheese
2 cups whipping cream
4 medium cucumbers
Watercress
French dressing

1. Soak gelatin in cold water five minutes; dissolve in hot water. 2. Press cottage cheese through sieve; add dissolved gelatin; mix until light, fluffy. 3. Whip cream until stiff; fold into cottage cheese mixture. 4. Rinse 2-quart mold with cold water; pour salad mixture into mold; chill until firm. 5. Peel

cucumbers; cut into slices ¼ inch thick; remove centers. 6. Place cucumber rings in ice water until crisp. 7. When ready to serve, unmold salad on bed of watercress; garnish with cucumber rings. 8. Serve with French Dressing.

DILL COLESLAW

4 servings

2 tablespoons chopped dill pickle
½ teaspoon prepared mustard
½ cup salad dressing
1½ cups shredded cabbage

1. Combine pickle, mustard, salad dressing. 2. Add to cabbage; toss lightly; chill.

MACARONI-MAYO SALAD

8 servings

8 ounces macaroni
1 cup diced Cheddar cheese
1 tablespoon prepared mustard
1 cup mayonnaise
1 can (1 lb.) peas, drained
¼ cup pickle relish
3 tablespoons pimiento strips

1. Cook macaroni according to package directions; drain. 2. Add cheese, mustard, ½ cup mayonnaise; cool. 3. Add remaining ½ cup mayonnaise, peas, pickle relish, pimiento; chill. 4. Serve on salad greens.

SPICED ORANGE MOLD

18 servings

3 11-ounce cans mandarin orange sections (4 cups)
¾ teaspoon salt
7 inches stick cinnamon
1½ teaspoons whole cloves
6 3-ounce packages orange-flavored gelatin
5½ cups cold water
½ cup lemon juice
1½ cups broken walnuts

1. Drain oranges, reserving syrup; add water to syrup to make 4¼ cups. 2. In saucepan combine syrup mixture, salt, cinnamon, cloves; cover; bring to a boil; simmer 10 minutes. 3. Remove from heat; let stand covered 10 minutes to steep; strain. 4. Dissolve gelatin in hot mixture. 5. Add cold water, lemon juice; chill until partially set. 6. Stir in oranges, nuts; pour into 3-quart mold; chill until firm.

AVOCADO RING SALAD

6 servings

3 avocados	1 tablespoon chopped parsley
2 3-ounce packages cream cheese	½ teaspoon salt
1 cup pecans, coarsely chopped	⅛ teaspoon pepper
1 cup chopped ripe olives	⅛ teaspoon cayenne pepper

1. Peel avocados; cut in half lengthwise; remove seeds.
2. Combine cheese, pecans, olives, parsley, seasoning; blend.
3. Fill avocados with cheese mixture; press halves together.
4. Wrap in Alcoa Wrap; chill thoroughly. 5. Slice crosswise; serve on crisp greens with French Dressing.

PEACH MELBA SALAD

14-16 servings

2 1-pound cans sliced peaches (4 cups)	2 3-ounce packages cream cheese, softened
¼ cup lemon juice	¼ cup finely chopped pecans
2 3-ounce packages lemon-flavored gelatin	2 10-ounce packages frozen red raspberries, thawed
2 cups hot water	¼ cup lemon juice
4 teaspoons milk	2 3-ounce packages raspberry-flavored gelatin
¼ cup mayonnaise	2 cups hot water

1. *Peach Layer:* Drain peaches; combine peach syrup, lemon juice, enough cold water to make 2 cups. 2. Dissolve lemon gelatin in hot water; add syrup mixture; refrigerate until partially set. 3. Blend in peaches; pour into 3-quart mold; refrigerate until almost set. 4. *Cheese Layer:* Combine milk, mayonnaise, cream cheese; blend well; stir in pecans. 5. Spread cheese mixture over peach layer in mold; refrigerate. 6. *Raspberry Layer:* Drain raspberries; combine raspberry syrup, lemon juice, enough cold water to make 2 cups. 7. Dissolve raspberry gelatin in hot water; add syrup mixture; refrigerate until partially set. 8. Blend in raspberries; pour over cheese layer in mold; refrigerate until set. 9. Unmold on bed of lettuce.

SENATE SALAD

4 servings

1 3-ounce package lemon-flavored gelatin
1 teaspoon salt
½ teaspoon garlic salt
⅛ teaspoon pepper
1½ cups hot water
1 tablespoon vinegar
½ pound cooked shrimp, cut in 1-inch pieces
1 package frozen artichoke hearts

1 cup Italian dressing
1 grapefruit, sectioned
1 cup diced tomatoes
1 cup thinly sliced celery
1 cup thin strips Cheddar cheese
½ cup sliced ripe olives
¼ cup chopped green onions
2 quarts salad greens (romaine, leaf lettuce, escarole, cabbage, watercress)
4 lettuce cups

1. Combine gelatin, salt, garlic salt, pepper; add hot water; stir until gelatin is dissolved; add vinegar. 2. Pour into 9 x 5 x 3-inch loaf pan; chill until slightly thickened. 3. Press shrimp pieces, one inch apart, into thickened gelatin; chill until firm. 4. Cook artichoke hearts as directed on package; drain; cut each heart in half. 5. Add Italian dressing; chill. 6. Combine grapefruit, tomatoes, celery, cheese, olives, onions, greens; toss together lightly in salad bowl; chill. 7. Just before serving, toss artichoke hearts and dressing with other ingredients. 8. Serve in lettuce cups; arrange shrimp squares on top.

STRAWBERRY SWEETHEART SALAD

6 servings

2 3-ounce packages cream cheese
1 cup mayonnaise
¼ pound marshmallows (15), cut fine
1 1-pound package frozen strawberries, thawed, drained

½ cup chopped pecans
1 cup crushed pineapple, drained
⅛ teaspoon red food coloring
1 cup heavy cream, whipped

1. Stir cream cheese to soften; add mayonnaise; blend well. 2. Add marshmallows, strawberries, pecans, pineapple, food coloring; blend well. 3. Fold in whipped cream. 4. Pour into 1-quart mold; chill until firm. 5. Unmold on bed of lettuce; garnish with sprig of mint.

EXOTIC CHICKEN SALAD

10 servings

4 cups chicken, cooked, cut in large chunks (4-pound fowl)
1 cup celery, cut on an angle
1 cup green pepper, minced (1 large or 1½ medium)
2 cups pineapple chunks, halved, (2½-pound can), drained
2 cups grapes, halved, seeded

1 cup almonds, toasted, slivered
⅔ cup mayonnaise
¼ cup light cream
1 teaspoon salt
⅛ teaspoon pepper
2 tablespoons vinegar
2 teaspoons grated onion

1. Combine chicken, celery, green pepper, pineapple, grapes, almonds in large bowl or pan.   2. Combine mayonnaise, cream, salt, pepper, vinegar, grated onion; blend thoroughly.   3. Chill both mixtures separately.   4. Just before serving, blend together, tossing lightly so as not to break up chicken chunks.

VEGETABLE-SEAFOOD SALAD

6 servings

1 pound cooked shrimp
1 pound cooked scallops
4 cups cooked rice
1 medium head cauliflower, broken into small pieces
1 cup thin green pepper strips
¾ cup chopped pimiento
½ cup chopped scallions

½ cup chopped ripe olives
1 tablespoon salt
¼ teaspoon pepper
1 cup mayonnaise
¼ cup French Dressing
Lettuce
Parsley
Ripe olives

1. Take double-thick, 18-inch square heavy duty Alcoa Wrap.
2. Place an 8-inch luncheon plate on top of foil.   3. Bring up foil around edge of plate; crimp 1-inch edge around container; remove plate.   4. Repeat procedure until 6 containers are made.   5. Combine shrimp, scallops, rice, cauliflower, green pepper, pimiento, scallions, ripe olives, salt, pepper; mix well.
6. Combine mayonnaise, French Dressing; pour over salad; toss lightly.   7. Place lettuce cup in each foil container.
8. Place salad on lettuce; garnish with ripe olives, parsley.   9. Cover each foil container with a sheet of Alcoa Wrap.
10. Chill until serving time.

PICKLED ASPARAGUS

Brine
3 quarts water
2 quarts white vinegar

10 tablespoons salt
1 tablespoon pickling spice
(omit clove)

1. Combine water, vinegar, salt, pickling spice in large saucepot.   2. Bring to a boil; boil 15 minutes; strain.

Asparagus

1. Just before starting to prepare asparagus, wash, rinse, and drain quart jars and covers; fill with boiling water; let stand until ready to fill.   2. Cut off tough stalk ends of asparagus spears (spears should be about 5½ inches long to fit into quart jar); wash spears.   3. Heat 2-3 quarts water to boiling; drop asparagus spears into boiling water (about 8-10 at a time); blanch 1½ minutes.   4. Remove from boiling water; immediately drop them into ice cold water for about 1-2 minutes.   5. Put chilled spears into jars, tip ends up; put 1 clove garlic in each jar; cover with hot brine; seal.   6. Let stand at room temperature about 2 weeks before using.   7. Chill thoroughly before serving.

Good to know: Each quart jar will hold approximately 16-17 (5½ inch) spears and 2 cups brine.

TOMATO FRENCH DRESSING   3½ cups

1 11-ounce can cream of tomato
soup, undiluted
1 cup salad oil
1 tablespoon dry mustard
1 teaspoon salt

1 teaspoon Worcestershire sauce
¾ cup white vinegar
1 cup sugar
1 small onion, grated

Combine all ingredients; beat with rotary beater until well blended.

BRAUNSCHWEIGER SALAD DRESSING   2 cups

¼ pound Braunschweiger
½ cup lemon juice
⅛ teaspoon pepper

¼ teaspoon prepared mustard
Dash of Tabasco sauce
1 cup salad oil

1. Mash Braunschweiger to soften; add lemon juice; mix until creamy. 2. Add pepper, mustard, Tabasco sauce. 3. Add salad oil slowly while beating with rotary or electric beater.

FRUIT SALAD DRESSING   2 cups

⅓ cup sugar
1 teaspoon flour
1 egg yolk
½ cup canned pineapple juice

2 tablespoons lemon juice
1 teaspoon celery seeds
1 cup whipping cream, whipped

1. Combine sugar, flour, egg yolk, pineapple juice in saucepan; stir until smooth. 2. Cook over low heat until thickened, stirring constantly. 3. Add lemon juice, celery seeds; chill. 4. Fold in whipped cream just before serving. 5. Serve with your favorite fruit salad.

Good to know: One pint commercial sour cream may be substituted for whipping cream.

HONEY FRENCH DRESSING   ¾ cup

½ teaspoon salt
1 teaspoon sugar
¼ teaspoon paprika

3 tablespoons vinegar
½ cup salad oil
1 tablespoon strained honey

1. Combine in jar; shake thoroughly until blended. 2. Serve with fruit salad.

WINE FRENCH DRESSING   1 cup

1 teaspoon salt
1 teaspoon sugar
¼ teaspoon dry mustard
Dash pepper

2 teaspoons grated onion
½ cup Sauterne or Rhine wine
¼ cup vinegar
¼ cup salad oil

1. Combine all ingredients in jar; shake well. 2. Chill slightly before using.

SOUR CREAM DRESSING

1½ cups

1 cup commercial sour cream
⅓ cup lemon juice
2 tablespoons sugar
1 tablespoon chopped chives or grated onion

1 teaspoon celery seeds
½ teaspoon dry mustard
½ teaspoon salt
⅛ teaspoon pepper

1. Combine all ingredients; beat with rotary beater until smooth. **2.** Chill several hours before serving.

HONEY-LIME DRESSING

1¼ cups

2 large limes
2 tablespoons honey

¾ cup salad oil
⅛ teaspoon salt

1. Juice limes; strain. **2.** Combine strained juice, honey, oil, salt in glass jar; shake well to blend thoroughly.

FRENCH DRESSING

1 cup

¼ cup sugar
¼ cup vinegar
¼ cup salad oil

¼ cup ketchup
½ clove garlic, peeled

1. Put ingredients in jar; add garlic, which has been placed on toothpick. Shake until blended. **2.** Let stand at room temperature at least one hour; chill until ready to serve; remove garlic.

VINAIGRETTE DRESSING

¾ cup

1 teaspoon salt
¼ teaspoon paprika
⅛ teaspoon pepper
1 tablespoon tarragon vinegar
2 tablespoons cider vinegar
6 tablespoons olive oil

1 tablespoon chopped green pepper
1 tablespoon chopped cucumber pickle
1 teaspoon chopped parsley
1 teaspoon chopped chives

Combine in a bowl all ingredients in order given; blend thoroughly.

A French Chef in Your Kitchen

The French chef's wonderful method of cooking en papillon—foods deliciously seasoned and oven-braised in a "butterfly" of parchment—is within the scope of any housewife whose papillon is aluminum wrap. What's really, truly new about home cooking? This is!

BUTTERFLY-BAKED FROZEN VEGETABLES

1. Remove any frozen vegetable from package. **2.** Place in center of large double-thick square of Alcoa Wrap. **3.** Place two pats of butter on top; sprinkle with salt, pepper. **4.** Bring two edges of the foil together over vegetable; fold, then fold again; fold over ends; leave a little space for steam expansion. **5.** Place on rack in 425° F. oven. **6.** Approximate baking time:

Asparagus spears	35-40 minutes
Broccoli cuts	35-40 minutes
Broccoli spears	30-35 minutes
Brussels sprouts	45-50 minutes
Cauliflower	45-50 minutes
Corn on the cob	20-25 minutes
Corn, cut	35-40 minutes
Green beans, cut	45-50 minutes
Green beans, French	35-40 minutes
Lima beans	45-50 minutes
Peas	30-35 minutes
Spinach, leaf	45-50 minutes
Squash	45-50 minutes

BAKED HAM SLICES
4 servings

2 medium ham slices, ½-inch thick

1. Brown ham slices; cut each slice in half. **2.** Place each piece of ham on double-thick sheet of Alcoa Wrap. **3.** Add a fruit or vegetable topping (see below). **4.** Fold torn edges up, using tight double folds. **5.** Place foil packages on baking sheet or in shallow pan. **6.** Bake 30 minutes at 425° F. **7.** Serve in open foil package.

BAKED HAM TOPPINGS

Pineapple Slice

4 slices pineapple
4 candied cherries
¼ cup brown sugar, firmly packed

1. Place a slice of pineapple with cherry in center on top of each slice of ham. **2.** Sprinkle one tablespoon sugar over pineapple. **3.** Proceed with Step 4, above.

Cherry-Pineapple Sauce

¾ cup sugar
¼ cup cider vinegar
½ cup cherry-pineapple juice
6 whole cloves
1 stick cinnamon
3 tablespoons flour

1 cup pitted sour cherries, drained
1 cup crushed pineapple, drained
1½ teaspoons lemon juice
Few drops red food coloring

1. Mix sugar, vinegar, ¼ cup cherry-pineapple juice together in saucepan. **2.** Add cloves, cinnamon stick. **3.** Bring mixture to a boil; simmer 15 minutes over low heat. **3.** Combine flour with remaining cherry-pineapple juice; blend into hot syrup, stirring constantly until thickened. **4.** Add cherries, pineapple, lemon juice, food coloring. **5.** Spoon over ham. **6.** Proceed with Step 4, above.

Onion or Cauliflower Topping

16 small whole onions or   **1 cup grated cheese**
cauliflower flowerettes

1. Place four onions or flowerettes on each piece of ham.
2. Proceed with Step 4, above. 3. Five minutes before ham is done, open foil, push down, away from meat. 4. Sprinkle cheese over vegetables; return to oven; leave in oven until cheese is melted.

BAKED POMPANO

4 servings

2 tablespoons butter or margarine
1 medium-size onion, finely
    chopped (½ cup)
½ teaspoon salt
    Few drops bottled hot-pepper
    sauce

½ pound cooked shrimp, finely
    chopped
4 pompano fillets (about ⅓
    pound each)

1. Melt butter in fry pan; sauté onions 5 minutes. 2. Add salt, hot-pepper sauce, shrimp; sauté 3 minutes. 3. Place each pompano fillet on a double-thick square of Alcoa Wrap; spread ¼ of shrimp mixture on top of each fillet. 4. Bring up sides of Alcoa Wrap; fold down in tight folds; fold ends up in tight double folds. 5. Place foil packages on baking sheet. 6. Bake 45 minutes at 375° F. 7. Serve in opened foil packages.

Good to know: Other fish fillets may be substituted for pompano.

FISH AND POTATO BAKE

4 servings

1 pound package frozen fish fillets
1 large onion
    Paprika
2 large potatoes

2 tablespoons chopped parsley
    Salt, pepper
2 tablespoons butter or margarine

1. Thaw fish until frozen block can be cut into 4 pieces.
2. Place each piece on a double-thick square of Alcoa Wrap.
3. Slice onion; arrange slices on top of fish; sprinkle with paprika. 4. Cut potatoes into Julienne sticks; arrange around

edge of fish.   5. Sprinkle with parsley, salt, pepper; dot with butter.   6. Bring up sides of Alcoa Wrap; fold down in tight double fold; fold ends up in tight double folds.   7. Place foil packages on baking sheet.   8. Bake 40 minutes at 425° F. 9. Serve in opened packages.

SAVORY FISH

4 servings

1 package frozen fish fillets, thawed	½ green pepper, chopped
2 medium onions, thinly sliced	4–5 tablespoons butter or margarine
2 tomatoes, quartered	Salt
1 4-ounce can mushroom buttons, sliced	Pepper

1. Divide fish fillets into 4 servings.   2. Place each serving on a 12-15-inch square of Alcoa Wrap.   3. Divide and arrange onions, tomatoes, mushrooms, green pepper on top of each serving.   4. Place 1 tablespoon of butter on each serving; sprinkle with salt, pepper.   5. Bring two edges of Alcoa Wrap together over fish. Make double fold; make double fold on each end.   6. Place package on baking sheet; bake 20-25 minutes at 375° F.   7. Serve in opened packages.

BAKED BROOK TROUT

4 servings

3 tablespoons butter or margarine	4 brook trout (½ pound each), split, boned (fresh or frozen)
½ pound mushrooms, thinly sliced	¼ cup Sherry wine
1 bunch green onions, sliced	Salt, pepper

1. Melt butter; add mushrooms; sauté 5 minutes.   2. Arrange sliced onions on four squares of Alcoa Wrap.   3. Place fish, skin side down, on onions; spread mushrooms over fish. 4. Pour 1 tablespoon Sherry over each package; sprinkle with salt, pepper.   5. Bring up sides of Alcoa Wrap; fold down in tight folds; fold ends up in tight double folds.   6. Place foil packages on baking sheet.   7. Bake 30-35 minutes at 375° F. 8. Serve in opened foil packages.

BAKED FILLET OF SOLE

4 servings

1 package frozen fillet of sole, thawed
1 8-ounce can button mushrooms
½ pound raw shrimp
1 can cream of mushroom soup, undiluted

½ teaspoon monosodium glutamate
1 tablespoon lemon juice
Paprika
Chopped parsley

1. Divide fillets into four servings. 2. Place each serving on double-thick square of Alcoa Wrap. 3. Place mushrooms on top of fish. 4. Peel, clean, de-vein raw shrimp; place on top of mushrooms. 5. Pour soup over fish mixture; sprinkle with monosodium glutamate, lemon juice, paprika, parsley. 6. Bring the two torn edges together over fish; fold, then fold again, bringing fold down close to food. Fold ends over and over, pressing close to food. 7. Place packages on baking sheet. 8. Bake 40 minutes at 425° F. 9. Serve in opened packages.

CLAM ROLLS

3 servings

3 wiener buns
3 tablespoons minced onion
3 tablespoons minced parsley
3 tablespoons butter or margarine

2 tablespoons pickle relish
1 10-ounce can minced clams (1 cup)
Salt, pepper

1. Scoop centers from buns; reserve 2 tablespoons bread crumbs. 2. Sauté onion, parsley in butter. 3. Add bread crumbs, relish, clams, salt, pepper; blend thoroughly. 4. Stuff buns with clam mixture. 5. Place each bun in center of a double-thick square of Alcoa Wrap. 6. Bring up sides of Alcoa Wrap; fold down in tight double fold; fold ends up in tight double folds. 7. Place foil packages on baking sheet. 8. Bake 15 minutes at 425° F. 9. Serve in opened foil package.

Convenience Cooking: Prepare Clam Rolls the night before or the morning before serving. Refrigerate the unbaked packages. When ready to serve, bake as directed, allowing 5 additional minutes for baking.

LEONE'S LOBSTER IN FOIL

1 serving

1 1¼-1¾-pounds live lobster
1 cup soft bread crumbs, browned in butter
3 tablespoons softened butter or margarine

½ teaspoon paprika
Salt
Pepper

1. Split lobster lengthwise; cut off legs, claws; remove entrails. 2. Combine browned bread crumbs, softened butter, paprika, salt, pepper; place in lobster cavity. 3. Place lobster in center of square of Alcoa Wrap; place small legs over filling; claws alongside tail. 4. Bring torn edges together over lobster; fold, then fold again, bringing fold down close to lobster. Fold ends over and over pressing close to lobster. 5. Bake 40 minutes at 400° F. 6. Serve in opened package; garnish with lemon wedges, parsley.

FOIL-BAKED LOBSTER TAILS

2 servings

1 1-pound package frozen lobster tails, thawed

2 tablespoons butter or margarine

1. Cut under shell around edge; remove membrane; loosen meat from shell. 2. Place tails in center of two double-thick squares Alcoa Wrap; dot with butter. 3. Bring torn edges together over tails; fold, then fold again, bringing fold down close to tails. Fold ends over and over, pressing close to food. 4. Place foil packages on baking sheet. 5. Bake 20 minutes at 425° F. 6. Serve in opened packages with lemon wedges.

ROQUEFORT SHRIMP BAKE

2 servings

1 12-ounce package frozen raw shrimp, thawed
1 3-ounce package cream cheese

3 ounces Roquefort cheese
⅓ cup chopped pimiento

1. Wash shrimp; remove shells, veins. 2. Combine cream cheese, Roquefort cheese, pimiento; blend thoroughly. 3. Place

cheese mixture in center of two double-thick squares of Alcoa Wrap; place cleaned shrimp on top of cheese mixture. **4.** Bring up sides of Alcoa Wrap; fold down onto shrimp in tight double fold; fold ends up in tight double folds. **5.** Place foil packages on baking sheet. **6.** Bake 20 minutes at 350° F. **7.** Serve in opened packages with wedges of lemon.

Convenience Cooking: Prepare Roquefort Shrimp Bake the night before or the morning before serving. Refrigerate the unbaked packages. When ready to serve, bake as directed, allowing 5 additional minutes for baking.

CHICKEN PICK-UPS
8 servings

2 tablespoons onion, finely diced	2 teaspoons vinegar
2 tablespoons green pepper, finely diced	½ teaspoon salt
	¼ teaspoon pepper
3 tablespoons butter or margarine	2 cups diced cooked chicken
2 8-ounce cans tomato sauce	¼ cup butter or margarine, melted
¾ cup water	¾ teaspoon garlic salt
2 tablespoons brown sugar	8 frankfurter rolls, split

1. Sauté onions, green pepper in butter until tender, lightly browned. **2.** Add tomato sauce, water, sugar, vinegar, salt, pepper; simmer uncovered 10 minutes. **3.** Add chicken; simmer 10 minutes longer. **4.** Combine melted butter, garlic salt. **5.** Brush inside of rolls with garlic butter; fill with mixture. **6.** Place each roll on a 6-inch square of Alcoa Wrap. **7.** Bring torn edges together over roll; fold, then fold again, bringing fold down close to roll. Fold ends over and over pressing in close to meat. **8.** Bake 10 minutes at 425° F.

BUNDLES OF CHICKEN
4 servings

1 frying chicken, quartered	Salt
2 large sweet potatoes, halved lengthwise	Pepper
	4 slices pineapple
½ cup softened butter or margarine	

1. Place each quarter chicken, half sweet potato, in center of square of heavy duty Alcoa Wrap. **2.** Spread softened butter over each serving; sprinkle with salt, pepper; top with pine-apple slice. **3.** Fold torn edges of foil together in tight double fold on top of food; fold ends up using tight double folds. **4.** Place on baking sheet. **5.** Bake 45-50 minutes at 425° F. **6.** Serve in opened packages.

Good to know: For outdoor cooking, place packages on grill over medium coals for 50 minutes, turning several times.

CHICKEN IN HERB SAUCE

4 servings

1 frying chicken, quartered	½ teaspoon pepper
¼ cup butter or margarine, softened	1 large carrot, quartered
1 tablespoon paprika	2 slices bacon, cut in half
2 teaspoons thyme	¼ cup canned consommé, undiluted
1 teaspoon salt	1 lemon, quartered

1. Wash, dry chicken quarters. **2.** Combine butter, paprika, thyme, salt, pepper; blend into a smooth paste. **3.** Rub paste onto both sides of chicken pieces. **4.** Place each coated piece in center of a large square of Alcoa Wrap. **5.** Place one piece of carrot under each chicken quarter, half slice of bacon on top. **6.** Pour 1 tablespoon of the consommé over each chicken quarter. **7.** Bring torn edges together over chicken; fold, then fold again, bringing fold down close to chicken. Fold ends over and over, pressing in close to meat. **8.** Place on baking sheet; bake 1 hour at 425° F. **9.** To serve: open packages; squeeze lemon quarters over each.

NESTED CHICKEN IN FOIL
4 servings

6 shredded wheat biscuits
½ cup flour
1 teaspoon salt
¼ teaspoon pepper
1 frying chicken, quartered
3 tablespoons shortening

½ cup butter or margarine
¼ cup minced onion
½ teaspoon salt
¼ teaspoon pepper
¼ cup chopped parsley

1. Crush shredded wheat biscuits into crumbs; set aside.
2. Combine flour, 1 teaspoon salt, ¼ teaspoon pepper; place in paper bag. 3. Wash, dry chicken pieces; drop into paper bag. shake until coated with flour. 4. Melt shortening in fry pan; brown chicken on both sides; remove; set aside. 5. In same pan, melt ¼ cup butter; add onion; cook until tender; remove from heat. 6. Add salt, pepper, parsley, shredded wheat crumbs; stir until mixed. 7. Place 1 cup of the shredded wheat mixture in the center of each of the four pieces of Alcoa Wrap; lay one quarter of the chicken on top of crumbs; dot each piece with 1 tablespoon of remaining butter. 8. Bring torn edges together over chicken; fold, then fold again, bringing fold down close to chicken. Fold ends over and over, pressing in close to chicken. 9. Place on baking sheet. 10. Bake 30 minutes at 375° F.

GRANADA CHICKEN WITH RICE
1 serving

¼ cup flour
½ teaspoon salt
⅛ teaspoon pepper
½ 2½ to 3 pound broiling chicken
2 tablespoons butter or margarine
⅛ teaspoon minced garlic
2 tablespoons green pepper, cut in ½-inch strips
2 tablespoons chopped onion

1 tablespoon chopped pimiento
1 chicken bouillon cube
½ cup water
¼ cup raw rice
Dash chili powder
Dash pepper
½ tablespoon chili sauce
¼ teaspoon salt

1. Combine flour, salt, pepper; roll chicken in seasoned flour.
2. Brown chicken in butter until golden brown on both sides; remove; set aside. 3. Sauté garlic, green pepper, onion in the fry pan until brown. 4. Add pimiento, bouillon cube, water,

rice, chili powder, pepper, chili sauce, salt; blend well.
5. Bring to a boil; simmer 5 minutes uncovered. 6. Place
rice mixture in center of double-thick square of Alcoa Wrap;
place chicken on rice, skin side up. 7. Bring torn edges together over chicken; fold, then fold again, bringing fold down
close to chicken. Fold ends over and over, pressing in close to
chicken. 8. Place on baking sheet. 9. Bake 1 hour at 425° F.

FRANKFURTER ROLL-UPS
6 servings

2 cups biscuit mix   mustard
6 frankfurters

1. Prepare dough for rolled biscuits according to directions on
package. 2. Roll dough in rectangle about ¼ inch thick.
3. Cut into strips ½ inch longer, twice the width of the
frankfurter. 4. Spread strips of dough with mustard; wrap
around frankfurter, pinching dough together to seal seams.
5. Place each frankfurter in center of double-thick square of
Alcoa Wrap; bring up torn edges tightly over top of frankfurter; fold in double folds; twist ends securely. 6. Place
packages on baking sheet. 7. Bake 25 minutes at 425° F.

*Good to know: For outdoor cooking, place packages on grill over
medium coals for 20 minutes, turning frequently.*

LITTLE MEAT LOAVES
6 servings

2 eggs, beaten   1 tablespoon salt
2 pounds ground beef   ½ cup milk
1 cup fine bread crumbs   ¼ cup ketchup
¾ cup minced onion   1 teaspoon dry mustard
¼ cup minced green pepper

1. Add eggs to meat; blend thoroughly; add remaining ingredients, but do not stir more than necessary, as it tends to toughen
meat. 2. Divide into six portions; shape each into little loaves
approximately 4½ x 3 x 1½ inches. 3. Place each loaf in
center of double-thick square of Alcoa Wrap. 4. Bring the
two torn edges together over meat; fold, then fold again,

bringing fold down close to meat. Fold ends over and over pressing in close to meat.   **5.** Place on baking sheet; bake 30 minutes at 425° F.

CHUCK WAGON SPECIAL   *1 serving*

2 tablespoons chili sauce	1 stalk celery, diced
2 teaspoons flour or 1 teaspoon quick-cooking tapioca	¼ pound beef sirloin tip, cut into 1-inch cubes
1 small baking potato, pared, halved	½ teaspoon monosodium glutamate
3 small onions, peeled	¼ teaspoon salt
1 medium carrot, quartered	⅛ teaspoon pepper

1. Combine chili sauce, flour; spread in center of double-thick square of Alcoa Wrap.   **2.** On sauce arrange potato, onions, carrot, celery; top with meat cubes.   **3.** Sprinkle monosodium glutamate, salt, pepper over top.   **4.** Bring the two torn edges together over food; fold, then fold again, bringing fold down close to food. Fold ends over and over pressing in close to meat.   **5.** Place on baking sheet; bake 1 hour at 450° F. **6.** Serve in opened packages.

SHORTRIBS IN BARBECUE SAUCE   *4 servings*

2 pounds shortribs	2 tablespoons shortening
Salt, pepper	2 cups Barbecue Sauce

1. Sprinkle shortribs with salt, pepper.   **2.** Fry shortribs in shortening until well browned.   **3.** Place each serving on a double-thick square of Alcoa Wrap.   **4.** Pour 2 tablespoons Barbecue Sauce over top of ribs.   **5.** Bring two edges of Alcoa Wrap together over ribs; make double fold; make double fold on each end.   **6.** Place on baking sheet; bake 1 hour at 375°F.

Good to know: *Shortribs in Barbecue Sauce may be prepared ahead of time, packaged in foil, refrigerated or frozen. Allow 15 additional minutes for baking if frozen.*

GOLD DISCOVERY
6 servings

6 medium to large yams	¼ cup butter or margarine
Lemon juice	6 slices bacon
Salt	6 whole chicken livers
Pepper	

1. Wash, dry yams. Slice off about ⅓ of each yam lengthwise.
2. From largest half of each yam, cut a cavity deep enough for chicken liver and bacon. 3. Brush each cavity with lemon juice to prevent discoloration; season with salt, pepper. 4. Place 2 teaspoons butter in each cavity. 5. Fry bacon until almost crisp; drain on absorbent paper. 6. Brown chicken livers; drain. 7. Wrap bacon around livers; place in each potato cavity. 8. Place each filled potato in center of a double-thick square of Alcoa Wrap. 9. Fit sliced-off portion of each potato over livers; bring up two sides of foil; double-fold ends up close to potato. 10. Place on baking sheet; bake 45-60 minutes at 425° F. 11. Serve hot in opened foil.

POTATO-VEGETABLE BAKE
4 servings

4 medium baking potatoes, pared	1 medium carrot, sliced thin
¼ cup butter or margarine, softened	Salt, pepper
2 medium onions, sliced	Paprika

1. Cut each potato in 4 crosswise slices. 2. Spread butter between and on top of slices. 3. Re-assemble potato, placing onion slices between potato slices; secure with toothpicks or skewers. 4. Slip thin slices of carrot between potato-onion slices. 5. Sprinkle with salt, pepper, paprika. 6. Place each potato in center of double-thick square of Alcoa Wrap; wrap, using tight double folds; twist ends securely; place on baking sheet. 7. Bake 60 minutes at 400° F. or until done.

Good to know: For outdoor cooking, place packages on grill over medium coals for about 1 hour, turning several times.

GRECIAN LAMB BALLS

4-5 servings

1½ pounds ground lamb
½ cup chopped onion
1 tablespoon chopped parsley
3 cups peeled chopped eggplant
1 teaspoon salt
⅛ teaspoon pepper
3 tablespoons fat
1 8-ounce can tomato sauce

¼ cup chopped onion
2 tablespoons vinegar
1 tablespoon brown sugar
¼ teaspoon salt
⅛ teaspoon pepper
⅛ teaspoon dry mustard
½ teaspoon cinnamon
¼ teaspoon ground cloves

1. Mix together lamb, onion, parsley, eggplant, salt, pepper.
2. Shape into 20 balls, using about ¼ cup mixture for each.
3. Brown on all sides in melted fat.   4. Place balls on squares of double-thick Alcoa Wrap (4-5 balls per square).   5. Combine remaining ingredients; pour over meat balls.   6. Bring torn edges together over meat; fold, then fold again, bringing fold down close to meat. Fold ends over and over pressing in close to meat.   7. Place in shallow baking pan.   8. Bake 45 minutes at 425° F.

DORIS' LAMB CHOPS

4 servings

2 hard-cooked eggs, shelled
½ cup butter or margarine
6 tablespoons fine bread crumbs
2 teaspoons minced onion
1 teaspoon salt

¼ teaspoon pepper
1 teaspoon Worcestershire sauce
4 loin lamb chops, cut 1-inch thick

1. Chop whites of eggs fine; rub yolks through sieve.   2. Melt butter in fry pan; add crumbs, onion; cook until lightly browned.   3. Add salt, pepper, Worcestershire sauce, eggs; blend well.   4. Sprinkle chops with salt, pepper.   5. Pat crumb mixture on one side of each chop; place a square of Alcoa Wrap on top; turn over; pat mixture on second side.   6. Bring torn edges together over meat; fold, then fold again, bringing down close to meat. Fold ends over and over pressing in close to meat.   7. Place in shallow baking pan; bake 1 hour at 400° F.

VEAL STEAKS PARMESAN

4 servings

2 pounds veal cutlet, ½ inch
thick
1 cup dry bread crumbs
½ teaspoon salt
⅛ teaspoon pepper

1 egg, beaten
¼ cup milk
¼ cup butter or margarine
1 8-ounce can tomato sauce
1 cup grated Parmesan cheese

1. Cut veal into serving pieces. 2. Combine crumbs, salt, pepper. 3. Combine egg, milk. 4. Dip veal into crumbs, into egg mixture, into crumbs again. 5. Melt butter in fry pan; add meat; brown well on both sides. 6. Place one serving in center of each of four squares of double-thick Alcoa Wrap, lightly greased. 7. Spread 2 tablespoons tomato sauce over each serving of meat. 8. Bring torn edges together over meat; fold, then fold again, bringing fold down onto meat. Fold ends over and over pressing in close to meat. 9. Place on baking sheet. 10. Bake 45 minutes at 425° F. 11. Open packages; sprinkle cheese over top; place under broiler 3-4 minutes or until cheese melts.

HOT HAM AND CHEESE ROLLS

12 servings

½ pound sharp Cheddar cheese
½ pound boiled or baked ham,
unsliced, or leftover ham pieces
⅓ cup sliced green onions
2 hard-cooked eggs, sliced

½ cup thinly sliced pimiento-
stuffed olives
3 tablespoons mayonnaise
½ cup chili sauce
12 frankfurter rolls, split

1. Cut cheese, ham into ¼ inch cubes. 2. Combine ham, cheese, onions, eggs, olives. 3. Mix mayonnaise, chili sauce; pour over ham mixture; toss until well blended. 4. Pile mixture into split rolls. 5. Wrap each roll in a 6-inch square of Alcoa Wrap; twist ends securely. 6. Place on baking sheet; bake 10 minutes at 400° F. 7. Serve each roll in its Alcoa Wrap.

Good to know: These can be made ahead; kept in refrigerator; heated at serving time.

PORK CHOPS WITH HAM STUFFING   6 servings

3 cups soft bread crumbs
1 cup cooked ham, finely chopped
¼ teaspoon salt
⅛ teaspoon pepper
¼ teaspoon nutmeg
1 beef bouillon cube
¼ cup boiling water

6 rib pork chops, 1-inch thick, cut with pockets
¼ cup all purpose flour
¾ teaspoon salt
Dash pepper
2 tablespoons shortening

1. Combine bread crumbs, ham, salt, pepper, nutmeg.   2. Dissolve bouillon cube in boiling water; pour over mixture; toss lightly.   3. Stuff pork chops; fasten with toothpicks.   4. Combine flour, salt, pepper; coat chops with mixture.   5. Melt shortening in heavy fry pan; sauté chops until well browned. 6. Place chops in center of 6 double-thick squares of Alcoa Wrap; bring up sides and ends in double folds; place on baking sheet.   7. Bake 1 hour at 450° F.

PORK CHOPS WITH BREAD STUFFING   4 servings

2 cups soft bread crumbs
¼ cup minced onion
1 tablespoon chopped parsley
½ teaspoon salt
½ teaspoon celery salt

3 tablespoons butter or margarine, melted
4 rib pork chops, 1-inch thick, cut with pockets
Salt, pepper
2 tablespoons shortening

1. Combine bread crumbs, onion, parsley, salt, celery salt, melted butter; toss lightly.   2. Stuff pork chops; fasten with

toothpicks. 3. Sprinkle chops with salt, pepper. 4. Melt shortening in heavy fry pan; sauté chops until well browned. 5. Place chops in center of 4 double-thick squares of Alcoa Wrap; bring up sides and ends in double folds; place on baking sheet. 6. Bake 1 hour at 450° F.

SPANISH PORK CHOPS
4 servings

4 loin pork chops, 1-inch thick
  Salt, pepper
2 tablespoons shortening
4 slices onion

¼ cup ketchup
½ cup diluted vinegar or sweet
  pickle juice

1. Sprinkle chops with salt, pepper. 2. Melt shortening in heavy fry pan; sauté chops until well browned. 3. Place chops in center of 4 double-thick squares of Alcoa Wrap; place slice of onion on each chop; top with ketchup. 4. Pour vinegar or pickle juice over chops. 5. Bring up sides and ends of foil in double folds; place on baking sheet. 6. Bake 1 hour at 450° F.

Variation: Eliminate vinegar or pickle juice and replace onion slices with lemon slices.

PORK CHOPS PIERRE
8 servings

1 tablespoon butter or margarine
⅓ cup finely chopped onion
¼ cup finely chopped celery
¼ cup water
½ cup ketchup
2 tablespoons vinegar
1 tablespoon lemon juice
1 tablespoon Worcestershire
  sauce

1 tablespoon brown sugar
½ teaspoon salt
⅛ teaspoon pepper
8 loin pork chops cut ½ inch
  thick
1 large onion, sliced thin
1 large green pepper, cut into
  rings

1. Melt butter in saucepan; add onion, celery; cook over low heat until tender. 2. Add water, ketchup, vinegar, lemon juice, Worcestershire sauce, sugar, salt, pepper; cover; simmer 20 minutes. 3. Brown pork chops on both sides in fry

pan.   **4.** Make 8 double-thick squares of Alcoa Wrap.   **5.** Pour 1 tablespoon of the sauce in the center of each square; place pork chops on top; place 2 slices onion, 1 tablespoon sauce, 2 green pepper rings on top of each chop.   **6.** Bring torn edges together over meat; fold, then fold again, bringing fold down close to meat. Fold ends over and over pressing in close to meat.   **7.** Place packages in shallow pan.   **8.** Bake 45-50 minutes at 425° F.

Staff of Life

Quick breads, yeast breads—polka-dotted with plump raisins or candied fruit, redolent with spices—as they bake, they smell like nothing else in the world ... when you bring them to the table, the happy faces will make you know you're the best cook in the whole, wide world!

QUICK BREADS

GARLIC BREAD

1 loaf

1 clove garlic
6 tablespoons butter or margarine
1 loaf French or Italian bread, unsliced
Salt
½ cup grated Parmesan cheese
Paprika

1. Peel, chop garlic fine. 2. Melt butter; add garlic; let stand 1-2 hours. 3. Cut bread into 2-inch slices down almost to bottom crust. 4. Place on sheet of Alcoa Wrap in shallow bake pan. 5. Brush top, sides and down in gashes with garlic-butter mixture. 6. Sprinkle top lightly with salt; sprinkle cheese over top. 7. Bake 10-15 minutes at 400° F. 8. Sprinkle with paprika; close foil up around bread to keep hot. 9. Serve at once.

CHOCOLATE-ORANGE LOAF

1 loaf

3 cups prepared biscuit mix
¾ cup sugar
1 egg, beaten
1¼ cups orange juice
¾ cup chopped nuts
1 6-ounce package semi-sweet chocolate bits

1. Combine biscuit mix, sugar. 2. Stir in egg, orange juice; beat well. 3. Fold in nuts, ¾ cup chocolate bits. 4. Pour

into a 9 x 5 x 3-inch loaf pan lined with lightly greased strips of Alcoa Wrap; allow strips of foil to extend up over edges of pan. **5.** Sprinkle remaining chocolate bits on top of batter. **6.** Bake 55-60 minutes at 350° F. **7.** Cool; wrap in foil; for short storage place in refrigerator; for longer storage place in freezer.

PUFF PASTE TWISTS
7½ dozen

6 egg yolks	1 tablespoon grated lemon peel
¼ cup sugar	½ teaspoon salt
1 tablespoon butter or margarine, melted	2 cups sifted all purpose flour
	Fat for frying
⅓ cup heavy cream, whipped	Confectioners sugar

1. Beat egg yolks until thick, lemon colored; beat in sugar. **2.** Gently stir in melted butter, whipped cream, lemon peel, salt, flour; mix only enough to blend ingredients to a soft dough. **3.** Chill. **4.** Roll dough (half at a time) ⅛-inch thick on lightly floured pastry cloth or board. **5.** Cut into rectangles 3 x ¾ inches; twist each one in the middle. **6.** Fry a few at a time in deep fat 375° F. until golden brown. **7.** Drain on absorbent paper. **8.** Sprinkle with confectioners sugar while still warm. **9.** Serve with jam and whipped cream.

VIENNESE COFFEE CAKE
16 servings

⅔ cup butter or margarine	2 teaspoons baking powder
⅔ cup sugar	5 tablespoons milk
3 egg yolks	½ cup chopped nuts
1 whole egg	1 tablespoon flour
1 cup sifted all purpose flour	

1. Cream butter until soft; add sugar gradually, continuing to cream until light, fluffy. **2.** Add egg yolks, egg; mix well. **3.** Sift flour, baking powder together; add alternately with milk. **4.** Coat nuts with remaining 1 tablespoon flour, fold into batter.   **5.** Pour into a 9 x 9 x 1¾-inch pan lined with Alcoa Wrap; extend foil up sides of pan allowing enough to grasp foil for easy removal of cake.   **6.** Bake 30 minutes at 350° F.   **7.** Cool; wrap in foil; for short storage place in refrigerator; for longer storage, place in freezer.

Good to know: Can be warmed in foil package.

HUNGARIAN COFFEE CAKE

8 servings

2 cakes compressed yeast
1 cup milk
½ cup sugar
1 teaspoon salt

2 eggs, well beaten
4½ to 4¾ cups sifted all purpose flour
½ cup shortening, melted

Topping

½ cup melted butter or margarine
1¼ cups sugar

2 teaspoons cinnamon
¾ cup finely chopped nuts
1 cup raisins

1. Crumble yeast into mixing bowl.   **2.** Scald milk; cool to lukewarm; add to yeast.   **3.** Add sugar, salt; let stand until thoroughly dissolved.   **4.** Add eggs; mix well.   **5.** Add ½ of the flour; beat until smooth, very elastic.   **6.** Add melted, cooled shortening.   **7.** Add remainder of flour—just enough so dough is soft, workable.   **8.** Round off and set to rise in a greased bowl in warm place until dough is double in bulk.   **9.** Punch dough down; divide in half; cut into pieces the size of walnuts; form into balls.   **10.** Roll each ball in butter; then in combined sugar, cinnamon, nuts.   **11.** Place one layer balls in greased 10 x 4-inch tube pan so that they barely touch.   **12.** Sprinkle with a few raisins.   **13.** Add another layer of balls, sprinkle more raisins in crevices; repeat, using all dough, raisins.   **14.** Cover; let rise in warm place until light (about 45 minutes).   **15.** Bake 35-40 minutes at 375° F.   **16.** Loosen from pan with spatula; invert.   **17.** To serve, break apart.

HOLIDAY FRUIT BREAD

2 small loaves

2 tablespoons grated orange rind
¾ cup orange juice (3 medium oranges)
¾ cup boiling water
1 cup sliced dates
1 cup chopped candied fruit
3 tablespoons melted shortening
2 teaspoons vanilla

2 eggs, slightly beaten
3 cups sifted all purpose flour
1½ cups sugar
1½ teaspoons baking powder
¾ teaspoon baking soda
¾ teaspoon salt
¾ cup slivered almonds

1. Combine orange rind, orange juice, boiling water; pour over dates, candied fruit. 2. Add shortening, vanilla, eggs; blend well. 3. Sift together flour, sugar, baking powder, baking soda, salt; add to fruit mixture; blend well. 4. Fold in almonds. 5. Pour into two lightly greased Alcoa Wrap loaf pans 8 x 4 x 2½ inches. 6. Bake 50-55 minutes at 350° F.

CARAWAY LOAF

1 loaf

½ cup butter or margarine
1 cup sugar
2 eggs
2 teaspoons caraway seed
2 cups sifted all purpose flour

1½ teaspoons baking powder
½ teaspoon salt
½ teaspoon mace
½ cup milk

1. Cream butter, sugar until light, fluffy. 2. Add eggs, one at a time, beating after each addition. 3. Add caraway seeds; blend. 4. Sift flour, baking powder, salt, mace together. 5. Alternately add in thirds—flour mixture, milk; blend well after each addition. 6. Pour into 9 x 5 x 3-inch loaf pan lined with lightly greased strips of Alcoa Wrap; allow strips of foil to extend up over edges of pan. 7. Bake 60 minutes at 350° F.

Good to know: *Loaf may be wrapped in Alcoa Wrap; stored in the freezer several months.*

ORANGE-PECAN MUFFINS
1½ dozen

Topping
¼ cup granulated sugar
3 tablespoons flour
½ teaspoon cinnamon
½ teaspoon nutmeg

2 tablespoons butter or margarine
1 14-ounce package orange muffin mix
½ cup chopped pecans

1. Combine sugar, flour, cinnamon, nutmeg, butter; blend together with 2 knives or pastry blender until mixture is crumbly; set aside. 2. Prepare muffin mix as directed on package; fold in chopped nuts. 3. Cut 18 6-inch squares of Alcoa Wrap; line muffin pans with foil, allowing edges of foil to extend up over edges. 4. Fill foil-lined muffin pans ½ full; sprinkle topping mixture over top. 5. Bake 20-25 minutes at 375° F.

Good to know: Extra muffins may be cooled; edges of foil folded over top of muffins; placed in the freezer for future use.

CRANBERRY BREAD
1 loaf

2 cups sifted all purpose flour
1 cup sugar
1½ teaspoons baking powder
1 teaspoon salt
½ teaspoon baking soda
1 tablespoon grated orange rind

Juice of 1 orange
2 tablespoons shortening
1 egg, well beaten
1 cup chopped walnuts
1 cup raw cranberries, cut in half

1. Sift flour, sugar, baking powder, salt, soda together into large mixing bowl. 2. Combine orange juice with enough boiling water to measure ¾ cup; add shortening; stir until dissolved; blend in egg. 3. Add to dry ingredients; mix until all dry particles are moistened. 4. Stir in nuts, cranberries, orange rind. 5. Turn into greased 9 x 5 x 3-inch loaf pan. 6. Bake 55-65 minutes at 350° F.; cool before slicing.

ROQUEFORT CHEESE BREAD *1 loaf*

1. Blend ½ pound butter or margarine with ¼ pound Roquefort cheese. 2. Add finely minced green onions, if desired. 3. Slash a loaf of French bread diagonally, cutting down to, but not through the bottom crust. 4. Spread butter mixture liberally between slices. Wrap in Alcoa Wrap; heat 15 minutes at 400° F., or on grill.

FRENCH COFFEE CAKE *9 servings*

½ cup shortening	1 teaspoon baking soda
1 cup sugar	1 teaspoon baking powder
3 eggs	½ teaspoon salt
1 teaspoon vanilla	1 cup commercial sour cream
2 cups sifted all-purpose flour	

Topping

2 tablespoons butter or margarine	¾ cup brown sugar
3 tablespoons flour	½ cup chopped nuts

1. Cream shortening; add sugar, gradually continuing to cream until light, fluffy. 2. Add eggs one at a time; beat well after each addition; add vanilla. 3. Sift flour, baking soda, baking powder, salt together. 4. Alternately add sifted dry ingredients, sour cream to mixture; blend together. 5. Prepare topping; cream butter, flour together; add sugar, nuts; mix until crumbly. 6. Line 8 x 8 x 2-inch pan with Alcoa Wrap; extend foil up sides of pan, allowing enough to grasp foil for easy removal of cake. 7. Pour half batter into pan; cover with half topping; pour remaining batter on top; sprinkle remaining topping over batter. 8. Bake 50-55 minutes at 350° F. 9. Cool; wrap in foil; for short storage, place in refrigerator; for longer storage, place in freezer.

Good to know: Can be warmed in foil package.

WEBSTER COFFEE CAKE

6-8 servings

½ cup shortening
1 cup sugar
3 eggs
1 teaspoon vanilla
2¼ cups sifted all purpose flour
1 teaspoon baking powder
1 teaspoon baking soda

½ teaspoon salt
1 cup commercial sour cream
½ cup chopped dates
½ cup sliced, candied cherries
½ cup chopped nuts
¼ cup chopped citron

Topping

1 tablespoon butter or
  margarine
1½ tablespoons flour

⅓ cup brown sugar
¼ cup chopped nuts

1. Cream shortening; add sugar, gradually continuing to cream until light, fluffy. 2. Add eggs one at a time; beat well after each addition; add vanilla. 3. Sift flour; set aside ¼ cup flour. 4. Sift remaining flour with baking powder, baking soda, salt. 5. Alternately add sifted dry ingredients, sour cream to mixture; blend. 6. Roll dates, cherries, nuts, citron in the ¼ cup flour; add to mixture; mix well. 7. Combine butter, flour, sugar, nuts for topping; mix well. 8. Pour mixture into greased, floured 8-inch tube cake pan; sprinkle topping over mixture. 9. Bake 55-60 minutes at 350° F. 10. Cool; wrap in Alcoa Wrap; for short storage, place in refrigerator; for longer storage, place in freezer.

Good to know: Can be warmed in foil package.

YEAST BREADS

ORANGE LATTICE COFFEE CAKE   2 *cakes*

1 cake compressed yeast
¼ cup lukewarm water
⅔ cup butter or margarine
⅓ cup sugar
1 teaspoon salt
4 eggs, beaten
¾ cup light cream
4 cups sifted all purpose flour

Orange Filling
⅔ cup butter or margarine
⅔ cup blanched chopped almonds
⅔ cup sugar
⅔ cup orange marmalade
¼ cup flour
1 egg, beaten

1. Crumble yeast into water; stir; let stand.   2. Cream together butter, sugar; add salt, eggs; beat well.   3. Combine yeast mixture with light cream.   4. Alternately add flour, yeast-cream mixture to butter-sugar mixture in thirds; mix well, but do not beat.   5. Reserve one cup dough. Spread remainder in two Alcoa Wrap-lined 9 x 9 x 2-inch pans; allow foil to extend up over edges of pan; lightly grease foil in pan. 6. Combine butter, almonds, sugar, marmalade; mix well. 7. Spread orange filling over dough.   8. Blend ¼ cup flour into reserved dough. Roll dough into rectangle; cut into twelve 9 x 1-inch strips.   9. Arrange six strips, lattice fashion, over filling in each pan; brush with beaten egg.   10. Cover with Alcoa Wrap; let rise in warm place until almost double (45-60 minutes).   11. Bake 30-35 minutes at 400° F.   12. Grasp edges of foil; remove coffee cake to serving platter; serve warm.

DANISH PASTRY   12-14 *servings*

1½ cakes compressed yeast
¼ cup warm water
1 cup butter or margarine
2¾ cups sifted all purpose flour
2 tablespoons sugar
2 eggs, beaten

Filling
½ cup butter or margarine
½ cup sugar
1 egg white, slightly beaten
½ cup slivered blanched almonds

1. Crumble yeast into water; stir, let stand.   2. Cut butter into flour until mixture resembles very fine crumbs.   3. Com-

bine sugar, eggs; add to flour-butter mixture; blend thoroughly. 4. Add yeast; mix until a sticky dough is formed. 5. Divide dough into fourths; roll one portion of dough on floured board into 9-inch circle; transfer to 9-inch pie pan; repeat using a second portion. 6. With palms of hands gently mold dough one inch up sides of pans. 7. Cream butter, sugar for filling; spread over circles of dough in pans. 8. Roll out other two portions of dough into 9-inch circles; cut into ¾-inch strips. 9. Place strips over filling to give a latticed effect. 10. Cover with waxed paper, dry cloth; let rise in warm place for two hours. 11. Brush top of strips with egg white; sprinkle with almonds. 12. Bake 15 minutes at 425° F.

CINNAMON TWISTS
2 dozen

1 cup commercial sour cream	1 egg, slightly beaten
3 tablespoons sugar	4 tablespoons melted shortening
⅛ teaspoon baking soda	3 cups sifted all purpose flour
1 teaspoon salt	⅓ cup brown sugar
1 cake compressed yeast	1 teaspoon cinnamon

1. Heat sour cream to lukewarm in saucepan. 2. Add sugar, soda, salt; blend. 3. Pour into mixing bowl; add crumbled yeast; stir until dissolved. 4. Add egg, 2 tablespoons shortening, flour; mix well. 5. Turn dough onto floured board; fold over several times until smooth. 6. Roll into oblong 24 x 6 inches; brush with remaining shortening. 7. Combine brown sugar, cinnamon; sprinkle over half dough. 8. Fold over dough, cut into 1 x 4-inch strips. 9. Hold strips at each end; twist; place on baking sheet; press ends onto baking sheet. 10. Cover; let rise in warm place 1 hour. 11. Bake 12-15 minutes at 375° F. 12. Frost with Confectioners Icing while still warm.

PEANUT BUTTER BREAD
1 loaf

1¼ cups warm water
1 cake compressed yeast
¼ cup chunk-style peanut butter
¼ cup finely chopped peanuts

2 teaspoons salt
¼ cup brown sugar, firmly packed
3 cups sifted all-purpose flour

1. Pour warm water into mixing bowl; add crumbled yeast; stir until dissolved. 2. Add peanut butter, peanuts, salt, brown sugar, half the flour; beat 2 minutes on medium speed of mixer or 300 vigorous strokes by hand, scraping sides and bottom of bowl frequently. 3. Add remaining flour; blend in with spoon until smooth; scrape batter down from sides of bowl. 4. Cover with damp cloth; let rise in warm place until double in bulk (30-40 minutes). 5. Stir batter vigorously about 25 strokes; spread evenly in greased 9 x 5 x 3-inch loaf pan (batter will be sticky). 6. Let rise in warm place until batter reaches 1 inch from top of pan (about 40 minutes). 7. Bake 45-50 minutes at 375° F. or until brown; cover loaf with Alcoa Wrap during last half of baking. 8. To test loaf, tap crust (it should sound hollow). 9. Immediately remove from pan; brush top with melted butter or margarine; place on rack to cool.

Superior Sandwiches

A sandwich—some rejected leftover slapped between two slices of bread—can be the cowardly cook's way out. On the other hand, a sandwich—perhaps made from that same leftover treated with imagination and know-how—can be a culinary triumph. Those you'll find here are triumphs, every one!

CREAMED CHICKEN SUPREME
12 servings

⅓ cup butter or margarine
⅓ cup flour
1 cup chicken broth
1½ cups milk
Salt, pepper

2 cups diced, cooked chicken
12 slices white bread
12 slices sharp cheese
Crumbled cooked bacon

1. Melt butter; blend in flour; gradually add broth, milk.
2. Cook over low heat, stirring constantly until thickened.
3. Add salt, pepper, chicken.   4. Toast bread; place in bottom of shallow baking pan lined with Alcoa Wrap.   5. Pile ⅓ cup creamed chicken on each slice; top with slice cheese.   6. Slide under broiler until cheese melts; top with crumbled bacon.

DEVONSHIRE SANDWICH
6 servings

18 slices bacon
1¼ cups flour
2 quarts milk, scalded
1 tablespoon salt
1 teaspoon dry mustard
½ teaspoon poultry seasoning
1 teaspoon monosodium glutamate

½ pound sharp cheese, diced
6 slices bread, toasted
1½ pounds cooked sliced chicken
or turkey
2 tablespoons grated Parmesan
cheese
1 teaspoon paprika

1. In fry pan cook bacon slowly until crisp; drain on absorbent paper.   2. Stir flour into hot fat; blend until smooth.   3. Add

180

milk gradually, stirring until sauce is smooth. **4.** Cook over low heat 10 minutes, stirring constantly. **5.** Add salt, mustard, poultry seasoning, monosodium glutamate, cheese; stir until cheese is melted. **6.** Place toasted bread in Alcoa Wrap lined baking pan. **7.** Place 3 strips bacon on each slice of toast. **8.** Arrange chicken or turkey over bacon on each sandwich; cover completely with sauce. **9.** Combine Parmesan cheese, paprika; blend. **10.** Sprinkle over each sandwich. **11.** Bake 10 minutes at 350° F.

Good to know: Thin ham slices may be substituted for part of the chicken or turkey. Sandwiches may be placed under the broiler for the last few minutes of baking time.

FIESTAS
8 servings

½ cup minced onion
¾ cup minced green pepper
3 tablespoons butter or margarine
1½ cups finely chopped left-over chicken or turkey
1 6-ounce can tomato paste

½ cup chopped stuffed olives
1 teaspoon Worcestershire sauce
1 teaspoon chili powder
⅛ teaspoon salt
Dash pepper
8 wiener buns

1. Sauté onion, green pepper in butter until soft. **2.** Add chicken, tomato paste, olives, Worcestershire sauce, chili powder, salt, pepper; simmer 10 minutes, stirring frequently. **3.** Fill buns generously with chicken mixture. **4.** Place each filled bun on a square of Alcoa Wrap; bring up foil in boat around bun. **5.** Place on broiler rack; broil 5-10 minutes, until buns brown lightly.

LUNCHEON SANDWICH
8 servings

½ cup butter or margarine
½ cup flour
1 teaspoon salt
4 cups milk
3 3¼-ounce cans deviled ham
Dash pepper

1 teaspoon prepared mustard
2 packages frozen asparagus spears
8 slices bread
6 hard cooked eggs, sliced

1. Melt butter in saucepan; add flour, salt; blend. **2.** Add milk; cook over low heat until thickened, bubbly, stirring constantly. **3.** Add deviled ham, pepper, mustard; blend. **4.** Cook asparagus according to directions on package. **5.** Cut 8 pieces Alcoa Wrap one inch larger than a slice of bread. **6.** Toast bread; remove crusts; place one slice toast on each piece of foil; fold up sides; pinch corners together to form four ears. **7.** Place asparagus, egg slices on toast; pour sauce over top; garnish with paprika.

Good to know: Canned peach halves filled with orange marmalade and lightly browned under the broiler make a good accompaniment.

TUNA CHEESE PUFFS
6 servings

2 6½ or 7-ounce cans tuna, drained	Salt to taste
1 hard cooked egg, chopped	½ pound Cheddar cheese, softened
¾ cup finely chopped celery	1 egg, well beaten
¼ cup pickle relish	2 tablespoons mayonnaise
¼ cup mayonnaise	1 tablespoon prepared mustard
	12 slices buttered white bread

1. Combine tuna, egg, celery, relish, mayonnaise, salt; blend well. **2.** Combine cheese, egg, mayonnaise, mustard; blend well. **3.** Spread tuna mixture on 6 slices bread; top with remaining bread. **4.** Line broiler with Alcoa Wrap; place sandwiches on foil; toast under broiler until golden. **5.** Turn sandwiches; pile cheese mixture on top. **6.** Broil 3-4 inches from heat 2-3 minutes, or until cheese has slightly browned, puffy.

BROILED MUSHROOM SANDWICH
4 servings

1 cup chopped fresh mushrooms	½ teaspoon salt
2 tablespoons butter or margarine	8 slices bread
1 cup grated sharp cheese	8 slices tomato
1 egg, slightly beaten	4 strips bacon

1. Sauté chopped mushrooms in butter. **2.** Add cheese, egg, salt; blend well. **3.** Trim crusts from bread; place tomato slice on each slice of bread. **4.** Spread mushroom mixture over tomato. **5.** Cut bacon strips in half; place ½ strip on each sandwich. **6.** Sandwiches may be prepared a few hours in advance; wrapped in Alcoa Wrap; stored in refrigerator. **7.** Open foil package; place under broiler; broil until bubbly and bacon is crisp.

BARBECUED TUNA ON BUNS   6 servings

½ cup tomato pureé
¼ cup wine vinegar
2 tablespoons soy sauce
¼ cup melted butter or
   margarine

1 clove garlic, finely chopped
½ teaspoon marjoram
2 7-ounce cans flaked tuna
6 sandwich buns
   Softened butter or margarine

1. Combine tomato purée, vinegar, soy sauce, butter, garlic, marjoram; simmer over low heat 15 minutes. **2.** Add tuna; let mixture stand 15 minutes to blend flavor. **3.** Split buns in half; butter lightly. **4.** Place buttered side down in hot fry pan to brown. **5.** Remove to hot serving platter with browned side up. **6.** Spread with tuna; serve immediately.

BAKED TUNA SANDWICHES   6 servings

1 7-ounce can tuna
2 hard cooked eggs, chopped
¼ cup sliced, stuffed olives
1½ tablespoons grated onion
⅓ cup mayonnaise

2 tablespoons softened butter or
   margarine
12 slices bread
4 tablespoons softened butter or
   margarine
¼ cup grated cheese

1. Drain tuna; place in mixing bowl; flake with fork. **2.** Add eggs, olives, onion, mayonnaise; toss lightly. **3.** Spread six slices bread with 2 tablespoons softened butter; spread with tuna mixture; top with remaining bread slices. **4.** Combine remaining butter, grated cheese; blend to form paste; spread over top of sandwiches. **5.** Place on baking sheet; cover with Alcoa Wrap; refrigerate. **6.** To serve; remove foil covering; bake 12-13 minutes at 400° F. or until nicely browned on top.

CRAB MEAT SALAD ON TOASTED BUN

6 servings

⅓ cup mushrooms, chopped
3 tablespoons butter or margarine
3 tablespoons grated onion
¼ cup chopped green olives

2 hard cooked eggs, chopped
2 6½-ounce cans crab meat
⅓ cup mayonnaise
6 sandwich buns

1. Sauté mushrooms in butter; cool. 2. Add grated onion, olives, chopped eggs, crab meat, mayonnaise; mix well; chill. 3. Split buns; toast under broiler; top with crab meat mixture; serve immediately.

FRENCH FRIED HAM SANDWICHES

10 servings

10 slices boiled or baked ham
20 slices of bread
3 tablespoons prepared brown mustard
10 slices American or Swiss cheese

1 egg, beaten
½ teaspoon salt
¾ cup milk
⅓ cup butter or margarine

1. Place slices of ham on bread; spread ham with mustard; cover with cheese slice; top with remaining slices of bread. 2. Combine beaten egg, salt, milk; blend well. 3. Dip sandwiches quickly into egg-milk mixture. 4. Fry in butter until delicately browned on both sides. 5. Garnish with pickles, olives.

MAGGIE'S SPECIAL SANDWICH
6 servings

6 slices rye bread
2 tablespoons soft butter or margarine
½ head lettuce
½ pound Swiss cheese
6 slices chicken

1 cup Thousand Island dressing
6 slices tomato
1 hard cooked egg
12 slices bacon, cooked crisp
6 ripe olives
6 sprigs parsley

1. Butter bread; place bread butter side up on dinner plate.
2. Put several lettuce leaves on bread; top with slice Swiss cheese; add large lettuce cup, reverse side up; cover with chicken slice. 3. Pour Thousand Island dressing over sandwich. 4. Top with tomato slice, egg slice. 5. Garnish with bacon, ripe olive, sprig of parsley.

CHICKEN PINEAPPLE TREATS
6 servings

1 No. 1 can pineapple slices
18 slices white bread
Softened butter or margarine
1 cup diced chicken or turkey
¼ cup finely diced celery
2 tablespoons chopped ripe olives

2 tablespoons chopped green stuffed olives
2 tablespoons pickle relish
1 3-ounce package cream cheese
2 8-ounce packages cream cheese, softened
Light cream

1. Drain 6 slices pineapple on absorbent paper until quite dry.
2. Cut bread into 18 rounds same size as pineapple slices; spread each round lightly with softened butter. 3. Cut six circles of Alcoa Wrap one inch larger than bread rounds. 4. Place one round of bread in center of each foil circle; bring foil up around bread; top each with a pineapple slice. 5. Combine chicken, celery, ripe olives, green olives, relish, 3 ounces cream cheese; blend well. 6. Spread 6 rounds of bread with chicken mixture; place on pineapple slices; top with remaining 6 rounds of bread, buttered side down. 7. Combine the two 8-ounce packages cream cheese with enough cream to spread easily. 8. Frost sides, tops of chicken-pineapple treats.

The Wonderful Smell of Baking

Of course, you don't have to remind your family that you love them. It doesn't hurt, though, to remind them . . . and what better way than by baking a pretty, delicious cake? And don't forget the bonus: that wonderful smell that comes from the oven while your cake is baking!

TO KEEP CAKES FRESH: All types of cake will stay fresh and moist if wrapped in Alcoa Wrap.

TO FREEZE CAKES: Butter, chocolate, spice, fruit and angel food cakes can be frozen successfully. These are baked before freezing. They may be iced or left un-iced, and should be cooled completely before freezing. Place cake on flat plate or cardboard, and wrap well in Alcoa Wrap. For best flavor, do not hold cakes in freezer for more than three months.

TO THAW FROZEN CAKES: Remove cakes from freezer. Let stand at room temperature, without removing wrapping, until thawed. If cake is unwrapped before thawing, beads of moisture will collect on icing and mar its quality.

JELLY ROLL
1 15½ x 10½ x 1-inch bake pan

3 eggs
1 cup sugar
5 tablespoons cold water
1 teaspoon vanilla

1 cup sifted cake flour
1 teaspoon baking powder
¼ teaspoon salt

1. Line bottom, sides of pan with waxed paper. 2. Beat eggs until thick. 3. Beat sugar in gradually. 4. Add water, vanilla;

beat. **5.** Sift flour, baking powder, salt together; add all at one time. **6.** Beat only until smooth. **7.** Pour into pan; spread evenly. **8.** Bake 12-15 minutes at 375° F. **9.** While cake is baking, sprinkle towel with confectioners sugar. **10.** When cake is done, remove from oven; loosen edges; turn at once upside down on towel. **11.** Quickly peel off paper. **12.** Spread at once with jam or jelly; roll up; wrap in towel until cool.

Good to know: To use special fillings, roll up plain jelly roll right after baking; let cool; unroll; spread with filling; reroll.

PLAIN TWO-EGG CAKE

2 8 x 1½-inch layer cake pans or
1 8 x 8 x 2-inch cake pan or
1 12-cup muffin pan

½ cup shortening	1¾ cups sifted cake flour
1 cup sugar	2 teaspoons baking powder
2 eggs, beaten	½ teaspoon salt
½ teaspoon vanilla	½ cup milk

1. Grease pan, dust lightly with flour. **2.** Cream shortening until soft. **3.** Add sugar gradually, continuing to cream until light, fluffy. **4.** Add eggs, vanilla; beat thoroughly. **5.** Sift flour, baking powder, salt together. **6.** Alternately add, in thirds, flour mixture, milk; beat well after each addition.
7. Pour into pans; spread evenly.
8. Bake:

Layers, 25-30 minutes 375° F.
Loaf, 50-60 minutes 350° F.
Cup cakes, 25-28 minutes 350° F.

9. When done, remove from oven; let stand 5 minutes.
10. Turn out onto cooling rack; turn, top side up; cool.
11. Frost as desired.

PRIZE SPICE CAKE

3 8 x 1½-inch layer cake pans or
2 9 x 1½-inch layer cake pans

¾ cup butter or margarine
2 cups light brown sugar, firmly packed
2 eggs
1 teaspoon vanilla
3 cups sifted cake flour
2 teaspoons cinnamon

1 teaspoon nutmeg
½ teaspoon cloves
1½ teaspoons baking soda
1 teaspoon baking powder
½ teaspoon salt
1 cup sour milk or buttermilk

1. Grease pans; dust lightly with flour. 2. Cream butter until soft. 3. Add sugar gradually, continuing to cream until light, fluffy. 4. Add eggs, vanilla; beat thoroughly. 5. Sift flour, cinnamon, nutmeg, cloves, baking soda, baking powder, salt together. 6. Alternately add in thirds, flour mixture, milk; beat well after each addition. 7. Pour into pans; spread evenly. 8. Bake 25-30 minutes at 375° F. 9. When done, remove from oven; let stand 5 minutes. 10. Turn out onto cooling rack; turn, top side up; cool. 11. Spread Sea Foam Frosting between layers, over top, sides of cake. 12. Sprinkle with chopped nuts if desired.

APPLESAUCE CAKE

1 13 x 9 x 2-inch baking pan

2½ cups sifted all purpose flour
2 cups sugar
¼ teaspoon baking powder
1½ teaspoons baking soda
1½ teaspoons salt
¾ teaspoon cinnamon
½ teaspoon cloves
½ teaspoon allspice

½ cup soft shortening
½ cup water
½ cup nuts, chopped
1 cup seedless raisins, chopped
1½ cups thick unsweetened applesauce
2 eggs

1. Grease pan; dust lightly with flour. 2. Sift into bowl, flour, sugar, baking powder, baking soda, salt, cinnamon, cloves, allspice. 3. Add shortening, water, nuts, raisins. 4. Beat 2 minutes. 5. Add applesauce, eggs; beat 2 more minutes.

6. Pour into pan; spread evenly. 7. Bake 45-50 minutes at 350° F. 8. When done, remove from oven; let stand 5 minutes. 9. Turn out onto cooling rack; turn, top side up; cool. 10. Frost as desired or sprinkle with confectioners sugar.

YELLOW CREAM CAKE

3 8 x 1½-inch layer cake pans or
2 9 x 1½-inch layer cake pans or
2 8 x 8 x 2-inch cake pans or
1 13 x 9 x 2-inch baking pan

¾ cup shortening
1½ cups sugar
3 eggs, beaten
1 teaspoon vanilla

3 cups sifted cake flour
3 teaspoons baking powder
¾ teaspoon salt
¾ cup milk

1. Grease pans; dust lightly with flour. 2. Cream shortening until soft. 3. Add sugar gradually, continuing to cream until light, fluffy. 4. Add eggs, vanilla; beat thoroughly. 5. Sift flour, baking powder, salt together. 6. Alternately add, in thirds, flour mixture, milk; beat well after each addition. 7. Pour into pans; spread evenly. 8. Bake at 375° F.:
    Layers, 25-30 minutes
    Loaf, 40-45 minutes
9. When done, remove from oven; let stand 5 minutes. 10. Turn out onto cooling rack; turn, top side up; cool. 11. Finish with desired filling and frosting.

HARLEQUIN CAKE

3 8 x 1½-inch layer cake pans

½ cup shortening
1½ cups sugar
3 eggs
1 teaspoon vanilla
3 cups sifted cake flour
3 teaspoons baking powder

½ teaspoon salt
1 cup cold water
1 square unsweetened chocolate, melted
Few drops red coloring

1. Grease pans; dust lightly with flour. 2. Cream shortening until soft. 3. Add sugar gradually, continuing to cream until light, fluffy. 4. Add eggs, vanilla; beat thoroughly. 5. Sift flour, baking powder, salt together. 6. Alternately add, in

thirds, flour mixture, water; beat well after each addition.
7. Divide batter into three parts.

Part one: stir in melted chocolate; blend.

Part two: add few drops red coloring to make deep pink; blend.

Part three: plain batter; no additions.

8. Pour chocolate batter into one pan, pink batter into second pan, plain batter into third pan; spread evenly. 9. Bake 20-25 minutes at 375° F. 10. When done, remove from oven; let stand 5 minutes. 11. Turn out onto cooling rack; turn, top side up; cool. 12. Assemble layers with chocolate layer on bottom, pink layer in middle, plain layer on top; spread Chocolate Butter Cream Icing between layers, over top, sides of cake.

BANANA NUT CAKE

1 8 x 8 x 2-inch cake pan

½ cup shortening
1 cup sugar
2 eggs
1 teaspoon vanilla
½ cup nuts, chopped
2¼ cups sifted cake flour

2 teaspoons baking powder
¼ teaspoon baking soda
¾ teaspoon salt
1 cup ripe bananas, mashed
(2-3 bananas)
2 tablespoons milk

1. Grease pan; dust lightly with flour. 2. Cream shortening until soft. 3. Add sugar gradually, continuing to cream until light, fluffy. 4. Add eggs, vanilla; beat thoroughly. 5. Add nuts; blend. 6. Sift flour, baking powder, baking soda, salt together. 7. Combine bananas, milk. 8. Alternately add, in thirds, flour mixture, banana mixture; beat well after each addition. 9. Pour into pan; spread evenly. 10. Bake 55-60 minutes at 350° F. 11. When done, remove from oven; let stand 5 minutes. 12. Turn out onto cooling rack; turn, top side up; cool. 13. Frost with Sea Foam Frosting or Vanilla Butter Cream Icing.

BLACK WALNUT CAKE

2 9 x 1½-inch layer cake pans or
3 8 x 1½-inch layer cake pans

½ cup butter or margarine	¾ teaspoon vanilla
1½ cups sugar	3 cups sifted cake flour
3 eggs	3 teaspoons baking powder
½ cup black walnuts, ground	½ teaspoon salt
1 teaspoon black walnut extract	1 cup milk

1. Grease pans; dust lightly with flour. 2. Cream butter until soft. 3. Add sugar gradually, continuing to cream until light, fluffy. 4. Add eggs, black walnuts, black walnut extract, vanilla; beat thoroughly. 5. Sift flour, baking powder, salt together. 6. Alternately add, in thirds, flour mixture, milk; beat well after each addition. 7. Pour into pans; spread evenly. 8. Bake 25-30 minutes at 375° F. 9. When done, remove from oven; let stand 5 minutes. 10. Turn out onto cooling rack; turn, top side up; cool. 11. Spread Double Boiler Frosting between layers, over top, sides of cake. 12. Sprinkle with chopped black walnuts.

MILK CHOCOLATE CAKE

2 8 x 1½-inch layer cake pans

½ cup shortening
1½ cups sugar
2 eggs
1 teaspoon vanilla
2 cups sifted cake flour
½ teaspoon salt

1 cup sour milk or buttermilk
2 squares unsweetened
 chocolate, melted
1 teaspoon baking soda
1 tablespoon cider vinegar

1. Grease pans; dust lightly with flour. **2.** Cream shortening until soft. **3.** Add sugar gradually, continuing to cream until light, fluffy. **4.** Add eggs, vanilla; beat thoroughly. **5.** Sift flour, salt together. **6.** Alternately add, in thirds, flour mixture, milk; beat well after each addition. **7.** Add chocolate; blend. **8.** Add baking soda to vinegar; stir; fold into batter. **9.** Pour into pans; spread evenly. **10.** Bake 25-30 minutes at 350° F. **11.** When done, remove from oven; let stand 5 minutes. **12.** Turn out onto cooling rack; turn, top side up; cool. **13.** Spread Chocolate Butter Cream Icing between layers, over top, sides of cake. **14.** Sprinkle with chopped nuts.

WELLESLEY FUDGE CAKE

2 9 x 1½-inch layer cake pans or
3 8 x 1½-inch layer cake pans

½ cup shortening
1½ cups sugar
2 eggs, beaten
1 teaspoon vanilla
4 squares unsweetened
 chocolate, melted

2 cups sifted cake flour
2 teaspoons baking powder
½ teaspoon salt
1½ cups milk
1 cup nuts, finely chopped

1. Grease pans; dust lightly with flour. **2.** Cream shortening until soft. **3.** Add sugar gradually, continuing to cream until light, fluffy. **4.** Add eggs, vanilla; beat thoroughly. **5.** Stir in melted chocolate; blend. **6.** Sift flour, baking powder, salt together. **7.** Alternately add, in thirds, flour mixture, milk; beat well after each addition. **8.** Fold in chopped nuts.

9. Pour into pans; spread evenly. 10. Bake 30-35 minutes at 350° F. 11. When done, remove from oven; let stand 5 minutes. 12. Turn out onto cooling rack; turn, top side up; cool. 13. Spread Wellesley Fudge Frosting between layers, over top, sides of cake.

MOCHA CHOCOLATE CAKE

2 9 x 1½-inch layer cake pans or
3 8 x 1½-inch layer cake pans

4 squares unsweetened chocolate
2 egg yolks
1 cup milk
½ cup shortening
1¼ cups light brown sugar, firmly packed

2½ cups sifted cake flour
1½ teaspoons baking soda
½ teaspoon salt
1 cup hot coffee
2 teaspoons vanilla

1. Grease pans; dust lightly with flour. 2. Melt chocolate in top of double boiler over boiling water. 3. Add egg yolks; stir; add milk slowly; cook until thick, smooth, beating constantly; set aside to cool. 4. Cream shortening until soft. 5. Add sugar gradually, continuing to cream until light, fluffy. 6. Sift flour, baking soda, salt together. 7. Alternately add, in thirds, flour mixture, coffee; beat well after each addition. 8. Stir in chocolate mixture, vanilla; blend thoroughly. 9. Pour into pans; spread evenly. 10. Bake 30-35 minutes at 350° F. 11. When done, remove from oven; let stand 5 minutes. 12. Turn out onto cooling rack; turn, top side up; cool. 13. Spread Mocha Icing between layers, over top, sides of cake.

MAGGIE'S MAHOGANY CAKE

2 9 x 1½-inch layer cake pans

½ cup cocoa
2 teaspoons baking soda
½ cup hot water
¾ cup butter or margarine
1¾ cups sugar

2 eggs
1 teaspoon vanilla
2½ cups sifted cake flour
½ teaspoon salt
¾ cup sour milk or buttermilk

1. Grease pans; dust lightly with flour. 2. Mix cocoa, baking soda together; add hot water, stir until blended; set aside. 3. Cream butter until soft. 4. Add sugar gradually, continuing to cream until light, fluffy. 5. Add eggs, vanilla; beat thoroughly. 6. Sift flour, salt together. 7. Alternately add, in thirds, flour mixture, milk; beat well after each addition. 8. Add cocoa mixture; stir until well blended. 9. Pour into pans; spread evenly. 10. Bake 35-40 minutes at 350° F. 11. When done, remove from oven; let stand 5 minutes. 12. Turn out into cooling rack; turn, top side up; cool. 13. Spread Sea Foam Frosting between layers, over top, sides of cake.

SPONGE CAKE

1 10 x 4-inch tubed cake pan

6 egg yolks
1 cup sugar
¼ cup cold water
1 teaspoon lemon extract
1 teaspoon grated lemon rind

1 cup sifted cake flour
¾ cup egg whites
½ teaspoon cream of tartar
½ teaspoon salt

1. Beat egg yolks until thick, about 5 minutes. 2. Beat sugar in gradually. 3. Combine water, extract, lemon rind; add alternately with flour; beat well after each addition. 4. Pour egg whites into large bowl; beat until frothy; add cream of tartar, salt; beat until stiff but not dry. 5. Fold egg yolk mixture gradually into beaten whites; continue to fold until the 2 mixtures are thoroughly blended. 6. Pour into ungreased pan; spread evenly. 7. Bake 60-65 minutes at 325° F. 8. When done, remove from oven; invert at once; let cake hang in pan until cold. 9. Frost or not as desired.

CHOCOLATE SPONGE ROLL

1 15½ x 10½ x 1-inch bake pan

4 egg whites	½ teaspoon baking powder
¾ cup sugar	¼ teaspoon salt
4 egg yolks, beaten	2 squares unsweetened chocolate,
1 teaspoon vanilla	melted
6 tablespoons sifted cake flour	

1. Line bottom, sides of pan with waxed paper. 2. Beat egg whites until stiff. 3. Fold sugar in gradually. 4. Fold in egg yolks, vanilla. 5. Sift flour, baking powder, salt together. 6. Fold gradually into egg-sugar mixture. 7. Add chocolate; blend gently until thoroughly mixed. 8. Pour into pan; spread evenly. 9. Bake 12-13 minutes at 400° F. 10. When done, remove from oven; loosen edges; turn upside down on towel sprinkled with confections sugar. 11. Peel off paper. 12. Spread with Double Boiler Frosting; roll as for jelly roll; cover with towel; cool. 13. Spread with Chocolate Butter Cream Icing.

CHOCOLATE CHIP ORANGE CAKE

1 9 x 9 x 1¾-inch cake pan

½ cup shortening	¼ cup chopped walnuts
½ cup brown sugar, firmly packed	Grated rind of 2 oranges
½ cup granulated sugar	2 cups sifted all purpose flour
2 eggs	¼ teaspoon salt
½ teaspoon vanilla	¼ teaspoon baking soda
1 6-ounce package chocolate bits, chopped	1 cup sour milk or buttermilk

1. Grease pan; dust lightly with flour. 2. Cream shortening until soft. 3. Add sugars gradually, continuing to cream until light, fluffy. 4. Add eggs one at a time, beating well after each addition. 5. Add vanilla, chocolate, nuts, orange rind; blend thoroughly. 6. Sift flour, salt, baking soda together. 7. Alternately add, in thirds, flour mixture, milk; beat well after each addition. 8. Pour into pan; spread evenly. 9. Bake

45-50 minutes at 350° F.   10. Serve warm; or cool and frost with Orange Butter Frosting.

APPLE CAKE WITH SHERRY CREAM

1 8 x 1½-inch layer cake pan

¼ cup shortening
½ cup sugar
½ teaspoon vanilla
1 egg
½ teaspoon lemon juice
1 cup sifted cake flour
1½ teaspoons baking powder
¼ teaspoon salt
⅓ cup milk

2 apples, peeled, sliced
1 tablespoon butter or margarine
¼ cup brown sugar, firmly packed
1 teaspoon cinnamon
½ cup cream, whipped
1 tablespoon Sherry wine

1. Grease pan; dust lightly with flour.   2. Cream shortening until soft.   3. Add sugar gradually, continuing to cream until light, fluffy.   4. Add vanilla, egg, lemon juice; blend.   5. Sift together flour, baking powder, salt.   6. Add dry ingredients alternately with milk in three additions.   7. Pour batter into pan.   8. Arrange apple slices over top of batter; dot with butter.   9. Combine brown sugar, cinnamon; sprinkle over top.   10. Bake 45 minutes at 350° F.   11. Top with whipped cream to which Sherry has been added.

CARAMEL CRUNCH CAKE

1 13 x 9 x 2-inch baking pan

1 package Caramel Cake Mix
½ cup finely crushed peanut brittle

1. Line bottom, sides of pan with Alcoa Wrap, allowing foil to extend up over sides.   2. Prepare cake mix as directed on package.   3. Pour batter into pan.   4. Sprinkle with crushed peanut brittle.   5. Bake 40-45 minutes at 375° F. (During baking candy melts to form crunchy topping.)   6. Cool 5-10 minutes in pan; lift cake from pan by the foil.

Good to know: Place peanut brittle between two sheets of Alcoa Wrap; crush with hammer or wooden mallet.

ORANGE SHELL FRUIT CAKES

16 cakes

¼ pound dates, coarsely chopped
½ pound seeded raisins
¾ pound candied cherries, cut in half—save 16 halves for decoration
2 ounces candied orange peel, cut fine
½ pound currants
6 ounces candied pineapple, coarsely cut
¼ pound citron, cut fine
2 ounces walnuts, coarsely broken
2 ounces pecans, coarsely broken
2 ounces blanched almonds, coarsely cut (save some whole almonds for decoration)
1½ teaspoons lemon juice
1½ teaspoons rose water
1½ teaspoons vanilla
½ cup whiskey or fruit juice
2 ounces grape or blackberry jelly
16 navel oranges

1. Combine all fruits, nuts; mix well.   2. Combine lemon juice, rose water, vanilla, whiskey or fruit juice, jelly; pour over fruit mixture; mix well.   3. Let stand over night to plump fruit.   4. Slice off tops of the oranges; remove pulp.

Batter

1 cup flour
½ cup butter or margarine
½ cup sugar
5 eggs
½ teaspoon cloves
½ teaspoon allspice
½ teaspoon cinnamon
¼ teaspoon ginger
¼ teaspoon mace
¼ teaspoon baking powder

1. Brown flour lightly in fry pan, stirring constantly; sift; measure after browning.   2. Cream butter until soft.   3. Add sugar gradually, beating until light, fluffy.   4. Add eggs, one at a time; beat after each addition.   5. Sift flour, cloves, allspice, cinnamon, ginger, mace, baking powder together; add in three additions; beat well after each addition.   6. Pour batter over fruit mixture; mix well, making sure every piece is covered.   7. Fill each orange shell with approximately ⅓ cup batter.   8. Tear off 16 pieces of Alcoa Wrap; place orange on foil; bring up around bottom of orange to make a cup; crimp edges of foil; set each orange on top of cups of muffin pan.   9. Bake 55-60 minutes at 325° F.   10. To glaze: Brush tops of cakes with dark or light corn syrup; return to oven for 5 minutes.

To Decorate: When cakes are cool, use shears to cut edge of orange shell into large points resembling petals. Place half cherry in center of cake, surround with half almonds to resemble a flower.

CHIFFON CAKE

1 10 x 4-inch tubed cake pan or
1 13 x 9 x 2-inch baking pan

2¼ cups sifted cake flour	¾ cup cold water
1½ cups sugar	2 teaspoons vanilla
3 teaspoons baking powder	2 teaspoons grated lemon rind
1 teaspoon salt	1 cup egg whites
½ cup salad oil	½ teaspoon cream of tartar
5 egg yolks, unbeaten	

1. Sift flour, sugar, baking powder, salt together into mixing bowl. 2. Make a "well" in center; add oil, egg yolks, water, vanilla, lemon rind. 3. Beat with spoon until smooth. 4. Place egg whites in large mixing bowl; add cream of tartar; whip together until whites form very stiff peaks. 5. Pour egg yolk mixture gradually over whites, gently folding until just blended. 6. Pour into ungreased pan; spread evenly. 7. Bake 10-inch tubed cake: 55 minutes, 325° F., then 10-15 minutes longer, 350° F. Bake 13 x 9 x 2-inch cake: 45-50 minutes, 350° F. 8. When done, remove from oven; invert at once; let hang in pan until cold. 9. Frost or not as desired.

Variations: Spice Chiffon Cake: Prepare Chiffon Cake, omitting vanilla, lemon rind. Add 1 teaspoon cinnamon, ½ teaspoon nutmeg, ½ teaspoon allspice, ½ teaspoon cloves to the dry ingredients. Bake as for Chiffon Cake. Frost with Sea Foam Frosting.

Chocolate Chip Chiffon Cake: Prepare Chiffon Cake, omitting lemon rind. Just before pouring into pan, sprinkle 3 squares grated semi-sweet chocolate over batter; fold in carefully with a few strokes. Bake as for Chiffon Cake. Frost with Chocolate Frosting.

ANGEL FOOD CAKE

1 10 x 4-inch tubed cake pan

1¼ cups sifted cake flour
1¾ cups sugar
½ teaspoon salt
1½ cups egg whites (12-13 eggs)

1 teaspoon cream of tartar
1 teaspoon vanilla
½ teaspoon almond extract

1. Sift flour, sugar, salt together 9 times; set aside. 2. Beat egg whites until frothy. 3. Add cream of tartar; continue beating until whites are stiff but not dry. 4. Beat in vanilla, almond extract. 5. Fold in flour mixture, about two tablespoons at a time; scrape down sides of bowl several times; continue folding until all of mixture has been added and batter is smooth. 6. Pour into ungreased pan; spread evenly. 7. Bake 65-70 minutes at 325° F. 8. When done, remove from oven; invert at once; let cake hang in pan until cold, at least 1 hour. 9. Ice or not as desired.

Good to know: ¾ *cup shredded coconut may be sprinkled over batter before baking if cake is not to be iced.*

Variations: Calico Cake: Prepare Angel Food Cake, omitting almond extract. Just before pouring into pan, fold in ½ cup semi-sweet chocolate bits. Bake as for Angel Food Cake. Frost with Chocolate Butter Cream Icing.

Chocolate Angel Food: Prepare Angel Food Cake, omitting almond extract and substituting ¼ cup cocoa for ¼ cup of flour. Sift cocoa with flour-sugar mixture. Bake as for Angel Food Cake.

Crowning Glories

That cake you baked will be delicious as it is—but many times more so if you put a luscious filling—tart-sweet or richly creamy—between the layers; if you pile the top high with frosting in your family's favorite flavor.

CARAMEL FROSTING

1½ cups dark brown sugar, firmly packed
1½ cups granulated sugar
1½ cups milk
2 teaspoons butter or margarine

1. Combine sugars, milk in sauce pan; bring to boil, stirring gently. 2. Boil without stirring until a little of mixture dropped in cold water forms a soft ball. 3. Add butter; stir until melted. 4. Beat until creamy. 5. To keep soft while spreading, set pan in hot water or add a little cream.

QUICK-TRICK FROSTING

White, chocolate or yellow cake
½–1 pound chocolate-covered peppermints

1. Leave cake in pan. 2. While still hot, arrange mints on top about ½ inch apart and out to within ½ inch of edge of pan. 3. As mints melt, spread evenly with spatula. This quick frosting is best on cakes baked in sheet or loaf pans but may be applied to layer cakes. Frost each layer while hot. Place one layer on top of the other before completely cooled.

PEPPERMINT CREAM FROSTING

1½ cups whipping cream
¼ cup confectioners sugar
Few drops peppermint extract
Dash salt

Few drops red food coloring
Slightly crushed peppermint
stick candy

1. Whip cream; add sugar, peppermint extract, salt, food coloring; blend well. 2. Swirl over sides, top of cake; sprinkle crushed candy onto sides of cake.

Good to know: This frosting is especially good on Angel Food Cake.

CHOCOLATE CREAM FROSTING

1 3-ounce package cream cheese
3 tablespoons milk
2 cups confectioners sugar, sifted

2 squares unsweetened chocolate, melted
⅛ teaspoon salt
1 teaspoon vanilla

1. Combine cheese, milk; blend until smooth. 2. Add sugar, ½ cup at a time; blend after each addition. 3. Add chocolate, salt, vanilla; blend. Spread on one 8- or 9-inch square cake.

Good to know: This frosting will keep several days if stored covered in refrigerator.

BROILED PRALINE FROSTING

3 tablespoons butter or margarine
5 tablespoons evaporated milk or light cream

½ cup brown sugar, firmly packed
½ cup shredded coconut
¼ cup chopped nuts

1. Combine butter, milk in saucepan; beat over low heat until butter melts. 2. Add remaining ingredients; blend. 3. Spread on warm 8- or 9-inch square cake. 4. Place cake low under broiler; broil until frosting bubbles and is lightly browned; cool in pan.

WELLESLEY FUDGE FROSTING

1 egg
1 pound sifted confectioners sugar
½ cup butter or margarine
2 squares unsweetened chocolate, melted
1 teaspoon lemon juice
1 teaspoon vanilla
1 cup nuts, chopped

1. Beat egg until thick. 2. Add sugar gradually. 3. Melt butter, chocolate; cool slightly; add to egg-sugar mixture. 4. Stir in lemon juice, vanilla. 5. Beat until creamy; fold in nuts.

PEANUT BUTTER FROSTING

¼ cup butter or margarine
½ cup peanut butter
1 cup sifted confectioners sugar
2 tablespoons cream or undiluted evaporated milk
¼ teaspoon vanilla

1. Cream butter, peanut butter until light, fluffy. 2. Add sugar, cream, alternately in 4 additions; beat well after each addition. 3. Add vanilla; blend.

MARTHA'S WHITE ICING

1⅔ cups sugar
½ cup water
¼ teaspoon cream of tartar
½ cup egg whites
1 teaspoon vanilla

1. Combine sugar, water, cream of tartar in saucepan; blend. 2. Cook over low heat, stirring until sugar is dissolved. 3. Continue cooking without stirring until a little of mixture dropped in cold water forms a hard ball. 4. Beat egg whites until stiff but not dry. 5. Slowly pour syrup over egg whites, beating constantly with hand or electric beater until all of syrup has been added and frosting is just stiff enough to spread. 6. Fold in vanilla.

LEMON FILLING

1 cup sugar	2 tablespoons grated lemon rind
3 tablespoons cornstarch	½ cup lemon juice
½ teaspoon salt	2 tablespoons butter or margarine
1 cup water	4 egg yolks

1. Combine sugar, cornstarch, salt, water, rind, juice, butter in saucepan. **2.** Bring to boil, stirring constantly; boil 1 minute, continuing to stir. **3.** Remove from heat; beat in egg yolks; cook 1 minute longer, stirring constantly. **4.** Chill before using.

Variation: Orange Filling: Make Lemon Filling, substituting orange juice for the water, grated orange rind for the lemon rind and 1½ tablespoons lemon juice for the ½ cup lemon juice.

BROILED COCONUT FROSTING

1¼ cups shredded coconut	¾ cup brown sugar, firmly packed
6 tablespoons butter or margarine, melted	⅓ cup light cream

1. Combine coconut, butter, sugar, cream; spread over top of 13 x 9 x 2-inch plain cake. **2.** Place under broiler, 3 inches from heat; broil 2-3 minutes or until lightly browned. **3.** Serve warm.

VANILLA CREAM FILLING

¼ cup sugar
1 tablespoon cornstarch
½ teaspoon salt

1 cup top milk or cream
4 egg yolks, slightly beaten
2 teaspoons vanilla

1. Combine sugar, cornstarch, salt, milk in top of double boiler. 2. Bring to boil over direct heat, stirring constantly; boil 1 minute; remove from heat. 3. Add 3 tablespoons of mixture to egg yolks; blend; add to remaining hot filling. 4. Cook over boiling water, stirring constantly until thickened, about 2 minutes. 5. Remove from heat; add vanilla. 6. Chill until set; then use.

Variation: Chocolate Cream Filling: Make Vanilla Cream Filling, using 2 teaspoons cornstarch instead of 1 tablespoon; add ¼ cup additional sugar and 2 squares grated unsweetened chocolate. Chill until set; then use.

DOUBLE BOILER FROSTING

2 egg whites, unbeaten
1½ cups sugar
5 tablespoons cold water

1½ teaspoons white corn syrup
1 teaspoon vanilla

1. Place egg whites, sugar, water, corn syrup in top of double boiler; beat until thoroughly blended. 2. Place over rapidly boiling water. 3. Beat constantly with hand or electric beater until frosting will stand in peaks on beater. 4. Remove from heat; add vanilla; blend.

Variations: Marshmallow Frosting: Make Double Boiler Frosting. After removing from heat, fold in 6-8 quartered marshmallows or 4 tablespoons marshmallow creme.

Chocolate Frosting: Make Double Boiler Frosting. Melt 3 squares unsweetened chocolate; cool slightly. Gently fold chocolate into frosting after removing from heat.

Sea Foam Frosting: Make Double Boiler Frosting. Substitute 1½ cups brown sugar, firmly packed, for granulated sugar; omit corn syrup; add speck of salt.

Orange Mist Frosting: Make Double Boiler Frosting. Substitute orange juice for water, add 1 tablespoon grated orange rind; omit vanilla.

Peppermint Frosting: Make Double Boiler Frosting. Substitute few drops peppermint for vanilla. Tint pale green or pink, or fold in ½ cup crushed peppermint stick candy.

VANILLA BUTTER CREAM ICING

5 tablespoons butter or margarine, melted	1½ teaspoons vanilla
3 tablespoons cream or undiluted evaporated milk	3 cups sifted confectioners sugar

1. Combine butter, cream, vanilla. 2. Add sugar gradually; beat until smooth.

Variations: Chocolate Butter Cream Icing: Make Vanilla Butter Cream Icing; add 3 squares unsweetened chocolate, melted, before adding sugar.

Mocha Icing: Make Chocolate Butter Cream Icing; substitute strong black coffee for cream; omit vanilla.

Orange Butter Cream Icing: Make Vanilla Butter Cream Icing; omit vanilla; substitute orange juice for part of cream; add 1 tablespoon grated orange rind.

Tutti Fruitti Icing: Make Vanilla Butter Cream Icing; substitute 1 tablespoon maraschino cherry juice for 1 tablespoon cream. Add ½ cup chopped maraschino cherries, ½ cup chopped nuts.

Prize Pies

A home-baked pie—as pretty as it is good to eat—is a perfect ending for any meal . . . it makes the simple supper a banquet, provides a fitting climax for a more elaborate dinner. Here's a wide variety of pies—fruit and cream and dozens of others—you can please your family with them whenever you feel the urge to bake something special.

Good to know: *Chiffon, custard and cream pies do not freeze well, but all other pies can be Alcoa Wrapped, frozen, and baked when you want them, without thawing; they'll taste fresh as new. Even when you don't wish to freeze a whole or leftover piece of pie, Alcoa Wrap it and it will keep several days in a state of maximum freshness.*

FLAKY PASTRY

2¼ cups sifted all purpose flour
1 teaspoon salt

¾ cup shortening, lard or vegetable
3–4 tablespoons cold water

1. Sift flour, salt together into bowl. 2. Cut in shortening with pastry blender or 2 knives until mixture resembles coarse meal; continue cutting until particles start to cling together in little balls about the size of peas. 3. Mark mixture off into thirds with fork. 4. Sprinkle about 1 tablespoon water on one part; quickly work it in with fork. Repeat operation on each part until particles will cling together when pressed

between fingers. Dough should not be wet or sticky. The amount of water may vary with flour but always use as little as possible. Empty contents of bowl onto Alcoa Wrap. 6. Place hands under foil, cup fashion; press dough into ball; wrap; chill 10-15 minutes before rolling. 7. Yield: 1 8- or 9-inch double-crust pie, 2 8- or 9-inch shells or one-crust pies, 8-10 medium tarts.

Cheese Pastry:
Add ¾ cup grated Cheddar cheese to flour, after cutting in shortening in recipe for Flaky Pastry.

ONE CRUST PASTRY

1½ cups sifted all purpose flour	½ cup shortening
½ teaspoon salt	3 tablespoons cold water

1. Follow mixing directions for Flaky Pastry. 2. Lightly roll pastry into circle 1¼ inches larger than inverted pie pan. 3. Fold in half; transfer to ungreased 9-inch pan; unfold. 4. Gently fit pastry to pan, patting out all air bubbles. 5. Trim overhang to ½ inch; fold under so edge stands up. 6. Press rim firmly between sides of index fingers until smooth. 7. Finish with desired edging. 8. Fill; bake according to recipe.

Baked Pie Shell No. 1
1. Prepare One Crust Pastry, steps 1 through 7. 2. Prick pastry on bottom, sides, closely and deeply with fork; chill 30 minutes. 3. Bake 12-15 minutes at 450° F. or until golden brown. 4. Cool in pan on rack before filling.
Good to know: After 5 minutes of baking, look into oven. If bubbles have appeared in pastry, prick with fork.

Baked Pie Shell No. 2
1. Prepare One Crust Pastry, steps 1 through 2. 2. Fold in half; place over outside of ungreased 9-inch pie pan. 3. Press

firmly to pan, working out all air bubbles. **4.** Trim off overhang. **5.** Prick pastry closely and deeply with fork; chill 30 minutes. **6.** Bake 12-15 minutes at 450° F. or until golden brown. **7.** Cool before filling.

Good to know: This method produces a better shaped shell but isn't as pretty because there is no special edging.

TART SHELLS

1. Prepare Flaky Pastry or use packaged pie crust. **2.** Make tarts in desired shape; prick well; chill 30 minutes before baking. **3.** Bake 10-15 minutes at 450° F. or until golden brown. **4.** Fill as desired.

Variations: Little Pies: Make one or two crust pies using small individual pie pans.

Tulip Cups: Cut pastry into 5-inch squares with sharp knife or pastry wheel. Snugly fit 1 square into each muffin cup; let corners stand upright.

Petal Tarts: Cut 6 circles 2¼ inches in diameter. Place 1 in bottom of custard or muffin cup. Wet edges; place 5 circles around sides so they overlap each other and bottom circle.

Fluted Tarts: Measure fluted tart pan with piece of cord—up one side, across bottom, down other side; cut cord to this length. Make Alcoa Wrap circle with diameter the length of cord; for example, if cord is 4-inches long, cut 4-inch circle; use as a pattern. Using pattern, cut desired number of circles with pastry wheel. Fit circles over outside of fluted shells; a wooden skewer will help fit pastry into grooves.

Pleated Tarts: Measure inverted muffin pan cup and cut pattern as in Fluted Tarts. Fit pastry circle over outside of every other muffin cup. Pinch pastry into pleats to make it fit snugly.

Shortcake Tarts: Cut pastry circles with 3½-inch biscuit cutter. Remove centers from half the circles with 1½-inch biscuit cutter. Place on ungreased cookie sheet; bake. Spread full circle with filling; top with the circle with hole in center to make shortcake.

GRAHAM CRACKER CRUST

1⅓ cups fine graham cracker crumbs (about 16 crackers)

¼ cup soft butter or margarine
¼ cup sugar

1. Mix all ingredients together with fork until crumbly. 2. Remove 3 tablespoons of mixture to use later as topping. 3. Pour into ungreased 9-inch pie pan. 4. With back of spoon press evenly, firmly to bottom, sides of pan. 5. Bake 8 minutes at 375° F. 6. Cool; fill as desired; top with remaining crumbs.

Variations: Vanilla Wafer Crust: Follow recipe for Graham Cracker Crust, substituting vanilla wafers (about 24) for graham crackers.

Chocolate Wafer Crust: Follow recipe for Graham Cracker Crust, substituting chocolate wafers (about 20) for graham crackers.

FRESH APPLE PIE

1 9-inch pie pan

Flaky Pastry
⅔ cup sugar
¼ teaspoon nutmeg
¼ teaspoon cinnamon
⅛ teaspoon salt

1 teaspoon lemon juice
6 cups pared, cored ¼-inch apple slices
1 tablespoon butter or margarine

1. Line ungreased pie pan with pastry. 2. Brush with slightly beaten egg white. 3. Combine sugar, nutmeg, cinnamon, salt, lemon juice; add apples; mix well; put into pastry lined pan. 4. Dot with butter. 5. Adjust top crust. 6. Bake 40-45 minutes at 425° F. 7. Serve slightly warm with wedge of sharp cheese or with vanilla ice cream or sprinkled with confectioners sugar.

FROZEN LIME PIE

9 x 9 x 1¾-inch cake pan

6 egg yolks	6 egg whites
1 cup sugar	2 cups heavy cream, whipped
Grated rind of 2 limes	1½ cups chocolate wafer crumbs
Juice of 3 limes	Green food coloring

1. Combine egg yolks, sugar, grated lime rind, lime juice in top of double boiler; cook over hot water, stirring until slightly thickened; cool. 2. Beat egg whites stiff; fold into cooled lime mixture. 3. Fold whipped cream into mixture. 4. Cover bottom of ungreased pan with half of crumbs. 5. Pour in lime mixture; sprinkle remaining crumbs on top. 6. Cover with Alcoa Wrap; freeze firm. 7. Place in refrigerator ½ hour before ready to serve.

MERINGUE PIE SHELL

1 9-inch pie pan

1 cup sugar	4 egg whites
¼ teaspoon cream of tartar	

1. Sift sugar, cream of tartar together. 2. Beat egg whites stiff but not dry. 3. Gradually add sugar mixture, continuing to beat until thoroughly blended and stiff. 4. Pile into greased pie pan. 5. Push out to sides, leaving a hollow in center; bottom should be about ¼-inch thick, sides should be 1-inch thick. 6. Bake 1 hour at 275° F.; cool.

FRESH BERRY PIE

1 9-inch pie pan

Flaky Pastry	⅛ teaspoon salt
⅔ cup sugar	1 teaspoon lemon juice
2 tablespoons flour	4 cups blackberries or black
¼ teaspoon nutmeg	raspberries
¼ teaspoon cinnamon	1 tablespoon butter or margarine

1. Line ungreased pie pan with pastry. 2. Brush with slightly beaten egg white. 3. Combine sugar, flour, nutmeg, cinna-

mon, salt, lemon juice, berries; blend thoroughly. **4.** Pour into pastry lined pan; dot with butter. **5.** Adjust top crust. **6.** Bake 40-45 minutes at 425° F.

DUTCH APPLE PIE

1 9-inch pie pan

One Crust Pastry
1 cup sugar
⅓ cup water
½ teaspoon cinnamon
⅓ cup cream

1 tablespoon butter or margarine
1 tablespoon flour
1 tablespoon sugar
6 cups pared, cored ¼-inch apple slices

1. Line ungreased pie pan with pastry. **2.** Combine sugar, water in saucepan. **3.** Bring to boil over low heat; boil 5 minutes. **4.** Add cinnamon, cream, butter; stir until melted; cool slightly. **5.** Combine flour, sugar; sprinkle over bottom of unbaked shell. **6.** Place apples in shell. **7.** Pour syrup over apples, being certain all pieces are coated. **8.** Bake 30 minutes at 400° F.; reduce heat to 300° F.; bake 30-35 minutes longer. **9.** Serve slightly warm with wedge of sharp cheese.

RAISIN PIE

1 9-inch pie pan

Flaky Pastry
3 cups seedless raisins
3 cups water
½ teaspoon grated lemon rind

⅔ cup sugar
3 tablespoons flour
¼ teaspoon cinnamon
1 tablespoon butter or margarine

1. Line ungreased pie pan with pastry. **2.** Combine raisins, water, lemon rind in saucepan; bring to boil; boil 5 minutes. **3.** Combine sugar, flour, cinnamon; add sufficient juice from raisins to make smooth paste; stir; add to raisins. **4.** Cook, stirring constantly until thickened, clear—about 5 minutes. **5.** Add butter; cool. **6.** Pour into pastry lined pan. **7.** Adjust top crust. **8.** Bake 30-35 minutes at 425° F. **9.** Sprinkle with confectioners sugar before serving.

STRAWBERRY PIE GLACÉ

Baked 9-inch Pie Shell

1 3-ounce package cream cheese
1 quart strawberries
1½ cups strawberry juice and water

1 cup sugar
3 tablespoons cornstarch

1. Mash cheese with fork. 2. Spread over bottom of cooled baked shell. 3. Wash, hull berries; place half of berries on cheese, using nicest ones. 4. Rub remaining berries through sieve to extract juice; add water to make the 1½ cups. 5. Pour juice into saucepan; bring to boil. 6. Combine sugar, cornstarch; gradually stir into boiling juice. 7. Bring to boil; boil 1 minute, stirring constantly; cool. 8. Pour over berries; chill 2 hours. 9. Just before serving, put border of sweetened whipped cream around edge.

FRESH CHERRY PIE

1 9-inch pie pan

Flaky Pastry
⅔ cup sugar
3 tablespoons flour
¼ teaspoon nutmeg
⅛ teaspoon salt

¼ teaspoon cinnamon
4 cups fresh sour cherries, pitted
1 teaspoon lemon juice
1 tablespoon liquid red coloring
1 tablespoon butter or margarine

1. Line ungreased pie pan with pastry. 2. Brush with slightly beaten egg white. 3. Combine sugar, flour, nutmeg, salt, cinnamon. 4. Add cherries, lemon juice, coloring; blend. 5. Pour into pastry lined pan; dot with butter. 6. Adjust top crust. 7. Bake 40-45 minutes at 425° F. 8. Sprinkle with confectioners sugar before serving.

Variation: Partially thawed and drained frozen cherries may be used; use ⅓ cup less sugar.

FRESH RHUBARB PIE

1 9-inch pie pan

Flaky Pastry
3 cups unpeeled rhubarb, diced
1 cup sugar
1 egg, beaten

2 tablespoons flour
Juice of ½ lemon
2 tablespoons butter or margarine

1. Line ungreased pie pan with pastry.   2. Brush with slightly beaten egg white.   3. Combine rhubarb, sugar, egg, flour, lemon juice; blend.   4. Pour into pastry-lined pan; dot with butter.   5. Adjust top crust.   6. Bake 45-50 minutes at 400° F.   7. Serve with wedge of sharp cheese or sprinkled with confectioners sugar.

FRESH PEACH PIE

1 9-inch pie pan

Flaky Pastry
2 tablespoons quick-cooking tapioca
⅔ cup sugar
¼ teaspoon nutmeg

⅛ teaspoon salt
¼ teaspoon cinnamon
4 cups peaches, sliced, peeled
1 teaspoon lemon juice
2 tablespoons butter or margarine

1. Line ungreased pie pan with pastry.   2. Brush with slightly beaten egg white.   3. Combine tapioca, sugar, nutmeg, salt, cinnamon.   4. Add peaches, lemon juice; blend.   5. Pour into pastry lined pan; dot with butter.   6. Adjust top crust.   7. Bake 45-50 minutes at 425° F.   8. Sprinkle with confectioners sugar before serving.

EGG CUSTARD PIE

1 9-inch pie pan

One Crust Pastry
4 eggs, slightly beaten
¾ cup sugar
½ teaspoon salt

3 cups milk
1 teaspoon vanilla
½ teaspoon nutmeg

1. Line ungreased pie pan with pastry. 2. Brush with slightly beaten egg white. 3. Combine eggs, sugar, salt; add milk, vanilla; blend. 4. Set pastry lined pie pan on rack in oven; fill with custard mixture. 5. Sprinkle nutmeg on top. 6. Bake 30-40 minutes at 450° F., or until knife inserted in center comes out clean.

Variation: Coconut Custard Pie: Follow recipe for Egg Custard Pie; add 1½ cups shredded coconut to mixture; omit nutmeg.

CHRISTMAS EGGNOG PIE

1 9-inch pie pan

Baked 9-inch Graham Cracker
  Crust
1 tablespoon plain gelatin
¼ cup cold water
3 egg yolks, beaten
1½ cups milk
½ cup sugar

⅛ teaspoon salt
4 egg whites
¼ teaspoon nutmeg
1 cup heavy cream
2 tablespoons sugar
2 teaspoons rum
½ square unsweetened chocolate

1. Stir gelatin into cold water; set aside. 2. Combine egg yolks, milk, ¼ cup of the sugar, salt in top of double boiler. 3. Cook over hot, *not boiling*, water, stirring constantly until mixture coats spoon. 4. Add gelatin; stir until dissolved; remove from heat. 5. Chill until slightly thickened. 6. Beat egg whites until frothy; add remaining ¼ cup sugar gradually, beating until stiff. 7. Fold in chilled mixture. 8. Pour into shell; sprinkle nutmeg over top; chill until set. 9. To serve: whip cream; fold in sugar, rum; spread over filling; grate chocolate over top.

LEMON CHIFFON PIE

1 9-inch pie pan

Baked 9-inch Pie Shell
1 tablespoon plain gelatin
¼ cup cold water
4 egg yolks, beaten

1 cup sugar
½ cup lemon juice
1 teaspoon grated lemon rind
4 egg whites, unbeaten

1. Stir gelatin into cold water; set aside. 2. Combine egg yolks, ½ cup of the sugar, lemon juice, rind in top of double boiler. 3. Cook over boiling water, stirring constantly until thickened. 4. Add gelatin; stir until dissolved; remove from heat. 5. Chill until slightly thickened. 6. Beat egg whites until frothy; add remaining ½ cup sugar gradually, beating until stiff. 7. Fold in chilled mixture. 8. Pour into baked shell; chill until set. 9. To serve, spread with whipped cream.

PUMPKIN CHIFFON PIE

1 9-inch pie pan

Baked 9-inch Pie Shell
1 tablespoon plain gelatin
¼ cup cold water
3 egg yolks
1 cup sugar
1¼ cups cooked pumpkin

½ cup milk
½ teaspoon salt
½ teaspoon nutmeg
½ teaspoon cinnamon
½ teaspoon ginger
3 egg whites

1. Stir gelatin into cold water; set aside. 2. Combine egg yolks, ½ cup of the sugar, pumpkin, milk, salt, nutmeg, cinnamon, ginger in top of double boiler. 3. Cook over boiling water, stirring constantly until thickened. 4. Add gelatin; stir until dissolved; remove from heat. 5. Chill until slightly thickened. 6. Beat egg whites until frothy; add remaining ½ cup sugar gradually, beating until stiff. 7. Fold in chilled mixture. 8. Pour into baked shell; chill until set. 9. To serve: spread with sweetened whipped cream; sprinkle with nutmeg.

MERINGUE

3 egg whites
¼ teaspoon cream of tartar

6 tablespoons sugar

1. Allow egg whites to reach room temperature. 2. Place egg whites in bowl; add cream of tartar. 3. With hand or electric beater, beat until frothy. 4. Start adding the sugar, a little at a time, continuing to beat until all sugar has been added and stiff peaks are formed. 5. With spoon place mounds of meringue around the edge of the filling, spreading so it touches inner edge of crust. 6. Pile remaining meringue in center; spread evenly. 7. Swirl meringue with spatula or use back of spoon to pull up points. 8. Bake 8-10 minutes at 400° F. or until delicately browned. 9. Cool pie on rack in kitchen, away from draft.

COCONUT CREAM PIE

1 9-inch pie pan

Baked 9-inch Pie Shell
⅔ cup sugar
½ teaspoon salt
2½ tablespoons cornstarch
1 tablespoon flour
3 cups milk

3 egg yolks, slightly beaten
1 tablespoon butter or margarine
1½ teaspoons vanilla
1½ cups moist shredded coconut

1. Combine sugar, salt, cornstarch, flour in saucepan. 2. Add milk gradually; stir until mixed. 3. Cook over medium heat, stirring constantly until mixture thickens, boils; boil 1 minute. 4. Remove from heat; stir a little of mixture into egg yolks; blend into hot mixture. 5. Return to heat; bring to boil; boil 1 minute longer; remove from heat. 6. Stir in butter, vanilla; cool. 7. Pour into baked shell. 8. Cover with meringue. 9. Sprinkle coconut over top. 10. Bake 8-10 minutes at 400° F. or until delicately browned.

Variations

1. Omit meringue; spread with sweetened whipped cream before serving.
2. Substitute chopped nuts for coconut.

BUTTERSCOTCH CREAM PIE

1 9-inch pie pan

Baked 9-inch Pie Shell
6 tablespoons butter or
margarine
1 cup dark brown sugar, firmly
packed
1 cup boiling water

3 tablespoons cornstarch
2 tablespoons flour
½ teaspoon salt
1⅔ cups milk
3 egg yolks, slightly beaten
1 teaspoon vanilla

1. Melt butter in fry pan; brown slightly. 2. Stir in sugar; cook 2-3 minutes, stirring constantly until bubbly; stir in water; remove from heat. 3. Combine cornstarch, flour, salt in saucepan; add milk gradually; mix until smooth. 4. Stir in brown sugar mixture. 5. Cook over low heat, stirring constantly until boiling; boil 1 minute. 6. Remove from heat; stir a little of mixture into egg yolks; blend into hot mixture. 7. Return to heat; bring to boil; boil 1 minute longer; remove from heat; add vanilla. 8. Cool, stirring occasionally. 9. Pour into baked shell. 10. Cover with meringue. 11. Bake 8-10 minutes at 400° F. or until delicately browned.

BANANA CREAM PIE

1 9-inch pie pan

Baked 9-inch Pie Shell
3 egg yolks, beaten
⅓ cup sugar
¼ teaspoon salt
2½ tablespoons cornstarch

2 cups milk
1 tablespoon butter or margarine
1 teaspoon vanilla
2 ripe bananas

1. Place egg yolks in top of double boiler. 2. Combine sugar, salt, cornstarch; beat gradually into eggs. 3. Add milk, butter. 4. Cook over boiling water, stirring constantly until thickened. 5. Remove from heat; add vanilla; cool. 6. Peel, cut bananas into thin slices. 7. Arrange in layer on bottom of baked shell. 8. Pour filling on top. 9. Cover with meringue. 10. Bake 8-10 minutes at 400° F. or until delicately browned.

CHOCOLATE CREAM PIE

1 9-inch pie pan

Baked 9-inch Pie Shell
1½ cups sugar
½ teaspoon salt
2½ tablespoons cornstarch
1 tablespoon flour
3 cups milk

3 squares unsweetened chocolate, shaved
3 egg yolks, slightly beaten
1 tablespoon butter or margarine
1½ teaspoons vanilla

1. Combine sugar, salt, cornstarch, flour in saucepan. 2. Add milk gradually; stir until mixed; stir in chocolate. 3. Cook over medium heat, stirring constantly until mixture thickens, boils; boil 1 minute. 4. Remove from heat; stir a little of mixture into egg yolks; blend into hot mixture. 5. Return to heat; bring to boil; boil 1 minute longer; remove from heat. 6. Stir in butter, vanilla; cool. 7. Pour into baked shell. 8. Cover with meringue. 9. Bake 8-10 minutes at 400° F. or until delicately browned.

Variations

1. Omit meringue; spread with sweetened whipped cream; top with chopped nuts.
2. Fold ½ cup chopped nuts into filling before pouring into pan.

STRAWBERRY CHIFFON PIE

1 9-inch pie pan

Baked 9-inch Pie Shell
1 tablespoon plain gelatin
¼ cup cold water
4 egg yolks, beaten
¾ cup sugar

1 tablespoon lemon juice
½ teaspoon salt
1 cup crushed fresh, canned or frozen strawberries with juice
4 egg whites

1. Stir gelatin into cold water; set aside. 2. Combine egg yolks, ½ cup of the sugar, lemon juice, salt in top of double boiler. 3. Cook over boiling water, stirring constantly until thickened. 4. Add gelatin; stir until dissolved; remove from heat. 5. Add berries; beat 1 minute. 6. Chill until slightly

thickened. **7.** Beat egg whites until frothy; add remaining ¼ cup sugar gradually, beating until stiff. **8.** Fold in chilled mixture. **9.** Pour into baked shell; chill until set. **10.** To serve: spread with whipped cream; place circle of sliced strawberries around edge.

CHOCOLATE CHIFFON PIE

1 9-inch pie pan

Baked 9-inch Pie Shell
1 tablespoon plain gelatin
¼ cup cold water
2 squares unsweetened chocolate
½ cup boiling water
3 egg yolks, beaten
1 cup sugar
¼ teaspoon salt
1 teaspoon vanilla
3 egg whites, unbeaten

1. Stir gelatin into cold water; set aside. **2.** Melt chocolate in saucepan over low heat; add boiling water; cook until smooth; remove from heat. **3.** Add gelatin; stir until dissolved. **4.** Combine egg yolks, ½ cup of the sugar; slowly beat in chocolate-gelatin mixture. **5.** Add salt, vanilla; chill until slightly thickened. **6.** Beat egg whites until frothy; add remaining ½ cup sugar gradually, beating until stiff. **7.** Fold in chilled mixture. **8.** Pour into baked shell; chill until set. **9.** To serve: spread with whipped cream; sprinkle with crushed peppermint stick candy or chopped nuts.

SOUTHERN PECAN PIE

1 9-inch pie pan

One Crust Pastry
½ cup butter or margarine
½ cup sugar
¾ cup white corn syrup
2 tablespoons strained honey
3 eggs, slightly beaten
1 teaspoon vanilla
2 cups pecans

1. Line ungreased pie pan with pastry. **2.** Cream butter until soft. **3.** Add sugar gradually, continuing to cream until light, fluffy. **4.** Stir in slowly syrup, honey, eggs, vanilla, 1 cup nuts. **5.** Pour into shell; place remaining 1 cup nuts on top. **6.** Bake 50-55 minutes at 350° F.; cool. **7.** Spread with sweetened whipped cream before serving.

MAGGIE'S LEMON PIE

1 9-inch pie pan

Baked 9-inch Pie Shell
2 cups sugar
4 tablespoons cornstarch
5 tablespoons flour
½ teaspoon salt

2 cups boiling water
4 tablespoons butter or margarine
4 egg yolks, beaten
2 lemons, juice and grated rind

1. Combine sugar, cornstarch, flour, salt in top of double boiler. 2. Add boiling water, slowly, stirring constantly; add butter. 3. Cook over boiling water 30 minutes until clear, thickened; stir. 4. Add egg yolks, lemon juice, rind; blend; cook 10 minutes longer, stirring twice; cool. 5. Pour into baked shell. 6. Cover with Meringue. 7. Bake 8-10 minutes at 400° F. until delicately browned.

BLACK BOTTOM PIE

1 9-inch pie pan

Vanilla Wafer Crust
1 tablespoon plain gelatin
¼ cup cold water
4 egg yolks, beaten
1 cup milk
1 cup cream
½ cup sugar
4 teaspoons cornstarch

1½ squares unsweetened chocolate, melted
½ teaspoon vanilla
1 tablespoon rum
3 egg whites, unbeaten
¼ teaspoon salt
¼ teaspoon cream of tartar
¼ cup sugar

1. Stir gelatin into cold water; set aside. 2. Combine egg yolks, milk, cream in top of double boiler. 3. Combine sugar, cornstarch; add. 4. Cook over boiling water, stirring occasionally, until mixture coats spoon heavily—about 20 minutes. 5. Remove 1 cup of the custard; add melted chocolate to it; beat until cool; add vanilla; blend. 6. Pour into shell. 7. Add gelatin to remaining custard; stir until dissolved. 8. Cool, but do not let it stiffen; stir in rum. 9. Beat egg whites, salt until frothy; add cream of tartar; beat until stiff. 10. Beat in sugar 1 tablespoon at a time. 11. Fold gelatin mixture into egg whites. 12. Pour on top of chocolate custard; spread evenly. 13. Chill until firm. 14. To serve: top with sweetened whipped cream.

DEEP DISH APPLE-CHEESE PIE

1 *8 x 8 x 2-inch cake pan*

One Crust Pastry
1½ cups thinly sliced apples
¼ cup sugar
¼ teaspoon cinnamon
¼ teaspoon nutmeg
2 eggs, slightly beaten

½ cup sugar
⅛ teaspoon salt
1 cup milk, scalded
1 teaspoon vanilla
1 cup creamed cottage cheese

1. Line ungreased pan with pastry. 2. Brush with slightly beaten egg white. 3. Combine apples, sugar, cinnamon, nutmeg. 4. Arrange apple mixture in pastry lined pan. 5. Bake 15 minutes at 425° F. 6. Meanwhile, combine eggs, sugar, salt, milk, vanilla, cottage cheese; blend thoroughly. 7. Remove baked apple mixture from oven. 8. Reduce heat to 325° F. 9. Pour custard mixture over apples. 10. Return to oven; bake 40-50 minutes at 325° F. 11. Cool before serving.

Cookie Craft

No self-respecting mother—or aunt or grandmother or even big sister—would be caught with her cookie jar empty. Here are dozens of ways to fill yours and keep the cookie-eating set—which, of course, includes fathers and grandfathers and brothers and boy-friends, as well as the kids—munching contentedly.

Good to know: *Wrapped in Alcoa Wrap, all types of cookies keep in your freezer. But if you don't want to freeze them, roll them in Alcoa Wrap, twist the ends, and they'll stay fresh for many days.*

REFRIGERATOR COOKIES

BLACK WALNUT COOKIES
12 dozen

1½ cups black walnuts	1 teaspoon vanilla
1½ cups shredded coconut	1 teaspoon black walnut extract
1¾ cups butter or margarine	6 cups sifted cake flour
1 pound brown sugar	1 teaspoon cream of tartar
½ cup granulated sugar	1 teaspoon salt
2 eggs	½ teaspoon baking soda

1. Grind nuts, coconut together in food chopper. **2.** Cream butter until soft. **3.** Add sugars gradually, continuing to cream until light, fluffy. **4.** Add eggs, vanilla, black walnut extract, ground nuts, coconut; beat well. **5.** Sift flour, cream of tartar, salt, baking soda together; add in 3 additions; beat well after each addition. **6.** Shape into rolls, 2 inches in diameter; wrap in Alcoa Wrap. **7.** Place in refrigerator; chill several hours or overnight. **8.** Slice thin; place on ungreased cookie sheet. **9.** Bake 10-12 minutes at 375° F.

RIBBON COOKIES

6 dozen

1 cup shortening
1½ cups sugar
1 egg
1 teaspoon vanilla
2½ cups sifted all purpose flour
1½ teaspoons baking powder

½ teaspoon salt
¼ cup candied cherries, chopped
¼ cup nuts, chopped
1 square sweet chocolate, melted
2 tablespoons poppy seeds

1. Cream shortening until soft. 2. Add sugar gradually, continuing to cream until light, fluffy. 3. Add egg, vanilla; beat well. 4. Sift flour, baking powder, salt together; add in 2 additions; beat well after each addition.
5. Divide dough into three parts:
  Part one: add cherries.
  Part two: add nuts, chocolate.
  Part three: add poppy seeds.
6. Line bottom, sides of 9 x 5 x 3-inch loaf pan with Alcoa Wrap. 7. Pat part one into bottom of pan; pat part two on top; pat part three on top of part two, pressing each layer down firmly; cover pan with aluminum foil. 8. Place in refrigerator; chill several hours or overnight. 9. Slice thin; place on ungreased cookie sheet. 10. Bake 10 minutes at 400° F.

VANILLA REFRIGERATOR COOKIES

4 dozen

½ cup butter or margarine
1 cup sugar
2 eggs
2 teaspoons vanilla

1 tablespoon milk
3 cups sifted all purpose flour
2 teaspoons baking powder
½ teaspoon salt

1. Cream butter until soft. 2. Add sugar gradually, continuing to cream until light, fluffy. 3. Add eggs, vanilla, milk; beat well. 4. Sift flour, baking powder, salt together; add in 3 additions; beat well after each addition. 5. Shape into a roll 12 x 2 inches; wrap in Alcoa Wrap. 6. Place in refrigerator; chill several hours or overnight. 7. Cut into ¼-inch

slices; place on ungreased cookie sheet. **8.** Bake 10-12 minutes at 400° F.

Variations: Butterscotch Cookies: Make Vanilla Refrigerator Cookies, substituting 1 cup dark brown sugar, firmly packed, for the white sugar.

Chocolate Cookies: Make Vanilla Refrigerator Cookies; add 2 squares melted unsweetened chocolate to sugar-egg mixture; one cup chopped nuts may also be added if desired. Bake 10-12 minutes at 375° F.

Spice Cookies: **1.** Make Butterscotch Cookies; add ½ teaspoon cinnamon, ½ teaspoon nutmeg, ¼ teaspoon cloves to dry ingredients before sifting.

DATE NUT PINWHEELS
5 dozen

2¼ cups pitted dates, cut into small pieces
1 cup sugar
1 cup water
1 cup nuts, chopped
1 cup shortening

2 cups brown sugar, firmly packed
3 eggs
4 cups sifted all purpose flour
½ teaspoon salt
½ teaspoon baking soda

1. Combine dates, sugar, water in saucepan; bring to boil; cook over low heat 10 minutes or until thick; add nuts; cool. **2.** Cream shortening until soft. **3.** Add sugar gradually, continuing to cream until light, fluffy. **4.** Add eggs; beat well. **5.** Sift flour, salt, baking soda together; add in 2 additions; beat well after each addition. **6.** Shape dough into ball; wrap in Alcoa Wrap; chill several hours. **7.** When dough is very firm, divide into three parts. **8.** Roll each part into rectangle ⅛-inch thick. **9.** Spread each with date-nut mixture. **10.** Roll each part up, jelly-roll fashion; wrap in Alcoa Wrap. **11.** Place in refrigerator; chill several hours or overnight. **12.** Cut into ¼-inch slices; place on ungreased cookie sheet. Bake 10-12 minutes at 375° F.

MOLDED COOKIES

FUZZY CAKES
3 dozen

1 cup butter or margarine	1 teaspoon vanilla
⅓ cup sugar	3 cups sifted cake flour
2 egg yolks	Jelly

1. Cream butter; add sugar gradually. 2. Add egg yolks, vanilla, flour; blend. 3. Roll into 1-inch balls. 4. Place on ungreased cookie sheet; make depression with finger; fill with jelly. 5. Bake 20-25 minutes at 375° F.

GINGER COOKIES
3 dozen

¾ cup shortening	1 teaspoon ginger
1 cup light brown sugar, firmly packed	1 teaspoon cinnamon
	½ teaspoon cloves
¼ cup molasses	2 teaspoons baking soda
1 egg, beaten	¼ teaspoon salt
2¼ cups sifted all purpose flour	36 blanched almonds

1. Cream shortening until soft. 2. Add sugar gradually continuing to cream until light, fluffy. 3. Add molasses, egg; blend well. 4. Sift flour, ginger, cinnamon, cloves, baking soda, salt together; add in 2 additions; beat well after each addition. 5. Chill dough. 6. Roll into 1-inch balls; place 2 inches apart on ungreased cookie sheet. 7. Flatten slightly; press almond in each. 8. Bake 12-15 minutes at 350° F.

RUM EASTER EGGS
3 dozen

2½ cups crushed vanilla wafers	1 cup finely chopped pecans
1 cup sifted confectioners sugar	2 tablespoons light corn syrup
2 tablespoons cocoa	5 tablespoons rum

1. Combine wafers, sugar, cocoa, pecans. 2. Stir in corn syrup, rum. 3. Make into egg-like shapes, using one level tablespoonful of mixture for each egg-shape. 4. Frost tops

with tinted Butter Cream Icing; swirl. **5.** Place in Alcoa Wrap cups, shaped like eggs. **6.** Decorate if desired. **7.** Place in refrigerator to set frosting.

To make foil egg-shaped cups:

36 4-inch squares Alcoa Wrap   1 bottle cap, size of cap on chili sauce bottle

1. Mold Alcoa Wrap over bottle cap to form cup. **2.** Pull out one end of cup to make container oval or egg-shaped. **3.** Turn under edges of foil to make cup ½ inch deep.

RUM BALLS
2½-3 dozen

2 tablespoons cocoa
1 cup confectioners sugar
¼ cup light or dark rum

2 tablespoons light corn syrup
2½ cups crushed vanilla wafers
1 cup chopped pecans

1. Sift cocoa, powdered sugar together. **2.** Combine rum, corn syrup; add; blend. **3.** Add crushed vanilla wafers, pecans; mix thoroughly. **4.** Roll mixture into balls about 1 inch in diameter; roll in confectioners sugar.

Variation: To make Bourbon Balls substitute bourbon for rum.

BAR COOKIES

ENGLISH TEA SQUARES   *2 dozen*

Pastry
½ cup shortening
¼ cup sugar
3 egg yolks
1 teaspoon vanilla
2 cups sifted all purpose flour

¼ teaspoon baking soda
¼ teaspoon salt
¼ cup water
1 cup jam

Meringue
3 egg whites
½ cup sugar

⅓ cup nuts, chopped

1. Cream shortening until soft. **2.** Add sugar gradually, continuing to cream until light, fluffy. **3.** Add egg yolks, vanilla; beat. **4.** Sift flour, baking soda, salt together; add alternately with water; beat well after each addition. **5.** Pour into greased 13 x 9 x 2-inch pan; spread evenly; spread jam over top of batter. **6.** Beat egg whites until stiff; add sugar a little at a time, beating constantly. **7.** Spread meringue over jam; sprinkle with nuts. **8.** Bake 25 minutes at 350° F. **9.** Cool slightly; cut into squares.

MAGGIE'S CHOCOLATE BROWNIES   5 dozen

1 cup plus 2 tablespoons butter
6 squares unsweetened chocolate, melted
2¼ cups sugar
5 eggs, beaten

2 teaspoons vanilla
1¾ cups sifted cake flour
1 teaspoon salt
1½ cups walnuts or pecans, chopped

1. Melt butter, chocolate. 2. Add sugar, eggs, vanilla; beat thoroughly. 3. Sift flour, salt together; add; beat until smooth. 4. Fold in nuts. 5. Pour into ungreased 15 x 10 x 1-inch pan; spread evenly. 6. Bake 20-25 minutes at 350° F. 7. Cool slightly; cut into 2-inch squares.

Good to know: These brownies have a shiny surface and fudge-like center.

DREAM BARS   4 dozen

Part One

1½ cups sifted cake flour
½ cup light brown sugar, firmly packed

½ cup butter or margarine, well chilled

1. Blend flour, sugar together. 2. Cut in butter with 2 knives or pastry blender until crumbly. 3. Spread evenly in greased 15 x 10 x 1-inch pan; press down firmly. 4. Bake 10 minutes at 375° F. 5. Remove from oven; spread Part Two over top.

Part Two

2 eggs
1 cup light brown sugar, firmly packed
1 teaspoon vanilla
2 tablespoons sifted cake flour

½ teaspoon baking powder
¼ teaspoon salt
1½ cups shredded coconut
1 cup nuts, chopped

1. Beat eggs; add sugar, vanilla; mix. 2. Sift flour, baking powder, salt together; blend with coconut, nuts. 3. Add to egg mixture; mix well. 4. Spread evenly over baked Part One. 5. Return to oven; bake 20 minutes. 6. Cool slightly; cut into bars 2½ x 1-inches.

CHERRY NUT BARS

3 dozen

¼ cup butter or margarine
½ pound marshmallows
½ cup chopped candied cherries
½ cup chopped pecans

½ teaspoon vanilla
1 5½-ounce package crisp rice cereal

1. Melt butter, marshmallows in top of double boiler. 2. Add cherries, pecans, vanilla; blend; pour over crisp rice cereal, stirring briskly. 3. Press into greased 9 x 9 x 1¾-inch pan. 4. To decorate, press extra candied cherries, pecans on top of mixture. Cut into 1 x 2¼-inch bars.

LEBKUCHEN

10 dozen

2 cups brown sugar, firmly packed
1 cup strained honey
¼ cup water
8 cups sifted all purpose flour
1 teaspoon salt
½ teaspoon baking soda
¼ teaspoon cloves
¼ teaspoon nutmeg
1 teaspoon cinnamon

2 eggs, beaten
¼ pound citron, chopped
¼ pound candied orange peel, chopped
½ pound blanched almonds, shredded
5 teaspoons boiling water
1 cup confectioners sugar
½ teaspoon vanilla

1. Combine brown sugar, honey, water in saucepan; bring to boil; boil 5 minutes; cool. 2. Sift flour, salt, baking soda, spices together; combine with sugar mixture; beat thoroughly. 3. Add eggs, fruits, almonds; mix well. 4. Shape into loaf; wrap in Alcoa Wrap. 5. Place in refrigerator 2-3 days to ripen. 6. Roll out to ¼-inch thickness; cut into bars 1 x 3-inches. 7. Place on greased cookie sheet. Bake 15-20 minutes at 350° F. When cool, spread with transparent icing made by adding boiling water to confectioners sugar, vanilla.

ROLL-OUT COOKIES

CHOCOLATE MINT SANDWICHES 2 dozen

½ cup butter or margarine
1 cup sugar
3 squares unsweetened chocolate, melted
1 egg, beaten

¼ cup milk
1 teaspoon vanilla
2½ cups sifted cake flour
2 teaspoons baking powder
½ teaspoon salt

Filling
⅓ cup cream
¼ teaspoon salt
1 teaspoon peppermint extract

4 cups confectioners sugar
24 walnut halves

1. Cream butter until soft. 2. Add sugar gradually, continuing to cream until light, fluffy. 3. Add chocolate; blend. 4. Combine egg, milk, vanilla. 5. Sift flour, baking powder, salt together. 6. Alternately add, in thirds, flour, liquid mixture; beat well after each addition. 7. Shape into loaf; wrap in Alcoa Wrap; chill several hours or overnight. 8. Roll out to ⅛-inch thickness on lightly floured board. 9. Cut with scalloped cutter; place on ungreased cookie sheet. 10. Bake 8-10 minutes at 400° F.; cool. 11. Combine cream, salt, extract, confectioners sugar; beat until smooth. 12. Spread one cooky with this mixture; place another cooky on top; put ½ teaspoon mixture in center; press a nut meat into it; repeat until all cookies have been used.

COTTAGE CHEESE COOKY STICKS 4½ dozen

1 cup cream-style cottage cheese
1 cup butter or margarine
2 cups sifted all purpose flour

¼ cup melted butter or margarine
¾ cup walnuts, chopped fine
¾ cup brown sugar, firmly packed

1. Blend cottage cheese, butter together with a pastry cutter. 2. Blend flour into mixture until dough holds together. 3. Roll out on lightly floured board to ⅛-inch thickness. 4. Brush

melted butter over dough; sprinkle brown sugar, walnuts over entire surface. **5.** Cut into equal strips, about 3 inches wide; cut each strip into triangles, each about 3 inches wide at the base. **6.** Beginning at base of triangle, roll dough into sticks; place on an ungreased cookie sheet, point side down. **9.** Bake 20 minutes at 400° F., or until golden brown.

SCOTCH SHORTBREAD
16 pieces

1 cup butter or margarine	1 egg yolk
½ cup plus 2 tablespoons sugar	3 cups sifted all purpose flour

1. Cream butter until soft. **2.** Add sugar gradually, continuing to beat until light, fluffy; add egg yolk. **3.** Add flour in 3 additions; beat well after each addition. **4.** Divide mixture into halves; on lightly floured board roll out each half to ½-inch thickness (about 7 inches in diameter); place in two 9-inch pie pans. **5.** Score each round into 8 pie-shaped pieces; pierce with fork in several places. **6.** Bake 25 minutes at 325° F.; remove from oven; separate sections with sharp knife; cool; remove from pan. **7.** Wrap in Alcoa Wrap for storage. **8.** Can be aged at room temperature for approximately 2 weeks or placed in freezer for several months.

FILLED COOKIES
2½ dozen

Part One

⅔ cup shortening	1 teaspoon vanilla
1 cup sugar	3½ cups sifted cake flour
1 egg, beaten	3 teaspoons baking powder
⅓ cup milk	1½ teaspoons salt

1. Cream shortening until soft. **2.** Add sugar gradually, continuing to cream until light, fluffy. **3.** Combine egg, milk, vanilla. **4.** Sift flour, baking powder, salt together; add alternately with egg-milk mixture; beat well after each addition. **5.** Shape into ball; wrap in Alcoa Wrap; chill several hours or overnight.

Part Two

2 tablespoons flour	½ cup nuts, chopped
½ cup sugar	½ cup dates or figs, chopped
½ cup water	1 teaspoon lemon juice
½ cup seedless raisins	

1. Combine in saucepan; cook until thickened; cool.

To finish cookies:

1. Roll out dough to ⅛-inch thickness on lightly floured board. 2. Cut into 2-inch circles with floured cutter. 3. Put together in pairs, with 1 teaspoon filling in center of each pair. 4. Press edges together with tines of fork. 5. Place on ungreased cookie sheet; use cake turner or broad spatula for lifting. 6. Bake 15-18 minutes at 375° F.

DROP COOKIES

CRISPY CRUNCHES
8 dozen

1 cup shortening	½ teaspoon salt
1 cup granulated sugar	½ teaspoon baking soda
1 cup brown sugar, firmly packed	1 cup uncooked rolled oats
2 eggs	1 cup rice flakes
1 teaspoon vanilla	½ cup nuts, chopped
2 cups sifted all purpose flour	½ cup shredded coconut

1. Cream shortening until soft. 2. Add sugars gradually, continuing to cream until light, fluffy. 3. Add eggs, vanilla; beat well. 4. Sift flour, salt, baking soda together; add alternately with rolled oats; beat well after each addition. 5. Combine rice flakes, nuts, coconut; fold into batter. 6. Drop from teaspoon, 2 inches apart, onto ungreased cookie sheet. 7. Bake 10-15 minutes at 375° F.

CHERRY COCONUT MACAROONS
3 dozen

4 egg whites	½ teaspoon vanilla
1¼ cups sugar	2½ cups moist shredded coconut
¼ teaspoon salt	½ cup candied cherries, chopped

1. Beat egg whites until stiff but not dry. 2. Gradually fold in sugar, salt, vanilla, coconut, cherries; blend well. 3. Drop from teaspoon, 2 inches apart, onto cookie sheet lined with Alcoa Wrap. 4. Bake 25-30 minutes at 325° F. 5. Remove from oven; cool slightly; peel off foil.

PECAN CRISPIES
6 dozen

½ cup shortening	1 teaspoon vanilla
½ cup butter or margarine	2½ cups sifted all purpose flour
2½ cups brown sugar, firmly packed	½ teaspoon baking soda
	¼ teaspoon salt
2 eggs	1 cup pecans, chopped

1. Cream shortening, butter until soft. 2. Add sugar gradually,

continuing to cream until light, fluffy. **3.** Add eggs, vanilla; beat well. **4.** Sift flour, baking soda, salt together; add in 2 additions; beat well after each addition. **5.** Fold in nuts. **6.** Drop from teaspoon, 2 inches apart, onto ungreased cookie sheet. **7.** Bake 15-17 minutes at 350° F.

CHOCOLATE CREAM DROPS
5 dozen

½ cup butter or margarine
2 1-ounce squares unsweetened chocolate, melted
1½ cups sugar
2 eggs
1 cup commercial sour cream

1 teaspoon vanilla
2¾ cups sifted all purpose flour
½ teaspoon baking soda
½ teaspoon baking powder
½ teaspoon salt
1 cup chopped nuts

1. Cream butter; add chocolate; blend. **2.** Add sugar gradually, continuing to cream until light, fluffy. **3.** Add eggs, one at a time; beat well after each addition. **4.** Add sour cream, vanilla; blend well. **5.** Sift flour, baking soda, baking powder, salt; add in 3 additions; beat well after each addition. **6.** Add nuts; mix. **7.** Chill at least 1 hour. **8.** Drop from teaspoon, 2 inches apart, onto lightly greased cookie sheet. **9.** Bake 10 minutes at 375° F.

CHOCOLATE STICKS
4 dozen

¾ cup butter or margarine
¾ cup sugar
2 eggs
¼ teaspoon salt
1 teaspoon vanilla

1¼ cups sifted all purpose flour
1 6-ounce package chocolate bits
1 cup shredded coconut, toasted

1. Cream butter until soft. **2.** Add sugar gradually, continuing to cream until light, fluffy. **3.** Blend in eggs, salt, vanilla; beat well. **4.** Gradually add flour; mix thoroughly. **5.** Fold in chocolate bits, toasted coconut. **6.** Fold two 36-inch pieces of Alcoa Wrap in half lengthwise; make pleated pan by folding foil crosswise in 1-inch pleats or troughs; open slightly to fit baking sheet approximately 17 x 14 inches. 7. Drop level teaspoonsful of dough into "troughs" in pan about 2 inches apart; do not use two outer troughs. 8. Bake 25-30 minutes at 325° F.; cool 5 minutes; pull edges of foil to flatten pleats; loosen sticks from foil.

PEANUT BUTTER LOLLYPOPS
1½ dozen

¼ cup shortening	1 egg
¼ cup butter or margarine	1¼ cups sifted all purpose flour
½ cup peanut butter	½ teaspoon baking powder
½ cup granulated sugar	¾ teaspoon baking soda
½ cup brown sugar, firmly packed	¼ teaspoon salt
	Raisins

1. Cream shortening, butter, peanut butter until soft. 2. Add sugars gradually, continuing to cream until light, fluffy. 3. Add egg; beat well. 4. Sift flour, baking powder, baking soda, salt together; add in 2 additions; beat well after each addition. 5. Drop 2 tablespoonsful three inches apart onto ungreased cookie sheet. 6. Crimp 10 x 12-inch sheet Alcoa Wrap to make a foil stick; flatten out one end; insert flattened end into cookie (lollypop fashion). 7. Flatten each cookie crisscross fashion with fork. 8. Make eyes, nose, mouth with raisins on each cookie. 9. Bake 8-10 minutes at 375° F.

PRALINE COOKIES
6 dozen

1¼ cups sweetened condensed milk	2 eggs
2 tablespoons instant coffee	½ teaspoon salt
⅔ cup dark brown sugar, firmly packed	½ teaspoon maple extract
	1 teaspoon vanilla
⅓ cup water	½ cup sifted all purpose flour
¼ cup butter or margarine	1 cup chopped pecans

1. Combine milk, coffee, brown sugar; bring to boil; remove from heat. 2. Add water, butter; stir until butter melts. 3. Combine eggs, salt, maple extract, vanilla; beat well; add coffee mixture slowly, stirring constantly. 4. Add flour, pecans; mix well. 5. Drop by half-teaspoonsful 2 inches apart onto ungreased cookie sheet. 6. Bake 10 minutes at 350° F.

FROSTED ORANGE COOKIES

3 dozen

½ cup shortening
1 cup sugar
2 eggs
½ cup commercial sour cream
2 tablespoons orange rind

⅓ cup orange juice
2⅓ cups sifted all purpose flour
½ teaspoon salt
½ teaspoon baking soda
¾ teaspoon baking powder

1. Cream shortening until soft. 2. Add sugar gradually, continuing to cream until light, fluffy. 3. Add eggs; beat well.
4. Add sour cream, orange rind, orange juice; blend well.
5. Sift flour, salt, baking soda, baking powder together; add to orange mixture; mix lightly until combined. 6. Drop from teaspoon 2 inches apart onto ungreased cookie sheet. 7. Bake 10-12 minutes at 375° F. until just light brown. 8. After cookies are cool, spread with Orange Butter Cream Frosting.

CHOCOLATE CHIP COOKIES

4 dozen

½ cup butter or margarine
½ cup granulated sugar
¼ cup brown sugar, firmly packed
1 egg
1 teaspoon vanilla
1 cup sifted cake flour

½ teaspoon salt
½ teaspoon baking soda
½ cup nuts, chopped
1 6-ounce package semi-sweet
chocolate bits

1. Cream butter until soft. 2. Add sugars gradually, continuing to cream until light, fluffy. 3. Add egg, vanilla; beat well.
4. Sift flour, salt, baking soda together; add; beat until smooth.
5. Fold in nuts, chocolate bits. 6. Drop from teaspoon 2 inches apart onto ungreased cookie sheet. 7. Bake 10-12 minutes at 375° F.

Grand Finale

Here are desserts plain and simple, elaborate and beautiful—all of them family-pleasers, all the kind you can serve to company with a flourish, because you'll be truly proud of them.

SPANISH CREAM

1 1½-quart mold

1 tablespoon plain gelatin	3 eggs, separated
3 cups milk	1 teaspoon vanilla
½ cup sugar	

1. Stir gelatin into milk in top of double boiler; let stand 5 minutes. 2. Add 2 tablespoons of the sugar, salt. 3. Cook over boiling water, stirring until gelatin is dissolved; remove from heat. 4. Beat egg yolks with 2 tablespoons of the sugar. 5. Add milk mixture gradually to egg yolks, stirring constantly. 6. Return to double boiler; cook over hot but not boiling water until slightly thickened; chill until thick, syrupy. 7. Beat egg whites until stiff; beat in remaining ¼ cup sugar. 8. Fold in vanilla, beaten egg white mixture. 9. Rinse mold with cold water. 10. Turn mixture into mold. 11. Chill until set; unmold. 12. Serve with whipped cream, Chocolate Sauce, or Butterscotch Sauce.

CHOCOLATE SPANISH CREAM

1. Make Spanish Cream, adding 1½ squares unsweetened chocolate, melted, to the milk-gelatin mixture; beat until smooth. 2. Serve with whipped cream.

APRICOT DELIGHT

10-12 servings

1 4-ounce package instant vanilla pudding
1 cup apricot nectar
1 small loaf angel cake
½ cup slivered almonds

12 peeled apricot halves, drained, chilled
6 egg whites
¾ cup sugar
½ teaspoon almond extract

1. Combine instant pudding, apricot nectar; beat with rotary beater one minute; chill in refrigerator until set. 2. Cut cake in three layers lengthwise. Place on Alcoa Wrap lined baking sheet. 3. Spread bottom layer of cake with half of pudding mixture; sprinkle half of slivered almonds over top; place apricot halves in two rows lengthwise on top of almonds. 4. Adjust second layer of cake; repeat Step 3 with remaining pudding mixture, almonds. 5. Top with third layer of cake; chill. 6. Beat egg whites until stiff, but not dry; add sugar, almond extract. Continue beating until meringue stands in peaks. 7. Spread meringue over top and sides of cake. 8. Bake 5 minutes at 450° F.

FLUFFY CHOCOLATE DELIGHT

20-24 servings

1 9-inch spring form pan

2 tablespoons unflavored gelatin
½ cup cold water
4 1-ounce squares unsweetened chocolate, grated
1 cup boiling water
6 eggs, separated

2 cups sugar
½ teaspoon salt
2 teaspoons vanilla
20 lady fingers or leftover sponge cake

1. Combine gelatin, cold water; let stand 5 minutes. 2. Melt chocolate in boiling water. 3. Add gelatin to mixture; stir until dissolved. 4. Beat egg yolks with 1 cup sugar until

light; add salt, vanilla; blend. **5.** Add eggs to chocolate mixture; blend; cool. **6.** Beat egg whites until they stand in peaks; gradually add remaining 1 cup sugar, beating constantly. **7.** Fold egg whites into chocolate mixture. **8.** Assemble pan using flat inset; line sides and bottom with split lady fingers or thin slices of sponge cake. **9.** Pour in chocolate mixture; chill until firm. **10.** Garnish with whipped cream, chopped nuts if desired.

NUT PIE
6 servings

1 9-inch pie pan

4 egg whites	1 teaspoon vanilla
½ cup granulated sugar	¾ cup crushed round crackers (21
½ cup light brown sugar, firmly	crackers)
packed	¾ cup nuts, chopped
½ teaspoon salt	1 teaspoon baking powder

1. Beat egg whites until stiff but not dry. **2.** Gradually add sugars; continue to beat until thoroughly blended, stiff. **3.** Add salt, vanilla; blend. **4.** Combine crushed crackers, nuts, baking powder; fold into egg white mixture. **5.** Pour into ungreased pan. **6.** Bake 30 minutes at 325° F. **7.** Serve with whipped cream or ice cream.

VANILLA SOUFFLÉ
6 servings

1 8 x 8 x 2-inch cake pan or
1 1½-quart casserole

4 tablespoons butter or margarine	3 eggs, separated
5 tablespoons flour	⅓ cup sugar
¼ teaspoon salt	1 teaspoon vanilla
1 cup milk	¼ teaspoon almond extract

1. Melt butter in top of double boiler over boiling water. **2.** Stir in flour, salt; blend; add milk. **3.** Cook, stirring constantly until thickened. **4.** Remove from heat; cool. **5.** Beat egg yolks until thick; stir in sugar; blend with milk mixture. **6.** Beat egg whites stiff; fold in milk-egg mixture, flavoring. **7.** Grease bottom only of pan or casserole. **8.** Pour in mixture; set in pan of warm water. **9.** Bake 1 hour at 325° F. or until knife inserted in center comes out clean. **10.** Serve at once with whipped cream, Rum Sauce or Vanilla Sauce.

Good to know: Soufflés should be timed to be done just the minute you are ready to serve the dessert as they have a tendency to fall.

CHOCOLATE NUT TORTE
10 servings

1 9-inch spring form pan

6 egg yolks	½ teaspoon baking powder
⅞ cup sugar	½ teaspoon cinnamon
½ cup fine cracker crumbs	¼ teaspoon cloves
¼ cup grated unsweetened chocolate	¼ teaspoon nutmeg
	¼ teaspoon salt
¾ cup walnuts, chopped	6 egg whites
2 tablespoons rum	

1. Beat egg yolks until light. **2.** Add sugar gradually, continuing to beat until well blended. **3.** Combine crumbs, chocolate, nuts, rum, baking powder, cinnamon, cloves, nutmeg, salt. **4.** Add to egg-sugar mixture; blend thoroughly. **5.** Beat egg whites until stiff; fold into batter. **6.** Pour into ungreased pan. **7.** Bake 1 hour at 325° F. **8.** When done, remove from oven; cool. **9.** Remove side section of pan. **10.** Spread Chocolate Butter Cream Icing over torte.

PARADISE PIE
12 servings

Meringue Shell
1 12 to 14-inch pizza pan

6 egg whites	1½ teaspoons vanilla
2 cups sugar	⅛ teaspoon salt
2 teaspoons vinegar	

1. Beat egg whites until stiff but not dry. **2.** Gradually beat in 6 tablespoons sugar; add vinegar, vanilla. **3.** Fold in remaining sugar, salt. **4.** Pour mixture into pan; spread mixture over bottom; shape so there is a 1-inch rim around edge.

5. Bake 1 hour at 275° F.   6. Remove from oven; let stand until cold.

Filling

2 squares unsweetened chocolate	1 cup confectioners sugar
½ cup sugar	4 egg whites
¼ cup cold water	1 cup whipping cream
4 egg yolks	1 teaspoon vanilla
1 cup butter or margarine	

1. Combine chocolate, sugar, water in top of double boiler; heat until melted.   2. Beat egg yolks until lemon-colored; gradually add to chocolate mixture; cook until thick, stirring constantly; cool.   3. Cream butter, confectioners sugar; add chocolate mixture; stir well.   4. Beat egg whites until stiff; fold into mixture.   5. Refrigerate until serving time.   6. Whip cream; add vanilla.   7. Fill meringue shell with filling; top with whipped cream.

CHEESECAKE
6 servings

1 9-inch pie pan

2 eggs	2 tablespoons sugar
½ cup sugar	¼ cup butter or margarine,
¾ pound cream cheese, softened	softened
½ teaspoon vanilla	1 cup commercial sour cream
1 teaspoon lemon juice	2 tablespoons sugar
20 graham crackers, crushed	½ teaspoon vanilla

1. Beat eggs until light, fluffy; add sugar gradually, beating after each addition.   2. Combine egg mixture, cheese, vanilla, lemon juice; beat thoroughly.   3. Set aside while making crust.   4. Combine cracker crumbs, sugar, butter; blend well; press onto bottom and sides of pan.   5. Pour in cheese mixture.   6. Bake 20 minutes at 375° F.   7. Remove from oven; cool completely.   8. Combine sour cream, sugar, vanilla; spread evenly over cooled cake.   9. Bake 5 minutes at 400° F. 10. Cool; chill.

MARY'S CHEESE CAKE SUPREME
10 servings

1 9-inch spring form pan

18 zwieback
2 tablespoons butter or margarine

2 tablespoons sugar

To make crust
1. Rub zwieback through food press or roll into fine crumbs.
2. Cream butter; add sugar, crumbs; blend. 3. Press onto bottom of pan to make crust.

To make filling
5½ 3-ounce packages cream
   cheese, softened
½ cup sugar
2 tablespoons flour
¼ teaspoon salt

1 teaspoon vanilla
4 egg yolks, unbeaten
1 cup light cream
4 egg whites, beaten stiff

1. Mash cream cheese. 2. Sift sugar, flour, salt together; add to cheese; blend thoroughly. 3. Add vanilla; blend. 4. Add egg yolks 1 at a time; beat well after each addition. 5. Add cream; blend thoroughly. 6. Fold in stiffly beaten egg whites. 7. Bake 60-70 minutes at 325° F. or until set. 8. Cool in pan; remove side section of pan.

INDIAN PUDDING
8 servings

1 2-quart casserole

4 cups milk
¾ cup corn meal
¼ cup molasses
¾ cup brown sugar, firmly packed
½ cup butter or margarine
4 eggs, well beaten

1 teaspoon ginger
1 teaspoon cinnamon
½ teaspoon nutmeg
½ teaspoon salt
1 cup sour milk or sour cream

1. Scald milk in saucepan over low heat. 2. Slowly stir in corn meal; remove from heat. 3. Add molasses, sugar, butter, eggs, ginger, cinnamon, nutmeg, salt; blend thoroughly.
4. Add sour milk gradually; blend. 5. Pour into Alcoa Wrap lined casserole. 6. Bake 2 hours at 275° F. or until knife inserted in center comes out clean.

Taste Tip: Serve warm with cream or Vanilla Sauce.

APRICOT REFRIGERATOR CAKE
8 servings

1 9-inch spring form pan

¾ cup undiluted evaporated milk
3 teaspoons plain gelatin
1 tablespoon cold water
1 teaspoon lemon juice
1 No. 2½ can apricot halves

¼ cup sugar
¼ cup orange juice
1 teaspoon grated orange rind
16 lady fingers

1. Scald milk in top of double boiler. 2. Combine 1 teaspoon gelatin with water; let stand 5 minutes. 3. Add gelatin to milk; stir until dissolved. 4. Pour into freezer tray; chill in freezing compartment until almost set. 5. Turn into chilled bowl; beat until 3 times original volume, adding lemon juice after it starts to thicken. 6. Drain apricots, reserving liquid. 7. Press apricots through fine sieve; add sugar; blend. 8. Combine remaining 2 teaspoons gelatin with ½ cup apricot juice; let stand 5 minutes; heat over boiling water until gelatin is dissolved. 9. Add mashed apricots to gelatin mixture; add orange juice, rind; chill slightly. 10. Fold in whipped milk mixture. 11. Line pan, individual molds or sherbet glasses with lady fingers. 12. Pile apricot mixture on top; chill until set. 13. Serve plain or with whipped cream.

RASPBERRY CREAM PARFAIT
4 servings

3 tablespoons quick cooking
tapioca
6 tablespoons sugar
¼ teaspoon salt

1⅓ cups milk
½ cup heavy cream
2 cups red raspberries

1. Mix tapioca, 4 tablespoons of the sugar, salt in saucepan. 2. Add milk gradually; stir. 3. Cook, stirring constantly, until mixture boils. 4. Remove from heat; cool. 5. Whip cream; fold into tapioca mixture; chill. 6. Crush raspberries slightly; add remaining sugar. 7. Pile raspberries, tapioca mixture in alternate layers in parfait glasses. 8. Serve plain or with whipped cream.

HOT FRUIT MEDLEY

6-8 servings

1 9 x 9 x 1¾-inch cake pan

2 cups crisp macaroon crumbs
(about 40 macaroons)
1 No. 303 can sliced peaches,
drained
1 1-pound can purple plums,
pitted, drained

1 No. 2 can pineapple chunks,
drained
1 1-pound can Bing Cherries,
pitted, drained
½ cup Sherry wine

1. Sprinkle ½ cup macaroon crumbs in bottom of buttered pan. 2. Combine peaches, plums, pineapple, cherries; toss lightly. 3. Place layer of fruit in pan; sprinkle with crumbs. 4. Continue layering fruit, crumbs, ending with layer of crumbs. 5. Pour Sherry over top of crumbs. 6. Bake 40-45 minutes at 350° F.

INDIVIDUAL CHERRY COBBLERS

6 servings

1 1-pound 5-ounce can cherry pie
filling

1 one-layer package yellow cake
mix (8¾ ounce)
¼ cup butter or margarine

1. To make foil cups: Cut six 8-inch circles of Alcoa Wrap; mold each circle over 10-ounce custard cup; crimp edges of foil; place foil cups on baking sheet. 2. Spoon pie filling into foil cups (about ⅓ cup per serving). 3. Sprinkle dry cake mix over cherries (about ¼ cup). 4. Top each with 4 very thin slices butter. 5. Bake 20-25 minutes at 400° F. or until golden brown. 6. Serve warm; may be topped with scoop of ice cream.

Variations: Other fruit pie fillings may be substituted.

FRUIT CURRY

6 servings

1 9 x 9 x 1¾-inch cake pan

⅓ cup butter or margarine
¾ cup light brown sugar, firmly packed
1 tablespoon curry powder
1 No. 2 can peach halves, drained

1 No. 2 can pear halves, drained
1 No. 2 can pineapple chunks, drained
12 maraschino cherries, drained

1. Melt butter; add brown sugar, curry; blend well. 2. Arrange peaches, pears, pineapple in pan; place cherries in peach and pear centers; spoon syrup over fruit. 3. Bake 45 minutes at 350° F. 4. Serve warm.

CHERRY-PEACH DUMPLINGS

6 servings

1 1-pound 5-ounce can cherry pie filling
Few drops red food coloring
½ cup water
1 tablespoon lemon juice
½ teaspoon cinnamon

⅛ teaspoon ground cloves
1 No. 303 can peach halves, drained
Milk
1 egg, beaten
1½ cups biscuit mix

1. Place cherry pie filling in 9-inch fry pan; add food coloring; stir. 2. Add water, lemon juice, cinnamon, cloves; stir. 3. Add peaches. 4. Cook over medium high heat until mixture comes to boil (about 3-5 minutes). 5. Add milk to egg to make ½ cup; stir into biscuit mix to form soft dough. 6. Drop by tablespoonfuls on top of boiling fruit. 7. Cook uncovered over low heat 10 minutes. 8. Cover; cook 10 minutes longer. 9. To serve: spoon fruit over dumplings.

NANAS GORENG

6 servings

2 tablespoons flour
1 egg, unbeaten
¼ teaspoon salt

6 pineapple slices, cut in half
3 tablespoons salad oil

1. Mix flour, egg, salt together to make batter. 2. Dip pineapple into batter; fry in hot oil in fry pan; brown both sides; serve hot.

BLUEBERRY BUCKLE

9 servings

1 9 x 9 x 1¾-inch cake pan

¾ cup sugar
¼ cup shortening
1 egg, slightly beaten
½ cup milk

2 cups sifted all purpose flour
2 teaspoons baking powder
½ teaspoon salt
1 cup blueberries, well drained

Crumb Mixture
½ cup sugar
⅓ cup sifted all purpose flour

½ teaspoon cinnamon
¼ cup soft butter or margarine

1. Grease pan; dust lightly with flour. 2. Mix together thoroughly sugar, shortening, egg; stir in milk. 3. Sift together flour, baking powder, salt; stir into sugar mixture; carefully blend in blueberries. 4. Pour into pan. 5. Mix together sugar, flour, cinnamon, butter; sprinkle over batter. 6. Bake 45-50 minutes at 375° F. 7. Top with Old Fashioned Lemon Sauce.

PEACH KUCHEN

6 servings

1 8 x 8 x 2-inch cake pan

2 cups sifted all purpose flour
¼ teaspoon baking powder
½ teaspoon salt
1 cup sugar
½ cup butter or margarine

12 peach halves, fresh or canned
1 teaspoon cinnamon
2 egg yolks, slightly beaten
1 cup commercial sour cream

1. Sift together flour, baking powder, salt, 2 tablespoons sugar. 2. Cut in butter with 2 knives or pastry blender until mixture looks like corn meal. 3. Pile into ungreased pan; pat an even layer over bottom, halfway up sides of pan. 4. Place peach halves over pastry. 5. Sprinkle mixture of cinnamon and remaining sugar over peaches. 6. Bake 15 minutes at 400° F. 7. Mix egg yolks, cream together; pour over kuchen. 8. Bake 30 minutes longer. 9. Serve warm.

JAMAICA PLANTERS CAKE

10-12 servings

¾ pound butter or margarine
3¾ cups confectioners sugar
9 eggs separated

½ cup strong coffee
1 large sponge cake
½ cup rum

1. Cream butter until soft; add 3 cups of the sugar gradually, continuing to cream until light, fluffy. 2. Add egg yolks, one at a time; beat well after each addition. 3. Add coffee; beat; set aside. 4. Beat egg whites until foamy; slowly add remaining ¾ cup sugar; beat until stiff. 5. Fold egg whites into butter mixture. 6. Slice sponge cake into thin layers. 7. Sprinkle layers of cake with rum. 8. Put layers together with frosting between and on top. 9. Chill at least 2 hours before serving.

PLANTATION FRITTERS

1½-2 dozen

3 ripe plantains or bananas
3¼ cups sifted cake flour
2 tablespoons sugar
2 teaspoons baking powder
¼ teaspoon salt
2 eggs, beaten

¼ cup sweetened condensed milk
1 teaspoon vanilla
¼ cup chopped salted peanuts
½ cup seedless raisins
Oil

1. Mash bananas with fork, leaving fairly small pieces. 2. Sift together flour, sugar, baking powder, salt. 3. Combine eggs, milk, vanilla; add to flour mixture; stir just to blend. 4. Fold in banana pulp, nuts, raisins. Batter should be the consistency of drop cookies. 5. Pour oil into pan to depth of 2 inches; heat to 365° F. or until hot enough to brown 1-inch bread cube in 1 minute. 6. Drop batter by teaspoonfuls into hot fat; fry 2-3 minutes until golden brown, cooked through. 7. If desired, roll in sifted confectioners sugar while warm.

SWEDISH TOSGAS

1 dozen pastries

Pastry Shells
6 tablespoons butter or margarine   1 cup sifted all purpose flour
¼ cup sugar

1. Cream butter until soft. 2. Add sugar gradually, continuing to cream until light, fluffy. 3. Add flour; blend thoroughly. 4. Divide mixture into 12 small ungreased muffin cups; press into bottoms and half way up sides of cups. 5. Bake 10 minutes at 350° F.

Filling
⅓ cup blanched almonds, slivered   1½ tablespoons cream
¼ cup sugar   2 teaspoons flour
  2 tablespoons butter or
    margarine

1. Combine almonds, sugar, butter, cream, flour in saucepan. 2. Cook over medium high heat, stirring constantly, until mixture boils. 3. Spoon into partially baked shells. 4. Bake 15 minutes at 350° F.; cool 5 minutes; remove from pan.

LINGONBERRY MOUSSE

6-8 servings

1½ cups water   1 14-ounce jar lingonberry
¼ teaspoon salt   preserves
¼ cup quick-cooking farina   Whipped cream

1. Combine water, salt in saucepan; bring to boil. 2. Add farina slowly to boiling water, stirring constantly. 3. Cook 2½ minutes over medium heat, stirring constantly to prevent sticking; remove from heat; set aside. 4. Press lingonberry preserves through fine sieve; add to cooked farina. 5. Cook to lukewarm; beat with electric mixer or rotary beater until thick, fluffy. 6. Pour into individual serving dishes; chill. 7. Serve with whipped cream.

Good to know: This mousse is delicious made with blackberry, black raspberry or red raspberry preserves. Line the serving dish with crisp vanilla wafers for an added treat.

That Extra Touch

Knowing how to make good sauces is something like having a fairy godmother's magic wand all your own. With the sauce-sorcery you'll find here, you can dress up a plain vegetable, make a chuck steak pretend it's Chateaubriand, turn a piece of plain cake into a culinary event!

BASIC STOCK

About 3 cups

2 pounds meat or poultry (including bones)
or
1 pound fish
6 cups water

1½ cups chopped carrots
1 cup chopped onions
1 tablespoon salt
1 teaspoon pepper

1. Add meat, poultry or fish to water in large saucepan. 2. Cook uncovered over medium heat 1 hour. 3. Add carrots, onions, salt, pepper; continue cooking 2 additional hours or until stock is reduced to 3 cups. 4. Use in sauce recipes that call for stock.

WHITE SAUCES I, II, III

Thin White Sauce I
1 tablespoon butter or margarine
1 tablespoon flour

¼ teaspoon salt
1 cup milk

Medium White Sauce II
2 tablespoons butter or margarine
2 tablespoons flour

¼ teaspoon salt
1 cup milk

Thick White Sauce III

3 tablespoons butter or margarine	¼ teaspoon salt
3 tablespoons flour	1 cup milk

1. Melt butter in saucepan; remove from heat. 2. Add flour, salt; stir; add milk. 3. Cook over low heat, stirring constantly until thickened.

FISH SAUCES

SAUCE BÉARNAISE
About 1 cup

1 teaspoon tarragon	¼ cup white wine
1 teaspoon chervil	3 egg yolks
2 tablespoons finely chopped scallions	1 tablespoon water
4 whole black peppercorns, ground	½ pound butter or margarine
	1 teaspoon salt
¼ cup tarragon vinegar	¼ teaspoon cayenne

1. Combine tarragon, chervil, scallions, ground pepper, vinegar, wine in sauce pan; blend well. 2. Cook over medium heat until reduced to a thick paste, stirring constantly; remove from heat; cool slightly. 3. Combine egg yolks, water; blend well; add to seasoned paste, beating until light, fluffy. 4. Place over low heat; add butter in thirds, beating well after each addition. 5. Add salt, cayenne; blend well. 6. Serve with broiled fish.

NEWBURG SAUCE
About 1 cup

2 tablespoons butter or margarine	¼ teaspoon cayenne
1 tablespoon flour	2 egg yolks, well beaten
1 cup light cream, heated	2 tablespoons Sherry wine
1 teaspoon salt	

1. Melt butter in saucepan; stir in flour; gradually add cream; blend well. 2. Cook over low heat until thick, smooth; stir constantly. 3. Add salt, cayenne; blend well. 4. Beat in egg yolks; continue cooking 2-3 minutes, stirring constantly. 5. Blend in sherry. 6. Serve with fish, shellfish.

CAPE COD SAUCE

About 1½ cups

- 2 tablespoons butter or margarine
- 4 tablespoons flour
- 1½ cups boiling water
- 3 tablespoons butter or margarine
- ½ teaspoon salt
- ⅛ teaspoon pepper
- 2 teaspoons lemon juice
- 1 tablespoon minced parsley

1. Melt butter in saucepan; blend in flour. **2.** Add boiling water gradually, stirring constantly; cook until thickened. **3.** Stir in butter, salt, pepper, lemon juice, parsley; blend well. **4.** Serve over fish cakes.

SAUCE BÉCHAMEL MAIGNE

About 4 cups

- ¼ cup butter or margarine
- 3 tablespoons minced onion
- ¼ cup flour
- 3 cups milk, scalded
- 3 cups Basic Fish Stock
- ½ teaspoon salt
- 5 whole white peppercorns
- ¼ teaspoon nutmeg
- Sprig parsley
- 2 tablespoons butter or margarine

1. Melt butter in large saucepan; add onion; sauté until lightly browned. **2.** Stir in flour; gradually add milk, fish stock; blend well. **3.** Add salt, peppercorns, nutmeg, parsley; cook uncovered over low heat about 1½ hours or until sauce is reduced to 4 cups; stir frequently. **4.** Strain; add butter. **5.** Serve with fish, shellfish.

MEAT SAUCES

CHATEAU SAUCE
About 4 cups

½ cup chopped onion
2 tablespoons pickled onions, chopped
¼ cup butter or margarine
¼ cup flour
6 beef bouillon cubes
3 cups boiling water

⅓ cup tomato purée
2 tablespoons bottled meat extract
¼ cup chopped mushrooms
¼ cup white wine
½ cup butter or margarine, melted

1. Sauté onions, pickled onions in butter in saucepan until lightly browned. 2. Add flour; cook over medium heat about 8-9 minutes or until deeply browned, stirring constantly. 3. Dissolve bouillon cubes in boiling water; stir in tomato purée, meat extract; add to sautéed onions; blend well. 4. Cook over medium heat about 10 minutes or until thickened; stir constantly. 5. Combine mushrooms, wine in saucepan; cook uncovered over medium heat 5-8 minutes or until liquid has evaporated; add to sauce. 6. Add melted butter; beat with rotary beater until thoroughly blended. 7. Serve with meat.

WESTERN HERB SAUCE
About 2 cups

¼ cup olive oil
¼ cup butter or margarine
2 tablespoons chopped scallions
1 8-ounce can sliced mushrooms, drained
2 tablespoons chopped chives

3 tablespoons chopped parsley
½ cup chopped walnuts
3 tablespoons bottled steak sauce
½ teaspoon salt
Dash pepper

1. Heat olive oil, butter in saucepan; add scallions, mushrooms; sauté until lightly browned. 2. Add chives, parsley, walnuts, steak sauce, salt, pepper; blend well; simmer uncovered about 5 minutes. 3. Serve with steak, ground beef patties.

SAUCE CHASSEUR
About 1 cup

2 tablespoons butter or margarine
2 tablespoons sliced mushrooms
1 teaspoon chopped scallions
½ cup white wine
1 tablespoon tomato purée

1 cup Brown Sauce (made with chicken stock)
2 tablespoons Sherry wine
1 tablespoon butter or margarine
½ teaspoon chopped parsley
½ teaspoon tarragon

1. Melt butter in saucepan; add mushrooms, scallions; sauté until lightly browned. 2. Add wine; cook uncovered over low heat about 10-15 minutes or until liquid is reduced about ½ in volume. 3. Blend in tomato purée, Brown Sauce, Sherry; bring to boil over medium heat; remove from heat. 4. Blend in butter, parsley, tarragon. 5. Serve with game.

ORANGE SAUCE FOR GAME
About 1½ cups

3 tablespoons butter or margarine
¼ cup flour
1⅓ cups Basic Chicken Stock
1 teaspoon salt

¼ teaspoon paprika
1 tablespoon grated orange rind
⅔ cup orange juice
2 tablespoons Sherry wine

1. Melt butter in saucepan; stir in flour; cook over low heat until lightly browned, stirring constantly. 2. Gradually add stock; blend well. 3. Cook over low heat until thick, smooth; stir constantly. 4. Blend in salt, paprika. 5. Just before serving, blend in orange rind, orange juice, Sherry; cook 1-2 minutes or until hot. 6. Serve over game.

BASIC BROWN SAUCE
About 1 cup

2 tablespoons butter or margarine
1 tablespoon chopped onion
2 tablespoons flour

1 cup Basic Stock (meat, poultry or fish)
1 teaspoon salt
¼ teaspoon paprika

1. Melt butter in saucepan; add onion; sauté until lightly browned; remove onion. 2. Stir flour into butter; cook over

low heat until lightly browned, stirring constantly.   **3.** Gradually add stock; blend well.   **4.** Cook over low heat until thick, smooth; stir constantly.   **5.** Blend in salt, paprika.   **6.** Use in sauce recipes that call for Brown Sauce.

SAUCE MILANESE
about 3 cups

1 large onion, thinly sliced
2 tablespoons butter or margarine
1 cup canned tomatoes
1 cup diced celery
1 cup diced green pepper
1 cup ketchup
2 tablespoons brown sugar
3 dashes Tabasco sauce

½ teaspoon dry mustard
2 cups beef stock
1 teaspoon salt
⅛ teaspoon pepper
⅛ teaspoon oregano
1 cup canned mushroom caps
1 green pepper, cut into ⅛-inch rings

1. Brown onion lightly in butter in saucepan.   **2.** Add remaining ingredients except mushroom caps, green pepper rings; cover; bring to boil.   **3.** Simmer over low heat 1 hour; add mushroom caps, green pepper rings; cook 10 minutes longer.   **4.** Serve over beef, pork or chicken; also may be used as a basting sauce for barbecued meats or fowl.

CIDER SAUCE
About 2 cups

2 tablespoons butter or margarine
⅓ cup flour

1¾ cups ham broth or water
½ cup cider
½ cup apple jelly

1. Melt butter; add flour; blend.   **2.** Add ham broth or water; stir; bring to boil.   **3.** Add cider, jelly; bring to boil.   **4.** Serve with ham.

BLACK BUTTER SAUCE
About 3 tablespoons

2 tablespoons butter or margarine
1 tablespoon lemon juice
1 teaspoon minced parsley or capers

⅛ teaspoon salt
Pinch of pepper
Pinch of paprika

1. Heat butter in fry pan until lightly browned.   **2.** Add remaining ingredients; stir.   **3.** Serve over steaks, chops.

DRAWN BUTTER SAUCE

About ¼ cup

¼ cup butter or margarine
2 tablespoons chopped parsley

Salt
Paprika

Melt butter; add remaining ingredients.

MINT SAUCE

About 1 cup

½ cup vinegar
1 cup water
¼ cup chopped fresh mint leaves
¼ cup lemon juice

½ cup water
2 tablespoons sugar
¼ teaspoon salt
¼ cup chopped mint leaves

1. Combine vinegar, water, mint leaves; simmer until liquid is reduced one half; strain.   2. Add lemon juice, water, sugar, salt; stir; chill.   3. Just before serving add remaining chopped mint.   4. Serve with cold roast lamb.

RAISIN SAUCE

About 2 cups

½ cup brown sugar, firmly packed
1½ teaspoons dry mustard
1½ tablespoons flour

½ cup seedless raisins
¼ cup vinegar
1¾ cups water

1. Combine dry ingredients in top of double boiler; add vinegar, water.   2. Cook 20 minutes over boiling water.   3. Serve over ham or fresh pork.

HORSERADISH SAUCE

About 2½ cups

1 cup whipping cream
1 tablespoon lemon juice

1½ tablespoons bottled horse-
    radish
⅛ teaspoon salt

1. Whip cream; add remaining ingredients; blend thoroughly.
2. Serve with ham.

STEAK SAUCE
About ¼ cup

3 tablespoons butter or margarine
3 tablespoons lemon juice
½ teaspoon dry mustard

1 tablespoon Worcestershire sauce
Salt
Pepper

1. Melt butter; add remaining ingredients. 2. Serve with broiled meat.

TOMATO SAUCE
About 1½ cups

2 cups canned tomatoes
1 sliced onion
2 stalks celery with leaves, chopped
1 tablespoon minced parsley
1 carrot, diced

½ green pepper, diced
3 tablespoons butter or margarine
3 tablespoons flour
¼ teaspoon salt
⅛ teaspoon pepper
¼ teaspoon sugar

1. Combine tomatoes, onion, celery, parsley, carrot, green pepper in saucepan. 2. Cover; bring to boil; simmer 15 minutes; strain, reserving liquid. 3. Melt butter in saucepan; remove from heat. 4. Add flour, salt, pepper, sugar; blend. 5. Add sufficient water, if necessary, to vegetable liquid to make 1½ cups. 6. Add to flour mixture; cook over low heat until bubbly, stirring constantly. 7. Serve over meat.

SUPER BARBECUE SAUCE
About 3 cups

1 large onion, sliced
2 tablespoons butter or margarine
1 cup canned tomatoes
1 cup diced celery
1 cup diced green pepper
1 cup ketchup
2 tablespoons brown sugar

3 dashes Tabasco sauce
½ teaspoon dry mustard
2 cups beef stock or 2 bouillon cubes dissolved in 2 cups boiling water
1 teaspoon salt
⅛ teaspoon pepper

1. Brown onion in butter in saucepan. 2. Add remaining ingredients; cover; bring to boil. 3. Simmer over low heat 1 hour. 4. Serve with hamburgers, ribs, fried chicken.

MUSTARD SAUCE

About 1 cup

1 tablespoon butter or margarine
2 tablespoons prepared mustard
2 teaspoons salt
2 teaspoons sugar
1 egg yolk, slightly beaten

1¼ cups cold water
5 teaspoons cornstarch
2 tablespoons cold water
1 tablespoon lemon juice

1. Melt butter in top of double boiler. 2. Stir in mustard, salt, sugar. 3. Combine egg yolk, water; stir into butter mixture. 4. Mix remaining cold water, cornstarch to a smooth paste. 5. Stir into sauce; cook over boiling water until thickened. 6. Remove from heat; add lemon juice.

VEGETABLE SAUCES

ALLEMANDE SAUCE
About 1 cup

3 tablespoons butter or margarine
3 tablespoons flour
1 cup Basic Chicken Stock
¼ teaspoon salt

¼ teaspoon paprika
1 egg yolk
1 teaspoon lemon juice

1. Melt butter in saucepan; stir in flour; gradually add chicken stock; blend well. 2. Cook over low heat until thick, smooth; stir constantly. 3. Add salt, paprika; blend well. 4. Beat in egg yolk; continue cooking 1-2 minutes, stirring constantly. 5. Blend in lemon juice. 6. Serve with asparagus or green beans.

PIQUANT CHEESE SAUCE
About 1 cup

2 tablespoons butter or margarine
2 tablespoons flour
1 cup buttermilk

½ teaspoon salt
¼ teaspoon dry mustard
½ cup grated Cheddar cheese

1. Melt butter in saucepan. 2. Stir in flour; gradually add buttermilk; blend well. 3. Cook over low heat, stirring constantly until thickened; (curdled appearance disappears when cheese is added). 4. Add salt, mustard, cheese; continue cooking until cheese is melted; stir constantly. 5. Serve with baked potatoes, vegetables.

EASY HOLLANDAISE SAUCE
About ½ cup

2 egg yolks
¼ teaspoon salt
  Dash cayenne pepper

½ cup melted butter or margarine
1 tablespoon fresh, frozen or
  canned lemon juice

1. Beat egg yolks until thick, lemon-colored; add salt, cayenne. 2. Very slowly, add ¼ cup melted butter, beating constantly. 3. Combine remaining ¼ cup butter, lemon juice; add slowly to yolk mixture, beating constantly. 4. Serve immediately.

DESSERT SAUCES

VANILLA SAUCE
About 2 cups

1 cup sugar
2 tablespoons cornstarch
⅛ teaspoon salt

2 cups boiling water
4 tablespoons butter or margarine
2 teaspoons vanilla

1. Combine sugar, cornstarch, salt in saucepan. 2. Add boiling water gradually, stirring constantly. 3. Cook over low heat, stirring constantly until clear, thickened—about 5 minutes. 4. Add butter, vanilla; blend. 5. Serve hot.

ORANGE SAUCE
About 3½ cups

1½ cups sugar
3 tablespoons cornstarch
¼ teaspoon salt
2¼ cups boiling water
3 tablespoons grated orange rind

6 tablespoons butter or margarine
¾ cup orange juice
3 tablespoons lemon juice

1. Combine sugar, cornstarch, salt in saucepan. 2. Add boiling water gradually, stirring constantly; add rind. 3. Cook over low heat, stirring constantly until clear, thickened—about 5 minutes. 4. Add butter, orange and lemon juices; blend. 5. Serve hot.

BANANA CREAM SAUCE
About 3 cups

2 egg whites
1 cup sugar
Dash salt

2 cups mashed bananas (about 4 medium bananas)

1. Have egg whites at room temperature. 2. Combine sugar, salt. 3. Beat egg whites until frothy; add sugar gradually, continuing to beat until stiff peaks are formed. 4. Fold egg whites into bananas. 5. Serve over Spice or Sponge Cake. 6. Garnish with banana slices.

SEMI-SWEET CHOCOLATE SAUCE

About 1 cup

4 squares unsweetened chocolate
½ cup honey
Dash salt

1 tablespoon yellow chartreuse
⅓ cup slivered almonds, toasted

1. Combine chocolate, honey in saucepan; melt over low heat, stirring constantly. 2. Add salt, chartreuse, almonds; blend well. 3. Cover; remove from heat; let stand 5 minutes; stir before serving. 4. Serve warm over ice cream.

NUTMEG SAUCE

About 2 cups

¼ cup butter or margarine
½ cup sugar
1 egg yolk
1½ tablespoons flour

1 teaspoon vanilla
1¼ cups boiling water
¼ teaspoon nutmeg

1. Cream butter; gradually add sugar; beat until light, fluffy. 2. Blend in egg yolk, flour, vanilla; gradually add boiling water. 3. Cook over medium heat, stirring constantly, until thickened. 4. Stir in nutmeg. 5. Serve warm over gingerbread, spice cake, etc.

ALMOND APRICOT SAUCE

About 2½ cups

2 cups dried apricots
2 cups water
½ cup sugar

1 teaspoon lemon juice
½ cup slivered blanched almonds

1. Combine apricots, water; simmer until apricots are tender, about 20 minutes. 2. Add sugar, lemon juice, almonds; stir. 3. Serve over plain sponge cake.

OLD FASHIONED LEMON SAUCE

About 1⅓ cups

½ cup butter or margarine
1 cup sugar
¼ cup water

1 egg, well beaten
3 tablespoons lemon juice
Grated rind of 1 lemon

1. Combine all ingredients in saucepan. 2. Cook over medium heat, stirring constantly just until mixture comes to a boil. 3. Serve warm over Blueberry Buckle.

FAVORITE CHOCOLATE SAUCE

About 1½ cups

2 squares unsweetened chocolate
1 can sweetened condensed milk

⅛ teaspoon salt
½ cup hot water

1. Melt chocolate over hot water in top of double boiler. 2. Add milk, salt; cook, stirring constantly until thickened—about 5 minutes. 3. Add hot water; beat until smooth.

RUM SAUCE

About 1½ cups

2 eggs, unbeaten
1 cup sugar

1 cup heavy cream, whipped
Rum or rum extract

1. Beat eggs until light. 2. Add sugar gradually, continuing to beat until mixture loses its grain. 3. Fold into whipped cream. 4. Flavor to taste with rum or extract.

HARD SAUCE

About 1 cup

⅓ cup butter
1 cup sifted confectioners sugar

1 teaspoon vanilla or brandy
Pinch salt

1. Cream butter until soft. 2. Add sugar gradually, continuing to cream until light, fluffy. 3. Add vanilla or brandy, salt; blend thoroughly. 4. Chill until needed.

CHOCOLATE FUDGE SAUCE
About 2 cups

½ cup light corn syrup
1 cup sugar
1 cup water

3 squares unsweetened chocolate
1 teaspoon vanilla
1 cup undiluted evaporated milk

1. Combine syrup, sugar, water in saucepan. 2. Cook over low heat until small amount forms soft ball in cold water; remove from heat. 3. Add chocolate; let stand until melted. 4. Add vanilla; add milk slowly, blending thoroughly.

RED RASPBERRY SAUCE
About 1 cup

2 cups red raspberries
½ cup currant jelly
½ cup sugar

1½ teaspoons cornstarch
1 tablespoon cold water

1. Crush berries in saucepan; add jelly, sugar; bring to boil. 2. Blend cornstarch, cold water to a smooth paste; add to berries. 3. Cook, stirring constantly until clear, thickened; strain; cool.

BUTTER CARAMEL SAUCE
About 1½ cups

¾ cup sugar
⅛ teaspoon salt
¼ cup butter or margarine

½ cup light corn syrup
1 cup light cream
½ teaspoon vanilla

1. Combine sugar, salt, butter, corn syrup and ½ cup of the cream in saucepan. 2. Cook over low heat until small amount forms a hard ball in cold water. 3. Add remaining cream; cook until syrup spins a thread; add vanilla; blend.

FOAMY SAUCE
About ⅔ cup

½ cup butter or margarine
1 cup sifted confectioners sugar

1 egg, beaten
1 teaspoon vanilla

1. Cream butter until soft. 2. Add sugar gradually, continuing

to cream until light, fluffy. **3.** Add egg, vanilla; blend. **4.** Heat over boiling water 2 minutes, stirring constantly.

ICE CREAM SAUCE
About 2 cups

1 egg, beaten
¾ cup sugar
Pinch salt

⅓ cup butter or margarine, melted
1 teaspoon vanilla
1 cup heavy cream, whipped

1. Combine egg, sugar, salt; beat well. **2.** Add melted butter gradually, continuing to beat; add vanilla. **3.** Fold egg mixture into whipped cream; chill thoroughly.

BUTTERSCOTCH SAUCE
About ⅔ cup

1 cup brown sugar, firmly packed
¼ cup light cream

2 tablespoons light corn syrup
3 tablespoons butter or margarine

1. Combine all ingredients in saucepan. **2.** Place over low heat; bring to boil; boil 3 minutes; cool.

MARSHMALLOW SAUCE
About ⅔ cup

½ cup sugar
¼ cup water
8 marshmallows

1 egg white, unbeaten
½ teaspoon vanilla

1. Combine sugar, water in saucepan; bring to boil; boil 5 minutes. **2.** Cut marshmallows into small pieces; add to syrup. **3.** Beat egg white until stiff. **4.** Fold marshmallow mixture, vanilla into egg white.

Good to know: Sauce may be tinted green: few drops pepper-mint oil may be substituted for vanilla.

CUSTARD SAUCE

About 2 cups

2 cups milk
3 eggs
4 tablespoons sugar

¼ teaspoon salt
1 teaspoon vanilla

1. Scald milk in top of double boiler. 2. Beat eggs slightly; add sugar, salt; blend. 3. Add milk gradually, stirring constantly. 4. Return to double boiler; cook over hot, not boiling, water, stirring constantly, until just slightly thickened—about 7-8 minutes. 5. Remove at once from hot water; add vanilla.

Good to know: If overcooked, custard sauce will curdle: set in pan of cold water; beat with rotary beater until smooth.

"A Very Small Rijsttafel"

INDONESIAN DINNER PARTY
for 8-10 guests

*How would you like to give a never-before party that
will have your guests talking about it—and about what
a good cook, what a clever hostess you are—for months
afterward? Here's how: menu, recipes, step-by-step directions. You can't go wrong—so have a wonderful
time!*

A Rijsttafel is, literally, a "rice table"—a buffet which centers around a great bowl of rice and may consist of as many
as twenty other dishes. A true Rijsttafel can occupy the better
part of an afternoon—and result in overstuffed guests!

However, the Surinamese have a scaled-down version which
they call "A Very Small Rijsttafel." This simplified feast, pro-
portioned for modern eating habits, can be a delightful ad-
venture in both cooking and eating without over-taxing either
the hostess or her guests. The cook gets a secret bonus, too:
this exotic menu can be prepared the day before and popped
into the oven just before serving time. So the hostess who
follows our step-by-step Rijsttafel guide ensures herself not
one but three happy days: the day of preparation, the day
of the party itself, and the day after, when all she does is sit
back and let the compliments come pouring in!

MENU

Relish Tray   Hot Rolls
Fluffy Rice
Dengdeng Ragi
Ajam Koening
Langosta Criolia
Sambel Goreng Oedang
Sambel Goreng Hatti Pitee
Satee Boemboe
Sambel Goreng Mushrooms
Gado Gado
Katjang Sauce
Coupe Curaçao
Coffee

PREPARATION DAY

1. Mold a double thickness of heavy duty Alcoa Wrap around the outside of a quart mixing bowl. Flatten the bottom, crush the edges firmly together. Make seven such bowls; then make one pint-size bowl for Katjang (Peanut) Sauce. Your party table will thus be set with attractive serving dishes that go right from the refrigerator to the oven to the table—and *out*. No serving dishes to wash!

2. Prepare the Coconut Water which you will need for most of the recipes.

3. Make Coupe crusts for Coupe Curaçao, increasing recipe as needed.

4. Prepare each recipe. Keep this in mind: for perfect results, do not omit or make substitutions for any ingredients.

PARTY DAY

1. Early in the day prepare a simple Relish Tray of celery, cut into 3 to 4-inch strips; carrots, scraped, cut into strips;

green pepper cut into strips; cucumbers, peeled, cut into 3 to 4-inch wedges. Wrap tray in Alcoa Wrap; refrigerate.

2. Set table. To enhance the East Indian atmosphere, use a gay paisley or bright all-over print tablecloth and pottery plates. Note that East Indian cookery uses little salt; be sure to put some out for guests who may prefer to add some to their own portions. And why not write out the name of each dish on a small card, attach to picks and tuck into the appropriate bowls? The exotic names will add to your party atmosphere.

3. Forty-five minutes before serving time:
   a. Remove foil covers from bowls prepared the previous day (see below). Place all bowls on a large oven-proof tray or platter. Lay sheet of Alcoa Wrap loosely over top. Place tray in oven; heat 45 minutes at 400° F.
   b. Cook rice.
   c. Make coffee; heat rolls.
   d. Set out relish tray; add olives if desired.

4. When ready to serve, spoon rice into large wooden salad bowl lined with Alcoa Wrap. Place rice bowl in center of table; surround with foil bowls taken from oven and set on salad plates along with serving spoons.

5. When ready to serve the dessert, place each coupe on dessert plate. Fill with ice cream; top with pineapple sauce.

6. Be sure to make *plenty* of coffee!

COCONUT WATER

4½ cups milk
1½ cups water

1½ teaspoons salt
¾ cup shredded coconut

1. Combine all ingredients in saucepan; bring to boil; cook over low heat 10 minutes. 2. Strain; use coconut water in recipes; reserve cooked coconut for Dengdeng Ragi.

RICE

2 cups raw rice
5 cups water

2 teaspoons salt

1. Add salt to water; bring to boil. 2. Add rice; stir; cover.
3. Cook over low heat 25-30 minutes, or until all water has
been absorbed. 4. Remove cover; fluff with fork; let stand
5 minutes before serving.

DENGDENG RAGI
(Spicy Meat in Fried Coconut)

¾ cup cooked coconut (reserved
    from coconut water recipe)
½ pound round steak, cut in 1-inch
    cubes
1 tablespoon olive oil
¼ cup grated onions
1 clove garlic, grated

2 teaspoons curry powder
2 tablespoons brown sugar
1 tablespoon lime juice
1 bay leaf, crushed
2 teaspoons salt
¼ cup water
1 tablespoon soy sauce

1. Brown cooked coconut in fry pan over very low heat until
dark golden brown, stirring frequently. 2. Sauté meat cubes
in oil, turning frequently; add grated onion, garlic clove; continue cooking 5 minutes. 3. Add curry powder, brown sugar,
lime juice, bay leaf, salt, water, soy sauce; blend well; cover.

4. Cook over low heat about 15-20 minutes or until meat is tender.   5. Add browned coconut; blend well; mixture should be dry.   6. Pour into foil bowl; cover with Alcoa Wrap; refrigerate.

AJAM KOENING
(East Indian Fried Chicken)

2 2½-pound chickens	2 tablespoons brown sugar
2 tablespoons salt	1 teaspoon lime juice
1 teaspoon pepper	1 teaspoon curry powder
½ teaspoon garlic salt	3 tablespoons olive oil
¼ cup olive oil	1 cup coconut water
2 small onions	2 bay leaves
2 cloves garlic	

1. Wash, dry chickens; cut into serving pieces.   2. Combine salt, pepper, garlic salt; rub into chicken pieces.   3. Brown chicken in olive oil; set aside.   4. Grind together onions, garlic; add brown sugar, lime juice, curry powder; fry 5-10 minutes in the 3 tablespoons olive oil.   5. Add coconut water, bay leaves; pour over browned chicken; cover.   6. Simmer about 30 minutes or until chicken is tender, sauce is thick.   7. Pour into foil bowl; cover with Alcoa Wrap; refrigerate.

LANGOSTA CRIOLIA
(Lobster Creole)

1 medium onion, chopped	⅛ teaspoon pepper
1 green pepper, chopped	1 8-ounce can tomato sauce
1 clove garlic, minced	1 pound cooked lobster meat,
¼ cup olive oil	diced
1 medium tomato, quartered	¼ cup white wine
¾ teaspoon salt	

1. Sauté onions, green pepper, garlic in olive oil until tender.   2. Add tomato; cook until soft.   3. Add salt, pepper, tomato sauce, lobster; cover; simmer 15 minutes.   4. Add wine; cook 2-3 minutes longer.   5. Pour into foil bowl; cover with Alcoa Wrap; refrigerate.

SAMBEL GORENG OEDANG
(Fried Shrimp in Hot Sauce)

1 cup finely chopped onions	1 teaspoon lime juice
1 clove garlic, grated	¾ cup raw shrimp, cleaned, cut in
2 tablespoons olive oil	½-inch pieces
½ teaspoon red pepper	2 bay leaves
1 tablespoon dark brown sugar	1 cup coconut water

1. Sauté onions, garlic in olive oil; add red pepper, brown sugar, lime juice; blend well. 2. Add shrimp, bay leaves; continue cooking 5 minutes. 3. Add coconut water; simmer 20 minutes or until shrimp is tender. 4. Pour into foil bowl; cover with Alcoa Wrap; refrigerate.

SAMBEL GORENG HATTI PITEE
(Fried Chicken Livers in Hot Sauce)

¾ cup chicken livers, cut into small pieces	½ teaspoon red pepper
	1 tablespoon dark brown sugar
2 tablespoons olive oil	1 teaspoon lime juice
1 cup finely chopped onion	1 bay leaf
1 clove garlic, grated	¾ cup coconut water

1. Sauté chicken livers in oil until nicely browned; add onion, garlic; continue cooking 5 minutes. 2. Add red pepper, brown sugar, lime juice, bay leaf, coconut water; blend well; cover. 3. Simmer 15-20 minutes or until chicken livers are tender. 4. Pour into foil bowl; cover with Alcoa Wrap; refrigerate.

SATEE BOEMBOE

4 small onions	½ teaspoon ground cloves
2 cloves garlic	½ teaspoon ground ginger
½ teaspoon red pepper	3 tablespoons warm water
1 tablespoon dark brown sugar	3 tablespoons soy sauce
1 teaspoon lime juice	1½ pounds round steak, cut into
1½ teaspoons curry powder	¾-inch cubes

1. Grind together onions, garlic; add red pepper, brown sugar, lime juice, curry powder, clove, ginger; blend well. 2. Com-

bine water, soy sauce; add to spices; mix thoroughly. **3.** Add meat cubes; knead meat with hands to absorb sauce; refrigerate 6 hours. **4.** Thread 5-6 pieces of marinated meat on 10 skewers; place on broiler rack 3 inches away from heat; broil 15-20 minutes, brushing meat with sauce, turning frequently. **5.** Place in foil bowl; cover with Alcoa Wrap; refrigerate.

SAMBEL GORENG MUSHROOMS

¾ cup mushrooms, diced
2 tablespoons olive oil
1 cup finely chopped onion
1 clove garlic, grated
½ teaspoon red pepper

1 tablespoon dark brown sugar
1 teaspoon lime juice
1 bay leaf
¾ cup coconut water

1. Sauté mushrooms in oil until nicely browned; add onion, garlic; continue cooking 5 minutes. **2.** Add red pepper, brown sugar, lime juice, bay leaf, coconut water; blend well; cover; simmer 10-15 minutes. **3.** Pour into foil bowl; cover with Alcoa Wrap; refrigerate.

GADO GADO WITH KATJANG SAUCE
(Vegetables with Peanut Sauce)

1 pound green beans, cut into 1½-
inch pieces
1 can bean sprouts

1 medium tomato, cut into eighths
2 hard cooked eggs, quartered

1. Cook beans in small amount of water slightly salted until just tender, 30-35 minutes; drain; add bean sprouts. **2.** Pour into foil bowl; cover with Alcoa Wrap; refrigerate. **3.** When ready to serve garnish with tomato wedges, eggs. **4.** Guests will help themselves to the Peanut Sauce.

KATJANG SAUCE
(*Peanut Sauce*)

2 tablespoons grated onion
2 tablespoons olive oil
1 tablespoon dark brown sugar
1 teaspoon lime juice

¼ cup peanut butter
1 cup coconut water
Dash salt

1. Sauté onions in olive oil 5-10 minutes; add brown sugar, lime juice, peanut butter; blend well. 2. Gradually add coconut water, stirring constantly; add salt. 3. Cook until sauce is thick, smooth. 4. Pour into small foil bowl; cover with Alcoa Wrap; refrigerate.

COUPE CURAÇAO
6 servings

Coupe Crusts

3 eggs whites
½ cup milk

¾ cup sugar
¾ cup all purpose flour

Filling:

1 quart vanilla ice cream

1½ cups Pineapple Sundae Topping

1. Combine egg whites, milk, sugar, flour; mix well. 2. Pour enough batter (approximately ¼ cup) to form a 5-inch "pancake" on a well-greased cookie sheet. 3. Bake two coupe crusts at a time for 4-5 minutes at 500° F. until edges of crust become golden brown. 4. Remove coupe crust *immediately* from cookie sheet. 5. Place crust over 4-ounce inverted custard cup; press another custard cup on top to make a coupe. 6. Remove custard cups immediately from coupe. 7. Cool. 8. Fill each coupe with vanilla ice cream. 9. Put Pineapple Topping on ice cream.

The Great Outdoors

There's Outdoor Cookery . . . and then, again, there's just cooking outdoors. The latter involves running up a bowl of potato salad in the morning, lugging it out to the yard at dinner time and slapping a couple of hotdogs on the grill. On the other hand, Outdoor Cookery is an art—and a pleasure for the cook and for the diners.

A MAGIC MUST

Heavy duty Alcoa Wrap is practically indispensable in outdoor cookery. Read these "magic must" hints, and you'll see why.

A sheet of foil, accordion pleated into one-inch pleats and placed under the charcoal, reflects the heat. When you use the pleated reflector, the charcoal can be placed about an inch apart—a real saving on fuel.

When cooking meat on the rotisserie, make the drip pan from heavy duty Alcoa Wrap—it catches all the fat, and when clean-up time comes it can be tossed away.

For greater heat reflection, line the sides and top of your barbecue with heavy duty Alcoa Wrap—that makes cleaning easier, too.

Shape double-thick squares of heavy duty Alcoa Wrap into little bowls for holding sauces or garlic butter to brush on the meat while cooking. Later on—no pans to wash.

When you're wrapping foods to be grilled, it's important

to make tight folds in the foil, since the packages must be turned during grilling.

If you're cooking for a crowd—so big a crowd that the grill can't take all the meat at one time—keep the cooked batches hot by wrapping them in foil.

Use heavy duty Alcoa Wrap to keep corn-on-the-cob and rolls hot during serving.

Line serving platters with foil, too— and there won't be soiled platters to wash later.

CANNED VEGETABLES ON THE GRILL

Peas with Celery Salt

1. Drain canned peas.   2. Place peas in center of large double-thick square of Alcoa Wrap.   3. Dot with butter; sprinkle celery salt over top.   4. Bring up sides of Alcoa Wrap; fold down onto peas in tight double fold; fold ends up in tight double folds.   5. Place package on grill; grill 8-10 minutes if placed at back or side of grill; 5-6 minutes over hot coals. 6. Serve in opened package.

Good to know: This same procedure will apply to any canned vegetable.

FROZEN VEGETABLES ON THE GRILL

1. Remove frozen vegetable from freezer package.   2. Place in center of double-thick square of Alcoa Wrap.   3. Season with two pats butter, salt, pepper or herb seasonings.   4. Bring up sides of Alcoa Wrap; fold down onto vegetable in tight double fold; fold ends up in tight double folds.   5. Place package on grill over hot coals; grill 25-30 minutes for vegetables still frozen when placed on grill; 20-25 minutes for vegetables that have defrosted in the package; turn several times.   6. Serve in opened package.

CHARCOAL ROTISSERIE TIME CHARTS

BEEF

	Thermometer Reading	Approximate Time
Standing Rib		
Rare	140° F.	2–2½ hours
Medium	140°–150° F.	2½–3 hours
Well Done	160°–170° F.	3–4 hours

Rolled Rib: Allow about 25–35 minutes longer. Thermometer reading will be the same.

LAMB

	Thermometer Reading	Approximate Time
Leg		
Medium	150°–160° F.	1½–2 hours
Well Done	175°–180° F.	2–2½ hours

Boned Shoulder: Same as for Leg of Lamb.

PORK

	Thermometer Reading	Approximate Time
Fresh Loin	170°–175° F.	2–2½ hours
Fresh Ham—12 lb.	170°–175° F.	4 hours

VEAL

	Thermometer Reading	Approximate Time
Rolled Roast—3-lb.	165°–170° F.	45–60 minutes

POULTRY

	Approximate Time
Chicken—3–4 lbs.	1–1½ hours
Turkey—15 lbs.	3–4 hours
Duck—4–6 lbs.	1–1½ hours
Goose—4–7 lbs.	1¾–2½ hours
Rabbit—3–5 lbs.	40 minutes–2 hours
Wild Duck—1–2½ lbs.	20–30 minutes
Cornish Hens—1–2 lbs.	1–1½ hours

CHARCOAL BROILING TIME CHARTS

BEEF

Steaks

Thickness	Very Rare	Rare	Medium	Well Done
1 inch	6– 8 min.	8–12 min.	12–15 min.	15–20 min.
1½ inches	8–12 min.	10–15 min.	14–18 min.	18–25 min.
2 inches	14–20 min.	18–30 min.	25–30 min.	45–60 min.
2½ inches	20–30 min.	30–35 min.	35–45 min.	60–75 min.

Hamburgers

Rare	Medium	Well Done
10–12 min.	14-15 min.	18–20 min.

LAMB

Chops and Steaks

Thickness	Med. Rare	Well Done
1 inch	6–14 min.	18–25 min.
1½ inches	8–16 min.	20–30 min.
2 inches	12–20 min.	25–30 min.

PORK

Chops and Steaks

Pork should always be cooked slowly until well done but not dry.

Thickness	Time
1 inch	25–35 min.
1½ inches	30–45 min.

HAM STEAKS

Thickness	Time
¾ inch	25–30 min.
1 inch	30–35 min.
1½ inches	35–45 min.
2 inches	45–60 min.

POULTRY

	Time
Chicken—split	25–45 min.
Duck—split	30–50 min.
Squab—split	25–35 min.

FISH

Thickness	Time
Fish Steaks 1 inch	6–9 min.
1½ inches	8–12 min.
2 inches	10–18 min.
Fish Fillets	6–18 min. depending on thickness.
Split Fish—small	8–12 min.
Whole Fish—small	12–18 min.
White Fish—large	30–60 min. or until flesh flakes.

ROTISSERIE ROASTED MEATS

1. Start charcoal fire early to have coals burning evenly for a low, steady heat.
2. Wipe meat with damp cloth; rub with cut side of clove of garlic; sprinkle with salt, pepper.
3. Insert spit rod completely through center of meat; insert spit fork into each end; tighten screws.
4. Check meat for balance by rotating spit between palms of hands.
5. If using a meat thermometer, insert it into thickest part, being sure bulb does not rest on bone, fat or gristle.
6. Arrange charcoal briquettes at back of fire box; knock off the gray ash.
7. Place a drip pan fashioned from heavy duty Alcoa Wrap in front of the coals.
8. Attach spit; start motor, having fire box at highest position until meat is seared.
9. Lower fire box 6-7 inches; continue roasting.
10. Roast according to Rotisserie Chart.

SHISH KEBAB

6 servings

¾ cup oil
½ cup white wine
1 tablespoon lemon juice
1 clove garlic, chopped
1 teaspoon salt
½ teaspoon pepper

3 pounds lean lamb, cut into 1½ inch cubes
12 small, egg-shaped tomatoes
6 small onions, cut in half
1 4-ounce can button mushrooms

1. Combine oil, wine, lemon juice, garlic, salt, pepper; blend well. 2. Place lamb cubes in large bowl; cover with marinade mixture; cover with Alcoa Wrap. 3. Marinate in refrigerator overnight; remove 1 hour before serving time; drain; save marinade. 4. Alternate meat, tomatoes, onion halves, mushrooms on each of 6 long skewers. 5. Broil over hot coals, turning and basting with marinade frequently. 6. Allow 20 minutes for medium, 25 minutes for well-done meat.

BARBECUED BROILERS

4 servings

2 2-pound ready-to-cook
   broilers, halved
2 teaspoons lime juice
¼ cup oil
2 tablespoons vinegar
1 tablespoon Worcestershire
   sauce

⅛ teaspoon Tabasco sauce
1 teaspoon salt
1 teaspoon sugar
½ teaspoon garlic salt
½ teaspoon paprika

1. Clean, dry broilers; place in Alcoa Wrap lined shallow pan.
2. Combine lime juice, oil, vinegar, Worcestershire sauce,
Tabasco sauce, salt, sugar, garlic salt, paprika; blend well;
pour over chicken. 3. Marinate 2 hours, turning once; remove; drain, saving marinade. 4. Place chicken on grill over
medium coals, skin side up. 5. Broil until well done, turning
and basting with marinade frequently. 6. Allow 35-40 minutes for well-done chicken.

CRUNCHY SHORT RIBS

4 servings

3 pounds beef short ribs
¾ cup water
½ cup Worcestershire sauce
2 tablespoons lemon juice

2 tablespoons oil
¼ teaspoon Tabasco sauce
½ teaspoon garlic salt
¼ teaspoon pepper

1. Wipe meat with damp cloth; place in large bowl. 2. Combine water, Worcestershire sauce, lemon juice, oil, Tabasco
sauce, garlic salt, pepper; blend well; pour over meat; cover
with Alcoa Wrap. 3. Marinate overnight in refrigerator, turning once. 4. Remove one hour before serving time; drain
when ready to broil, saving marinade. 5. Broil over medium
coals, turning and basting with marinade frequently. 6. Allow
35-45 minutes for well-done meat.

CHICKEN TEXAS

4 servings

2 2-pound ready-to-cook
broilers, halved
2 chicken bouillon cubes
1 cup boiling water
¼ cup oil
2 tablespoons ketchup
1 tablespoon Worcestershire
sauce

1 teaspoon prepared horseradish
1 teaspoon sugar
1 teaspoon salt
½ teaspoon chili powder
½ teaspoon cayenne pepper
1 clove garlic, minced
1 small onion, chopped

1. Clean, dry broilers. 2. Dissolve bouillon cubes in boiling water. 3. Add oil, ketchup, Worcestershire sauce, horseradish, sugar, salt, chili powder, cayenne pepper, garlic, onion; blend well. 4. Pour into saucepan; bring to a boil; cook 10 minutes over low heat. 5. Brush chicken with sauce; place on greased grill, skin side up. 6. Broil until well done, turning and basting with sauce frequently. 7. Allow 35-40 minutes for well-done chicken.

GRILLED LAMB STEAKS

4 servings

4 lamb steaks cut from leg,
1-inch thick
¾ cup olive oil
¼ cup vinegar
1 clove garlic, crushed

1 teaspoon salt
¼ teaspoon pepper
¼ teaspoon chopped fresh mint or
½ teaspoon crushed dried mint

1. Wipe meat with damp cloth; place in Alcoa Wrap lined shallow baking pan. 2. Combine oil, vinegar, garlic, salt, pepper, mint; blend well; pour over meat; cover with Alcoa Wrap. 3. Marinate in refrigerator 3-4 hours, turning once. 4. Remove when ready to broil; drain, saving marinade. 5. Grease grill well before placing steaks. 6. Broil, turning and basting with marinade frequently. 7. Allow 20-22 minutes for medium to well-done steaks.

SHRIMP KEBAB

6-10 servings

1 pound raw shrimp, washed,
  cleaned
1 1-pound can pineapple chunks

¼ cup soy sauce
4 slices bacon, cut into 2-inch
  pieces

1. Place shrimp, pineapple chunks in bowl; top with soy sauce; cover with Alcoa Wrap; let stand 30 minutes. 2. Alternate shrimp, pineapple, bacon pieces on small skewers. 3. Place each filled skewer in center of lightly greased square of Alcoa Wrap; bring up two sides of foil; fold over top of skewers, using double fold. Fold each end over twice, being careful not to pierce foil on tips of skewers. 4. Place foil packages on grill; broil, turning once. 5. Allow 12-14 minutes to thoroughly cook shrimp, bacon. 6. Serve each skewer in opened foil package.

Good to know: These kebabs are delicious served as appetizers while broiling steaks, chops.

GRILLED OYSTERS

5 servings

1 pint can frying oysters
  (about 30 oysters)
  tablespoons oyster liquor
  tablespoon lemon juice
  blespoons grated onion

1 tablespoon minced celery
1 teaspoon salt
¼ teaspoon pepper
1 tablespoon butter or margarine,
  softened

ain oysters; save liquor. 2. Place 6 oysters in center of
  of 5 squares of Alcoa Wrap. 3. Combine oyster liquor,
  juice, onion, celery, salt, pepper, butter; blend well;

pour over oysters. **4.** Bring up sides of Alcoa Wrap; fold down onto oysters in tight double fold; fold ends up in tight double folds. **5.** Place each package in center of another square of Alcoa Wrap; wrap in same way with double folds. **6.** Place packages directly on coals; grill 10-12 minutes, turning once. **7.** Serve in opened packages.

LOBSTER FANTANS
4-5 servings

1 6½-ounce can lobster, drained
½ cup cubed Swiss cheese
3 tablespoons chopped green pepper
2 tablespoons minced onion
½ teaspoon salt

¼ cup mayonnaise or salad dressing
1 teaspoon lemon juice
4–5 sandwich buns, unsliced
¼ cup butter or margarine, softened

1. Break lobster in chunks; add cheese, green pepper, onion, salt; toss lightly. **2.** Blend mayonnaise, lemon juice; add to lobster mixture; toss lightly. **3.** Cut buns crosswise in 4 slices, not quite through to bottom crust. **4.** Spread cut sides with butter; fill in between with lobster mixture. **5.** Place each bun on square of Alcoa Wrap; bring sides together over top of bun; make double fold; double fold ends. **6.** Place packages on grill over medium coals; grill 15-20 minutes; turn once. **7.** Serve in opened packages.

SKEWERED LIVER AND BACON
6 servings

2 pounds calves liver, cut 1½ inches thick
12 mushroom caps

12 slices bacon
2 tablespoons oil

1. Wipe liver with damp cloth; cut into 12 1½-inch cub **2.** Place liver, bacon, mushroom caps on skewers, altern ing in order given; put 2 pieces of each on a skewer; v bacon strips around liver-mushrooms, spiral fashion. **3.** I each piece with oil. **4.** Place skewers on grill; broil bacon is crisp. **5.** Allow 10-12 minutes broiling time.

Worcestershire sauce, Tabasco sauce, sugar, salt, pepper; add ¾ cup marinade; heat. **6.** Place steak on greased grill over coals. **7.** Broil until done to taste, basting twice with the hot sauce. **8.** Allow 8 minutes each side for rare; 10 minutes each side for medium; 12-14 minutes each side for well done. **9.** Cut into serving pieces; serve with hot sauce.

BARBECUED HAM STEAKS
4-6 servings

2 uncooked smoked ham steaks, 1-inch thick
1 cup cider

3 tablespoons brown sugar
1 tablespoon dry mustard
3 whole cloves, crushed

1. Trim excess fat from ham; score edges at 1-inch intervals. **2.** Place in large fry pan; cover with boiling water; parboil 5 minutes. **3.** Pour water off steaks. **4.** Combine cider, brown sugar, mustard, cloves; blend well. **5.** Pour over steaks; marinate 15 minutes; drain, saving marinade. **6.** Grease grill with fat trimmings. **7.** Broil over medium coals until brown on both sides, turning and basting with marinade frequently. **8.** Allow 30-35 minutes for well-done, browned meat.

BARBECUED SPARERIBS
4 servings

4 pounds spareribs, cut into serving pieces
2 tablespoons salt
½ cup melted butter or margarine
½ cup chili sauce
2 tablespoons vinegar

1 tablespoon Worcestershire sauce
½ teaspoon garlic salt
½ teaspoon chili powder
¼ teaspoon pepper

1. Rub meat with salt. **2.** Place in Alcoa Wrap lined shallow roasting pan. **3.** Bake 1 hour at 350° F.; baste 3 or 4 times with meat drippings. **4.** In saucepan, combine melted butter, chili sauce, vinegar, Worcestershire sauce, garlic salt, chili powder, pepper; blend well; cook 10 minutes over low heat. **5.** Remove meat from oven; place on grill; broil, basting with sauce frequently. Turn only once. **6.** Allow 30 minutes for well-done meat.

CHICKEN FIRECRACKERS

8 sandwiches

2 cups diced cooked chicken
1½ cups diced celery
¼ cup slivered almonds, toasted
1 tablespoon diced onion
1 tablespoon lemon juice

1 teaspoon salt
⅛ teaspoon pepper
½ cup mayonnaise
¼ pound grated Cheddar cheese
8 French rolls

1. Combine chicken, celery, almonds, onion, lemon juice, salt, pepper, mayonnaise, cheese; blend well. 2. Scoop out center of each French roll; fill with chicken mixture. 3. Wrap each roll in Alcoa Wrap, twisting ends to resemble firecrackers. 4. Place on grill; heat about 20 minutes, turning several times.

BARBECUED HALF TURKEY

1. Wash, dry turkey; sprinkle body cavity with salt. 2. Skewer wing to body; tie leg to tail; brush with parsley sauce. 3. Place bony cavity side down on grill about 8 inches from glowing coals. 4. Turn occasionally; baste with sauce. 5. Total cooking time will be approximately 1½ hours.

Parsley Sauce:

½ cup salad oil
½ cup white wine
½ cup finely minced parsley

2 cloves garlic
Salt, freshly ground pepper

1. Combine all ingredients; let stand one hour before using. 2. Baste turkey frequently with sauce. 3. Remaining sauce may be heated, served with sliced turkey.

GRILLED SALMON WITH HERB BUTTER   *8 servings*

2–2½ pounds salmon fillet
4 tablespoons butter or margarine
1 clove garlic, minced
1 small onion, finely chopped
3 tablespoons minced parsley

3 tablespoons lemon juice
½ teaspoon sweet basil
1 teaspoon salt
½ teaspoon pepper

1. Place salmon fillet on double-thick square of Alcoa Wrap.
2. Combine butter, garlic, onion, parsley, lemon juice, basil, salt, pepper; blend. 3. Spread over salmon. 4. Bring up sides of Alcoa Wrap; fold down in tight double fold; fold ends up in tight double folds. 5. Place package on grill over medium coals; grill 20-25 minutes; turn once. 6. Open foil; place on platter to serve.

FISH BARBECUE   *6 servings*

2 1-pound packages frozen fish
    fillets

Prepared barbecue sauce

1. Allow fish to defrost enough to separate fillets. 2. Divide fillets into six servings. 3. Place each serving in center of double-thick square of Alcoa Wrap. 4. Brush each fillet generously with a favorite barbecue sauce. 5. Bring up sides of Alcoa Wrap; fold down onto fish in tight double fold; fold ends up in tight double folds. 6. Place package on grill over medium coals; grill 20-25 minutes. 7. Serve in opened packages.

FISH AND POTATO GRILL   *4 servings*

1 pound package frozen fish fillets
1 large onion
    Paprika
2 large potatoes

2 tablespoons chopped parsley
    Salt, pepper
2 tablespoons butter or margarine

1. Thaw fish until frozen block can be cut into 4 pieces.
2. Place each piece on a double-thick square of Alcoa Wrap.
3. Slice onion; arrange slices on top of fish; sprinkle with paprika. 4. Cut potatoes into Julienne sticks; arrange around

edge of fish.   **5.** Sprinkle with parsley, salt, pepper; dot with butter.   **6.** Bring up sides of Alcoa Wrap; fold down in tight double fold; fold ends up in tight double folds.   **7.** Place packages on grill over medium coals; grill 20-25 minutes; turn once.   **8.** Serve in opened packages.

ORANGE BEETS

4 servings

1 No. 2½ can sliced beets, drained
2 medium size oranges, peeled, sectioned

2 tablespoons orange juice
1 tablespoon grated orange rind
2 tablespoons butter or margarine

1. Place sliced beets in center of double-thick sheet of Alcoa Wrap.   **2.** Add orange sections, orange juice, orange rind; dot with butter.   **3.** Bring up sides of Alcoa Wrap; fold down over beets in tight double fold, leaving some space for steam expansion; fold ends up in tight double folds.   **4.** Place package on grill over medium coals; grill 15-20 minutes, turning once.

GRILLED CORN ON THE COB

Fresh corn on the cob
Melted butter or margarine

Salt
Pepper

1. Husk corn; brush with melted butter; season with salt, pepper.   **2.** Wrap each ear in a dampened paper towel; place in center of square of Alcoa Wrap.   **3.** Bring up sides of Alcoa Wrap; fold down onto corn in tight double fold; twist ends securely.   **4.** Place on grill over medium coals; grill 20-25 minutes, turning frequently.   **5.** Serve in opened packages.

CREOLE BARBECUED ZUCCHINI

4 servings

½ pound zucchini squash
1 medium tomato, cut in wedges
½ cup celery, cut in ¼-inch pieces

1 small onion, thinly sliced
Salt, pepper
2 tablespoons butter or margarine

1. Wash zucchini squash; do not peel. 2. Cut crosswise in ¼-inch pieces. 3. Place on double-thick sheet of Alcoa Wrap. 4. Add tomato wedges, celery, onion rings; sprinkle with salt, pepper; dot with butter. 5. Bring up sides of Alcoa Wrap; fold down over vegetables in tight double fold, leaving some space for steam expansion; fold ends up in tight double folds. 6. Place package on grill over medium coals; grill 30-35 minutes, turning once.

HERB FLAVORED CARROTS

4 servings

8 small, tender carrots
Salt, pepper
Thyme

1 teaspoon minced parsley
2 tablespoons butter or margarine
3 tablespoons water

1. Wash, scrape carrots. 2. Place in center of double-thick sheet of Alcoa Wrap. 3. Sprinkle with salt, pepper, thyme, minced parsley. 4. Dot with butter; add water. 5. Bring up sides of Alcoa Wrap; fold down over carrots in tight double fold, leaving some space for steam expansion; fold ends up in tight double folds. 6. Place package on grill over medium coals; grill 35-45 minutes or until carrots are tender, turning packages several times.

SMOTHERED ONIONS

1 serving

1 medium size onion, sliced
1 tablespoon butter or margarine

Salt
Pepper

1. Place sliced onion in center of double-thick square of Alcoa Wrap. 2. Place butter on top; add salt, pepper to taste. 3. Bring up sides of Alcoa Wrap; fold down onto onions in

tight double fold; fold ends up in tight double folds. **4.** Place package on grill over medium coals; grill 25-30 minutes; turn several times. **5.** Serve in open packages.

SKILLET BARBECUED ONION BISCUITS
5 servings

2 tablespoons butter or margarine
1 medium onion, thinly sliced
2 teaspoons poppy seeds

1 package oven-ready refrigerated biscuits (10 biscuits)

1. Line fry pan with double-thick sheet of heavy duty Alcoa Wrap, allowing excess foil to extend up sides of pan. **2.** Melt butter in fry pan; sauté onion slices until soft, transparent, but not brown. **3.** Sprinkle poppy seeds over onions. **4.** Dip each biscuit in onion-butter mixture; place biscuits on top of onions, buttered side up. **5.** Bring excess foil over top of biscuits in tight double folds. **6.** Place pan on grill 6-8 inches from glowing coals; grill 20-30 minutes or until biscuits are "set," bottoms brown. **7.** Turn packages out onto serving plate, onion side up. **8.** Slit foil across top of package; fold back for serving.

GRILLED FRESH PEACHES
4 servings

4 medium size peaches
Juice of 1 lemon

3 tablespoons brown sugar

1. Peel; slice peaches onto double-thick sheet of Alcoa Wrap. **2.** Sprinkle with lemon juice, brown sugar. **3.** Bring up sides of Alcoa Wrap; fold down over peaches in tight double fold; fold ends up in tight double folds. **4.** Place package on grill over medium coals; grill 10-15 minutes, or until peaches are heated through. **5.** Serve warm over ice cream or cake.

OUTDOOR SMOKE OVEN COOKERY

This is the simplest and easiest method of Outdoor Cooking. While the food cooks you are free to enjoy your guests. The result, the most delicious meat, fish or fowl you ever tasted, all delicately seasoned with a true smoky flavor.

Any outdoor Barbecue or Grill can be converted into a Smoke Oven by making a hood from Alcoa Wrap.

Here's how:

1. Before starting the fire, completely line the bowl or fire box with double-thick sheets of heavy duty Alcoa Wrap, allowing each strip to extend about three inches over the rim. Depending on size, you will have one to three double-thick sheets running from north to south and one to three double-thick sheets running from east to west.
2. Press overhang tightly to form a firm rim. The hood now looks like an umbrella. Remove from bowl or fire box.
3. Cut a hole about 2 inches in diameter in the center of the top. This makes the vent necessary for good browning.
4. The hood is now ready to use. It can be used over and over again—any time you want to do Smoke Oven Cookery.

To Do Smoke Oven Cookery

1. Line fire box or bowl with Alcoa Wrap.
2. Build fire in usual way; put grill in place.
3. When coals start to turn gray, set a portable oven thermometer on the grill; cover with the Alcoa Wrap hood; let Smoke Oven pre-heat.
4. Prepare food according to recipe; place on grill; add hood; bake as directed in recipe.

Good to know: *Alcoa Wrap hood may be removed by inserting the tines of a barbecue fork into the vent.*
If Smoke Oven gets too hot, prop hood up slightly.

RODEO CHICKEN

5-6 servings

1 pint commercial sour cream
1 tablespoon lemon juice
1 teaspoon salt
1 teaspoon monosodium glutamate
¼ teaspoon pepper
½ teaspoon paprika
½ teaspoon celery salt
2 broiler-fryers, cut into serving pieces
¾ cup butter or margarine, melted

1. Combine sour cream, lemon juice, salt, monsodium glutamate, pepper, paprika, celery salt; blend well. 2. Place chicken pieces in shallow bake pan; pour marinade over chicken; cover with Alcoa Wrap; refrigerate. 3. Let stand several hours or overnight. 4. Pre-heat charcoal grill with Alcoa Wrap hood to 350° F. 5. Remove chicken pieces from marinade; scrape off excess with spatula; place skin side down in greased bake pan. 6. Pour half of melted butter over tops of chicken pieces; place uncovered bake pan on grill; add hood; bake 30 minutes. 7. Turn chicken pieces; add remaining butter; bake additional 30 minutes or until tender, golden brown. 8. Remove chicken pieces; add marinade to browned butter; blend well; serve with chicken.

ORIENTAL PORK CHOPS

8 servings

1 cup salad oil
½ cup soy sauce
⅔ cup wine vinegar
¼ cup lemon juice
2 tablespoons Worcestershire sauce
2½ tablespoons chopped parsley
2 teaspoons dry mustard
1½ teaspoons pepper
8 pork chops, ½ inch thick

1. Combine oil, soy sauce, vinegar, lemon juice, Worcestershire sauce, parsley, mustard, pepper; blend well. 2. Place pork chops in shallow bake pan; pour marinade over chops; cover with Alcoa Wrap; refrigerate. 3. Let stand several hours or overnight; spoon marinade over chops occasionally. 4. Pour off all but ½ cup marinade; reserve rest for basting. 5. Pre-heat charcoal grill with Alcoa Wrap hood to 350° F. 6. Place

uncovered bake pan with chops on grill; add hood; bake 1-1¼ hours or until chops are tender; baste occasionally with marinade.

FLANK STEAK BOURBON   *4-6 servings*

2 cups tomato sauce
¼ cup chopped chives
1 teaspoon seasoned salt
¼ teaspoon pepper
½ teaspoon celery salt

¼ cup bourbon
4 ounce can chopped mushrooms plus liquid
1 flank steak, 1-1¼ pounds

1. Combine tomato sauce, chives, seasoned salt, pepper, celery salt, bourbon, mushrooms plus liquid; blend well. 2. Score flank steak with criss cross cuts, on both sides; place in shallow bake pan; pour marinade over steak; cover with Alcoa Wrap; refrigerate. 3. Let stand several hours or overnight; spoon marinade over beef occasionally. 4. Pre-heat charcoal grill with Alcoa Wrap hood to 350° F. 5. Place uncovered bake pan with steak on grill; add hood; bake 1½ hours or until tender; baste occasionally with marinade.

BEEF BURGUNDY
8 servings

1½ cups red wine
1 garlic clove, minced
1 tablespoon pickling spice
2½–3 pounds bottom round beef, about 1 inch thick

¾ cup sliced carrots
1 medium onion, sliced into rings
½ cup celery, cut into ½-inch pieces

1. Combine wine, garlic, pickling spice; blend well. 2. Place beef in shallow bake pan; pour marinade over beef; cover with Alcoa Wrap; refrigerate. 3. Let stand at least 12 hours or overnight; spoon marinade over beef occasionally. 4. Strain marinade; pour over beef once again; add carrots, onions, celery. 5. Pre-heat charcoal grill with Alcoa Wrap hood to 350° F. 6. Place uncovered bake pan with beef on grill; add hood; bake 2-2½ hours or until tender; baste occasionally with marinade.

MARINATED LOBSTER TAILS
4 servings

6 tablespoons lemon juice
1½ tablespoons soy sauce
½ teaspoon ginger
½ teaspoon salt
½ teaspoon tarragon

1 clove garlic, minced
½ teaspoon hot pepper sauce
1 cup Sherry wine
8 frozen lobster tails

1. Combine lemon juice, soy sauce, ginger, salt, tarragon, garlic, hot sauce, Sherry; blend well. 2. Thaw lobster tails; cut under-shell around edge; remove membrane. 3. Place lobster tails in shallow bake pan; pour marinade over lobster; cover with Alcoa Wrap; refrigerate. 4. Let stand several hours or overnight; spoon marinade over lobster occasionally. 5. Pre-heat charcoal grill with Alcoa Wrap hood to 350° F. 6. Remove lobster from marinade; place directly on grill above charcoal with shell side on grill; add hood; grill 6-9 minutes, basting occasionally with marinade.

HERB LAMB CHOPS 5 servings

1 cup olive oil
1 cup chopped onions
½ cup chopped parsley
½ cup lemon juice
1½ teaspoons salt
1½ teaspoons marjoram

1½ teaspoons thyme
¾ teaspoon pepper
¼ teaspoon garlic salt
5 shoulder lamb chops, ½ inch thick

1. Combine olive oil, onions, parsley, lemon juice, salt, marjoram, thyme, pepper, garlic salt; blend well. 2. Place lamb chops in shallow bake pan; pour marinade over chops; cover with Alcoa Wrap; refrigerate. 3. Let stand several hours or overnight; spoon marinade over chops occasionally. 4. Preheat charcoal grill with Alcoa Wrap hood to 350° F. 5. Remove chops from marinade; place directly on grill above charcoal; add hood; grill 8 minutes per side. 6. Heat marinade; serve with grilled chops.